# FISHING WITH MY FLY DOWN

Sunbelt Editions
An imprint of Sunbelt Shows, Inc.
Albuquerque, New Mexico
www.FieryFoodsCentral.com

Printed in the U.S.A.
Cover design by Marcus Casman
Interior design by Lois Manno

ISBN 978-0-9832515-6-9

# FISHING
# WITH
# MY FLY
# DOWN

## A FLY FISHING CAREER
## RUINED BY ROCK RADIO

TJ Trout

# SUNBELT
# EDITIONS

Published by Sunbelt Editions

# CONTENTS

Bob Gerding and me at the Cimarron in northern New Mexico; the man most
responsible for getting me into this fly fishing racket!

# DEDICATIONS AND ACKNOWLEDGMENTS

THIS WORK OF LITERARY ART (?) is dedicated to two of the people who were responsible for putting my life on the proper road, so I was able to have all these experiences. Tragically, we lost both of them recently, and I continue to mourn their loss:

Bob Gerding, my mentor, my teacher, and above all, my friend.

He started me on this flyfishing journey, and it has taken me all over the world. When I was still fishing with worms and Panther Martin's (nothing wrong with that, by the way), he gently chided me until I bought my first fly rod. Then to seal the deal, he built me a beauty of a 4-weight, which 25 years later, after several rod tip repairs and tune-ups, is still my favorite. Bob and I have fished all over the state of New Mexico, and I have been honored to have been included in his flyfishing seminars. Every year I eagerly awaited his Outdoor Adventures Hunting and Fishing Show at Expo New Mexico. Thank you for your guidance and your friendship. I miss you terribly, as does all of New Mexico.

And to Bill Swortwood.

Bill and I were kindred spirits. We used to sit on his front porch in the afternoon talking about life, and joking how we'd probably be on the same porch doing the same thing when we were 80. How I wish that were true. Through our many travels, Bill showed me the wonder that New Mexico is. We'd go on hikes all over the state. Bill was part Cherokee, and through him I was introduced to the Native American culture when we'd visit his friends on the Zuni Pueblo. And we'd fish. He loved to fish, and

Bill Swortwood in the lodge on the Kvichak River in Alaska. We shoulda fished more!

even after he hurt his back and shoulder, he vowed he'd soon be well enough to cast a fly rod again and wade a stream. You are missed and loved by many.

I want to thank my wife, Marti for her love and support, and everyone who made the final cut in this book, especially Jer, Mo, Roger, Milt, and David. These are the guys I've done most of my fishing with, and they will tell you that all of this stuff is true, and for the most part, not exaggerated! I hope you enjoy it.

Marti amidst flowers with a mountain backdrop. Can you say Julie Andrews? Heidi?

# FOREWORD BY BOB GERDING (1938-2013)

SOME YEARS AGO, CHARLES RITZ, heir to the Ritz Hotels, wrote a book *My Life as a Fly Fisher*. It was a serious work about his life and experiences flyfishing all over the world. We can now add another angler to the list of those who share their experiences. Within these pages you can travel with TJ Trout on his life as a fly fisher.

TJ and Charles Ritz shared a passion for flyfishing but the similarities end there. TJ loves to fish and may be found fishing for Blues with bait as well as going after Stripers with big Streamers. He has even been known to use chicken skin as bait.

Flyfishing is a combination of skill and passion. You may have one but you will never be an accomplished angler without the other. You have to pay your dues. TJ has paid his dues. You can always tell a passionate angler by how excited he gets when landing a six-inch trout. My father gave me some valuable advice: choose your hunting and fishing partners more carefully than your friends. It gives me great pleasure to count TJ as both friend and fishing partner.

It has been my honor and pleasure to have shared many pleasant days on the water and finishing with a good bottle of wine. I can only hope for many, many more. Whether alive or in spirit, I will look forward to many more days of a special bond between two people who share the same passion for fishing.

# PREFACE

I GREW UP IN A WORKING CLASS NEIGHBORHOOD in Cleveland, Ohio and in 1977, graduated from Bowling Green State University with a degree in Journalism. Bob Woodward and Carl Bernstein's exposé on the Watergate affair which ultimately brought down President Richard Nixon inspired me to become an investigative reporter. I was intent on finding my own Watergate and making a name for myself as a watchdog of big government and slayer of corrupt businessmen. But during those same years, something happened that I wasn't expecting. Rock radio was trying to seduce me. With its anti-establishment nature and rebellious appeal acting as aphrodisiacs, it finally succeeded in luring me away from print media. I changed my major to Broadcast Journalism and started working for my campus radio station. After graduating, I found that getting that first radio job was not easy. However, after short stints as a greeting card salesman, working for a leather shop, and selling bongs and rolling papers at a Cleveland head shop and record store, I finally landed my first radio gig and began a career that lasted thirty-plus years.

After four radio jobs, two of which I got fired from, I ended up in Albuquerque, New Mexico as the morning show host of KZRR-94 Rock, where I remained for 25 years. While there, journalistic writing still appealed to me. It seemed so...legitimizing... to see your ideas and opinions in black and white. So, for a while I wrote a weekly column for the local paper, but I knew I would have to write more. Finding the proper subject would be the trick.

Some of my first memories involved fishing, but it took me thirty years to even think about fly- fishing. Nobody fly-fished in Cleveland when I was growing up. It took moving to the western U.S. to finally become indoctrinated, and when I did, it changed my life. I liked every-thing about it; the skill and mental concentration required to perform, the beautiful places it took me, its solitary nature. I started meeting like-minded people who became friends of mine, took part in seminars, trade shows, and even started to become politically active involving en-vironmental issues that affected my sport. In short, I was a lifer!

xii   Fishing with My Fly Down

Then it dawned on me. This would be the subject that I would write about.

This book is an anecdotal account of things that have happened to me over the years while fishing. Most of it involves fly-fishing but not all of it, because there are instances where using a fly rod makes no sense at all, despite what some purists might think! It covers a time span of over forty years, most of it occurring during my stay in Albuquerque which began in 1986. But not all the stories are about the Southwest. My travels took me all over the United States including Alaska, plus Canada, Mexico, Belize, and Argentina.

You will meet several fishing buddies of mine, including my dear departed friend, Bob Gerding, who I have called the fly-fishing Yoda of the Southwest. Bob did the fishing report on the 94 Rock Morning Show for over twenty years and was personally responsible for transforming me from a bait slinger to a fly caster. Then there's Jer, who was my partner on the air for several years, and now lives in Salida, Colorado. Up until recently, he was a guide on the Arkansas River, and is now a talented furniture maker, among other things. Then there are my buddies Mo, Roger, Milt, and Bill, who we also lost this year. All accomplished fly-fishers. Taylor Streit is an amazing fly-fisher, author, owner of Taos Fly Shop in New Mexico, and was my partner in crime in Argentina. David Mangum is a saltwater fly- fishing guide and owns Shallow Water Expeditions on the Florida panhandle, who I've fished with for over a decade. David and Jer, probably more than anyone have seen me at my best and also my lowest points of humiliation.

There are several places I've fished, especially in New Mexico and Colorado that are not in these pages, but should be. Two that deserve special mention are the Brazos River Ranch in northern New Mexico, run by Bo Prieskorn and his family*, and the Rio Culebra in southern Colorado which is managed by Van Beacham. Bo's place is on my top five list of all the places I've fished for trout, and Van's is right up there with it. My hat's off to both of you guys for providing me with some of the best fishing experiences! Now that I think about it, the reason you didn't warrant a chapter is because nothing particularly weird or dangerous happened at either of your places.

So, to all my buddies in the book, I hope I didn't piss any of you off. To many of you that I didn't include, we either hardly fished together, or there are several valid reasons you weren't included, legal and otherwise, and you probably should be damned happy you didn't make the final cut!

*I take part of that back!  Now in the latest expanded edition of this book, there is a chapter on the Brazos River Ranch. Sadly, Bo has sold the property, so now as far as I know, it is not accessible to losers like me!  And Van, the Culebra still ain't in here. SORRY! Next book!

*Then I heard the words a son would never EVER*
*want to hear from his father:*
*"Take your pants off."*

# 1 IN THE BEGINNING

IMUST HAVE BEEN FIFTEEN OR SIXTEEN. It was the early 1970's, Richard Nixon was the president and the Vietnam War raged on. But none of that mattered because the mid-morning Montana sun was bathing everything in a golden yellow light, and the willows lining the stream were almost glowing in shades of green that subtly changed as the leaves moved in a light breeze. It was warm for May, yet the water in the Blackfoot was still cold from the melting snow from up top. My father and I were armed with our 5-weights and wading slowly upstream when he stopped and quietly said, "Son, do you see that backwater eddy up about a hundred feet on the left side of the main channel?"

"Yeah, Pop, I see it!"

"Look closely because there are several trout taking bugs off the surface. Let's slowly and carefully wade to within casting distance and see if we can get one."

We took our time and got to within about thirty feet of the rainbows, which were still lazily rising to the hatching mayflies. My father put his hand on my shoulder and said, "It's your cast and your fish. Make your old Pop proud!"

"I will, Pop! I won't let you down!"

I took some line off my reel and with my father standing to the right of me, I laid a parachute adams directly in front of a large rainbow. It slowly swam towards my fly, and with the same leisurely nonchalance that it took the real bugs, it took mine. The water exploded as the fish realized it made a mistake, and with an acrobatic jump, the fight was on.

Old pic of my barechested dad with a stringer of Canadian bass. Kinda makes me feel small and insignificant!

It shot upstream into the main channel, taking me quickly to my backing. With my father's gentle, yet persistent instruction and encouragement, I brought the fish to bay, and he unclipped his net from the back of his wading vest, and landed a beautiful, deeply colored 20-incher.

"You did it!" he beamed. I am so proud of you! You fought that fish like a master, and it is obvious our time fishing together has paid off!"

With that he put his arm around me, and with tears in both of our eyes, he said, "I love you, son!"

"I love you too, Pop!"

And with that, a bluebird landed on my shoulder and the skies opened up and a chorus of heavenly angels began to sing songs of praise and...and...and...

Oh, who the hell am I kidding with this bullshit? I WISH my childhood was like that! Want the real story?

I must have been 15 or 16. It was still the early 1970's and I was standing knee-deep in black, smelly, slimy swamp bottom, unable to move, after my dad and I both leaned the same way in a canoe and fell into a Lake Erie backwater where we were shooting carp with bows and arrows. Most of the contents of the canoe were now floating in about a foot of toilet-brown water, next to where I was stuck. The stringer full of impaled dead carp somehow stayed with the boat. I don't remember how my dad got loose, but we were in a narrow channel, and cursing with a vileness even more repulsive than usual, he got the canoe over to the cat-tail lined bank, and came back to get me loose.

Me with a stringer of unrecognizable fish. God, what a little dweeb!

"Try raising one of your feet up again!"

"I did but I lost my shoe!"

"Shit! Well, try the other leg!"

I did, and lost my other shoe.

"I'm stuck! Every time I try, I get even more stuck!"

"Son of a bitch!"

Then I heard the words that a son would never EVER want to hear from his father:

"Take your pants off."

"What?"

"Unzip your pants and pull them down as far as you can. You're not gonna get out of this any other way!"

At that moment, I swore I heard the twang of banjos in the distance. With visions of Ned Beatty about to get buggered in the movie "Deliverance," I complied. To make matters worse, anytime in the past my dad got angry or excited about something, his face would set into a strange grimace, which to us as kids, actually looked like a maniacal smile. Any time my brothers and I were about to get the crap beat out of us for something we did to Mom or each other, he'd get this same look on his face like he was really looking forward to the pain he was about to inflict. To my horror, at that moment he had the same look on his face, grimacing with determination, his face contorted into that hideous leer.

So, he wrapped both of his big burly arms around me from behind, and as the imaginary banjos increased in tempo and volume, he pulled as hard as he could. With a long, loud sucking noise, the muck gave way and he actually pulled me free, pants-less, out of the swill. Luckily, my bell-bottoms were still half laying half standing where I was stuck, and we were able to retrieve them so I wouldn't have to ride back to Cleveland in just my underwear. Again, not a way I would have wanted to arrive home, with Mom coming out the side screen door and greeting us in the driveway:

"So how was your trip? Oh my God! What happened to you? Where are your pants?

"Uhhh, Dad made me take them off."

"Again? Steve! I told you to stop doing that! I mean, he's your son! Do I have to call the priest again?"

It really wouldn't have happened like that, but as an impressionable adolescent, your mind tends to occasionally go places it shouldn't. Well, maybe yours didn't but mine did.

Dad enjoying a smoke with his prized skewered carp.

So wet, stinking of decaying animal and plant matter, and somewhat humiliated, we made it back to our Cleveland home with the trunk of our 1963 bronze Chevy Impala weighted down with probably a couple dozen carp, some twenty pounds or bigger. Later we would bury them in the garden as fertilizer, and get a bumper crop of tomatoes come mid-summer. Dad then insisted on having his picture taken with his quarry, all laid out on the backyard lawn, dead, bloody, bloated, and, well, looking like you would imagine a lawn full of skewered carp would look like.

We did this every spring during carp spawning season, and the older I got, I started to think there's got to be something better than this. Yeah, I know, it's bonding with the old man, but Jesus! Can't we bond on a golf course, or maybe actually fish with a rod and reel for something less disgusting? And what did these poor carp do that they deserved to be shot through the head and buried behind my house? I mean, if we were going to eat them, that's one thing, but to just shoot them for the sport of it, which is really what we were doing, just wasn't right. And really, you could go to the store and buy Miracle Gro for the garden and probably get the same results.

That was the year I stopped going. Everything I just mentioned, plus the pants-less incident convinced me to stop before something REALLY bad happened, and I ended up being permanently sucked under the muck, with archaeologists finding my mummified remains a thousand years from now. I tried to explain my thought process to Dad, who pretended he was listening until his eyes started to glaze over. The next Spring he went with my Uncle Jack instead of me and never missed a beat.

I didn't know it at the time, but events like this set the tone for the rest of my fishing life, because for some reason, even to this day, stuff like this continues to happen to me and whomever I'm fishing with.

And by the way, I never called my dad "Pop."

Speaking of living in the muck and filth...

I've worked in rock and roll radio for over thirty years. In 2011 it was my twenty-fifth anniversary as the top-rated morning show host at KZRR-94 Rock in Albuquerque, and I decided I'd had enough. I quit for a number of reasons:

—I was too old to be acting like Bevis and Butthead. Dick and fart jokes are funny to a point, but when you start worrying about your dignity (like I had any to begin with), it's time to go.

—I'd seen too many people in this business turn into alcoholics, drug addicts, or die, for that matter. I didn't want to push my luck because it was possible that any of those things could still happen to me.

—Getting up at 3:45am started to take its toll. I was constantly sleep-deprived, and my hours were at complete odds with the way the rest of humanity lived, including my wife. Naturally, getting up that early made you want to go to bed early. I'd be nodding off in the 8PM hour and was asleep by nine. Needless to say, my love life was, shall we say, critically bereft.

—Radio as I'd always known it, was being systematically murdered by corporate America. Huge soul-sucking companies were buying up hundreds of stations...no...make that THOUSANDS of stations until there were virtually no Mom and Pop stand-alones left in the country. The thing that made radio relevant and appealing radio was its localism. Each town had its own quirks and idiosyncrasies and its stations were a reflection of the community they broadcasted in. That was, until the corporate pigs came to town.

In my case, they fired 60% of the staff in our building, forcing the remaining skeleton crew to each do the job of three people. On top of that, they replaced most of the on-air personalities with piped-in syndicated bullshit. So instead of your afternoon announcer being able to tell you about the headaches the new construction was causing at I-25 and San Mateo, or that he just went to the local concert venue to see the Screaming Muskrats and got thrown-up on, you'd get a guy who couldn't care less about your local town. He might try to fake it, and you might even be fooled for a while. But if you listened closely you'd be able to tell he was a poser, most likely broadcasting from New York or L.A., or maybe even from the studio he built in an upstairs bedroom in his home in Destin, Florida. (Sorry about the male pronoun...It could have easily been a female under the same circumstances.) In conclusion, I had to get out before I killed someone.

This really wasn't a reason that I left: Some of you might think that being a rock jock on a successful station might be the coolest thing ever.

Think again.

In the pecking order of the music/entertainment industry, we are the weak link, the red-headed stepchild, the annoyingly yet necessary evil. One might have visions of hanging out with Guns and Roses at backstage parties, buddying up to all the musicians and being treated to all the accompanying perks. Forget it. At concerts, we were tolerated at best, demeaned and dismissed at worst. As an example, we would be ushered back for a quick meet and greet, with or without a contest-winning listener. Mick Jagger or some other guy depending on the band, would come out, didn't look at anyone, smiled and said something that really wasn't saying anything, MAYBE consented to have his picture taken with you and your listener and then left, taking all of one minute. Then we'd be hustled back out.

If, on the rare occasion we had a hot and willing female groupie with us, we might get two minutes, and if she played her cards right, she might get more time, most likely doing things her mother warned her not to do. If we were going to do stage announcements, the stage manager, normally a needle-dicked moron with a large stick up his ass, would push you over to the side of the stage, tell you what you could and couldn't say, usually concluding with, "And don't touch the fuckin' mic!" I remember once being told I could come to a backstage "party" with food, drinks, etc...and ended up being led into an 8 by 10 windowless room with a bunch of other media types and local business people, no band members in sight, and we all sheepishly stood around, eating picked over snacks and wilted salad, while being handed one beer, and then told to leave. It was not anything close to anyone's idea of "cool." There were exceptions to this, but they were few and far between. At least I was never told to take my pants off.

Yeah, I know...blah, blah, blah...I have no right to complain about anything. I could have been shoveling up rhino dung at the zoo for 25 years. On the grand balance sheet of life, what I did for a living comes out big on the plus side:

I HAVE hung out with some rock stars, many of which were quite cool. I smoked a joint with Tommy Chong. I talked politics with George Carlin. I found out that Jeff Bridges is a fly fisherman and we spent about an hour telling each other fishing stories. I had a deep philosophical conversation with '60s activist and LSD advocate Timothy Leary. When I asked him, "OK...What's it all about? What is the meaning of life? Does our existence serve any purpose?" he said, "I have no idea."

That crushed me. But it HAS been a real trip.

When you do morning radio, you can bring the world into your studio. Virtually anything you have an interest in, you can invite an expert or a practitioner to the show and if you're fortunate enough, you can occasionally get invited to actually do some of these things. For instance:

I've gone on archaeological digs. I've dug up dinosaurs. I've partic- ipated in ghost hunts. I've gone on diving trips and swam with sharks. I've learned all about the Native American culture. I've gone to the Adult Video Convention and Awards in Las Vegas, which is another book in itself. I've climbed mountains, learned to snow ski, and yes, because of my radio connection, I've learned to fly fish, which was something that people just didn't do in Cleveland, Ohio when I was growing up, or even much now, for that matter.

My first fishing memory happened five minutes from where we lived, which was in a typically small cookie-cutter single story ranch house built in the fifties in the working class town of Parma. In Ohio, not Italy, unfortunately. I was four years old, and my dad took me to State Road Park Lake, which really wasn't a lake at all. It was a con- crete-lined, perfectly round, man-made pond, sitting near the entrance to State Road Park which was located up the street and across State Road. It was the same lake that as teenagers, we would shovel off the winter snow and play hockey. The park had several softball fields as well as one baseball field, where I played my high-school baseball on the Par- ma High team. On that particular day, my dad had just gotten home from work and with a bamboo pole and a box of night crawlers that my grandfather "farmed" behind our garage, we walked up the street.

We hadn't had the line in the wa- ter more than a couple minutes when I caught a fairly sizeable catfish which delighted me and surprised my dad. After releasing the fish, Dad, being an impatient man, figured he accomplished what he set out to do, and we walked home. In retrospect, he was right, because from that moment on, I was hooked, so to speak.

Dad was a hunter/fisher- man, and fancied himself an am- ateur wildlife painter Our family was definitely blue-collar work- ing class, and my parents were loud, boisterous, smoking and

Reasons why NOT to go into radio.

drinking, fun-loving people, both having the propensity to use healthy doses of profanity when the situation called for it. You might draw similarities to Ralph and Alice in "The Honeymooners." They were good parents, successfully raising their three sons, with none of the three having spent more than one night in jail (as far as I know). Dad worked a miserable job as a machinist, and often had to supplement his income by working other jobs to make ends meet. But every year, he and my mother made sure they had enough money saved to take us on a summer vacation that usually involved fishing. In lean years, we'd stay close to home and go to the Lake Erie Island and fish for perch and walleye. In the good years, our destination was Canada for northern pike.

We'd stay at fishing cabins at various locations in southern Ontario that were usually recommended by someone my dad worked with. Most of these places had the word "Lodge" associated with them, but in reality, they were drafty ramshackle cabins resembling what Jed Clampett lived in before he packed up the truck and moved to Beverly Hills. Sometimes we'd be lucky and get a cabin with indoor plumbing, but other times we'd have to tough it out with pump water and an ancient outhouse. Mom would cook breakfast, and Dad and I, sometimes with Mom, would head out in our 12-foot aluminum boat with a five-horsepower motor early in the morning, and then after an early dinner, we'd go back out for evening of fishing. In those days we'd troll a Johnson's silver spoon with a frog patterned pork rind attached, or maybe a daredevil behind the boat. When we reached our destination, we'd either keep those on, or throw on a Mepps buck tail spinner and cast into the weed beds where the pike would be hiding.

I got married in 1977, and for some insane reason, I thought it'd be a great idea to take Marti up to one of the old places we used to fish, not really thinking about the less than rustic accommodations, or the fact that she really liked hotels and had a thing about doing something that might "break a nail." I also decided it'd be a great idea to go in the middle of October, the last week the cabins were open. But we were newlyweds, and she felt an obligation to at least humor me and try. After crossing the St. Lawrence River at the Thousand Island Bridge on a beautiful fall morning, we arrived at our location at lunchtime, met Duncan and Laura, the owners, and were led over to our cabin which turned out to be an improvement over what I remembered. And to my supreme relief, we had indoor plumbing. Since it was late in the year, the rest of the cabins were empty, so as a bonus, we ended up eating all of our meals with Duncan and Laura in the main house, which was also a plus.

What could possibly go wrong?

The trip started to go bad when the weather turned abysmal the next day and we ended up fishing in a sleet storm. As it often happens in crappy weather, the fish were enthusiastically biting and at least I was catching something. So not thinking of my wife's comfort, I made the decision to keep fishing. I mean, what fisherman in their right mind would come back in when they're getting at least a strike on every cast? Who cares about a little sleet?

I'll tell you who cares.

The woman you are with.

Cold, damp, and one of us being quite happy, and the other one close to hypothermia, we finally boated back across the lake with a stringer-full of pike, and Marti shivering and miserable, and looking forward to a hot shower. Under normal circumstances this would merely require a walk from the bedroom to the bathroom. Unfortunately, that was not the case. The cabins might have had toilets, but all eight shared a shower house which was about a one-hundred-foot-walk to the edge of the woods. In the sleet. At dusk. So, she made the walk and commenced to take her shower.

All seemed to be going well until I heard her anguished screams coming from the shower house. Still dressed in my fishing clothes I ran over, thinking she had fallen or worse. As I entered the steamy building, I saw her cowering in a corner with a towel wrapped around her as dozens of large hornets are dive-bombing her head. She was desperately trying to keep them away by flailing one hand at them and covering up with the other. Apparently since the shower had not been used for a while, the heat and steam had awakened the slumbering nest of hornets, who either thought was spring, or were just angry because some naked blonde chick had disturbed their peaceful sleep, resulting in the relentless attack. So, I gathered up her clothes and her generous supply of toiletries, make-up, and girlie stuff, and with her only wrapped in a towel, we made a quick exit and ran back to our cabin. Somehow, Duncan dispatched the hornets, we showered in peace, had dinner, and left the next morning.

Did I learn any valuable lessons about married life that day? Oh yeah. In fact, I'll share some of those later on.

*"Yeah but I just had this moment of existential enlightenment over at the Piggly Wiggly."*

# 2 WAIT! WHAT THE HELL JUST HAPPENED? DATELINE SEPTEMBER 4, 2021

SITTING HERE AT MY DESK, BACK AT WORK. In Albuquerque. After a seven-year hiatus. Retirement seemed like a good idea back in 2011. I put in 25 years—a respectable career—as the Morning Show Host at KZRR-94 Rock. This book reflects not only fishing stories, but also some of the fun and games and debauchery from those years. But I knew it was time to leave. I spent over three of those years following the sun, travelling from beach to beach each year, Florida in the winter like a good aging Snowbird, then up to the Delaware shore during the summer months. I wrote the first edition of this book back then, and then spent time travelling from bookstore to bookstore, flyfishing shop to flyfishing shop, signing books, and doing things new authors do to sell their wares. It was a good retirement. I was successfully settling into the groove of it all, as life began to slow down and new activities not involving a daily grind began to fill up my days. I remember having to run to the Piggly Wiggly in Destin, Florida because I forgot to pick up some shrimp for dinner that night. I still had on my swim trunks and a bright green Pompano Joe's t-shirt on and my flip-flops, as I pulled into the parking lot and parked under a palm tree. I exited the car and the entirety of it hit me. I was doing EXACTLY what I wanted to do at the perfectly exact moment. Dressed in beach garb, sand and salt still on my beach body, getting out of my vehicle on a beautiful late spring day to pick up some shrimp just caught in one of the local bayous. I stopped, closed my eyes for a second, and took it all in, and smiled. This was what I worked for all those years. I had found my bliss in a fucking Piggly Wiggly parking lot. I guess it doesn't matter where it hits you. At least for that moment, I was IN the moment. Perfectly living in the present. And it was good. I went in to the store, bought my shrimp and another six pack of Corona and a lime, just in case, and went home, cracked open a beer, cleaned and skewered the shrimp and grilled them outside next to the pool, listening to the mockingbird perched on one of my house's gables sing me a song. I almost wept with gratitude. Then the conversation happened.

My wife: "You know, my parents have reached the point where they can't manage on their own anymore. We have to figure out what needs to be done."

Me: "Uhh. OK. What are your sisters in California doing?"

Wife: "You know they're both working and can't just drop everything and interrupt their careers right now."

Me: "So I guess that means it's up to us. Would they be willing to move down here?"

Wife: "Maybe a few years ago but they're too old for that now, to tear them away from their friends and their church."

Me: "Yeah but I just had this moment of existential enlightenment over at the Piggly Wiggly."

Wife: "What are you talking about?"

Me: "Never mind. We need to do the right thing. I guess we'll move back to-to-to-Ohio and take care of them."

Wife: "Are you sure?"

Me: "You got a better idea?"

So, in the fall of 2014, we sold the Florida house, moved to Hudson. Ohio and bought a nineteenth-century bungalow along with a snow shovel, and spent the next four years taking care of Pat and Zim (Weird name, I know, short for Zimmerman. Weird dude too. Long story, not book-worthy). Zim died first, and Pat lasted another year. Sadly, her dementia was so bad at the end, the real Pat had left us shortly after Zim's passing, leaving us with a sometimes lucid, but mostly not, mother of the woman I love. Pat died at the end of the year, and we spent a good part of the next year getting all their affairs in order. Then, almost all of a sudden, after four years of pretty much a full-time job which often times was 24-7...Nothing. Done with that. So now what? As I said, we sold Florida...in retrospect, dumb, so what's the next chapter? At about the same time, politics in the country was heating up to the point of lunacy. We all know what happened. Trump got elected, half the country freaked, the other half appointed him the second coming of Jesus Christ. And it was getting close to the campaign season...so I was getting antsy. The only outlet I had to express myself was Facebook, and that was proving stultifying and soul-killing. And then the phone rang. It was Jeff Berry, the general manager of Cumulus Media in Albuquerque.

"So, dude! What are you doing?"

"Nothing much."

"You want back in the game?"

"Maybe."

"You wanna talk about it?"

"Uhh...Let me go ask my wife."

So, after an actually not-so-lengthy discussion, she goes, "Look. You've spent the last several months screaming at the TV, so you may as well do it and get paid for it."

Done deal. We packed up the truck, put the cats in cages, and moved back to New Mexico. And which began my second radio career. In all honesty I was itching to get back on the air anyway, be it my huge ego, or something that happened to me in my early childhood while I was being toilet-trained. I guess that perfect beach moment of Zen was fleeting, and temporary. Fuck.

So here we are. In the beginning it was great, re-acquainting ourselves with old friends, adjusting again to the Southwest culture and food, and lack of a decent Jewish deli, and then finding out that talk radio required a crushing amount of prep time to do it right, unlike 94 Rock, where yeah, I did prep, but nothing like this. No music to use as a crutch when nothing else was going on. I found myself working several hours more a day, which left me little time to do a lot of other stuff, like fish for instance. When I did my old job, I'd keep my fly-fishing accoutrement in the back of the truck. I could get off the air at 10A, do a small amount of prep for the next day, and then drive up to the Jemez Mountains, or the Pecos River, and be on the stream with a fly in the water in about an hour. Or if I didn't have that much time, go down to the south catch-and-release lake at Tingley Beach in the city and play around for an hour or two.

But not now.

NOW...I'm working Afternoon Drive, meaning, 3-6 p.m. So instead of being done early, my entire day is filled with radio. Prep all morning and then on the air. Not complaining, but my fly-fishing lifestyle was altered when I took this job, to my dismay. I guess I didn't think to clearly about it when I accepted the gig.

And then Covid hit, and everything shut down. No more friends, no more going out, and sadly, the paltry amount of fishing I was able to get in also was diminished. You all know what I'm talking about. We all had to do our radio shows from home, and after about six months of that I started to hate my little home office. I have a large movie poster of "A River Runs Through It" on my office wall, and I'd find myself staring at Brad Pitt, standing on that damned rock, making the absolutely worst cast imaginable. Seriously. Look at the poster. That cast would have fallen in a heap right at his feet.

Then it kind of opened up. A little. So, we made a trip to the San Juan River, which was an almost dystopianly bizarre experience. We ate in our rooms, talked to no one, and there was apprehension about how open to be with the guide. Do we wear our masks in his truck on the way to the river? Yes. Do we wear our masks in the boat? Yes, and then fuck it. No. Do we shake hands? Nope. Fist bump. Do we have streamside lunch with the other guides and anglers at Betis Bend? Decided against that. The one good thing? The river on a weekend is usually like Wal-Mart after the unemployment checks come out. But in Covid, the river, although there WERE people fishing, was nothing like it usually is. And because of less pressure, fishing was fantastic.

Now as of this writing, and hopefully when you read this, everything is open. More opportunities have presented themselves and I've been back to the Juan a couple more times, fished the Rio Costilla above Taos, as well as the Rio Culebra, in southern Colorado, all with mixed results. Our friends Holly and Marcus, who you'll meet later in the book, just bought a delightful little riverfront cottage on the Los Pinos River above Durango, which I was fortunate enough to test the waters. Sadly, that weekend, the water was very warm and high for some reason, considering the drought conditions out here. It's a beautiful stream that enters above and exits below Vallecito Reservoir, and maybe the water was being released for irrigation downstream. Regardless, fishing was... mehhh. You've had those days. You try everything. Dries, nymphs, terrestrials, a shotgun, nothing really worked. There was a beautiful riffle directly in front of their house, which was about a hundred yards below a large, swiftly moving riffle where the river picked up speed and by the time it reached their property. The conditions, hypothetically, were perfect. Except for those two days. And as luck would have it, or stupidity, I blew it with the only large fish I hooked. Marcus was doing yard work, clearing brush from his property, watching me fish, mostly unsuccessfully. I would occasionally hook and land a dink, but that was it. Until I put a large yellow humpy on and cast into the faster water before it fell into the pool under their riffle. The take was instantaneous. The fish rolled and turned its belly upward and sideways, and I and saw the girth, and thought to myself," Holy shit! It's about time!" The fight was on. I knew it would be tough because it was in the fast-moving current, but I've successfully landed fish out of the same type of water before. It was a large brown, 20+ inches, and I was desperately trying to keep it out of the stronger current down below the house. At some point I thought it was beginning to tire, and I had the situation pretty much under control, so I turned back to Marcus and yelled, "Hey! Look at thi..." Of course, before I could finish the sentence, the line went limp. Gone. So, when something like that happens, I am not shy at expressing my displeasure, especially if it was my fault. I slammed the rod down onto the surface of the water and yelled "FUUUUUUUUUUUCK ME!" at the top of my lungs. This caused Holly and Marti to come running out of the house, thinking that something horrible happened, like I fell and broke my hip. Nope. Just me being an idiot. So, they went back in, brought out a bottle of wine, sat down on the Adirondack chairs and decided to start drinking and see if I might further entertain them with my sophomoric antics. The other thing was, Marcus didn't even hear me when I tried to make him aware that I was this big alpha-male mighty angler. He sauntered over and goes, "So what happened dude? Did I just miss something?" Yeah, I thought, you missed me missing a giant trout because I mistakenly tried to get your attention mid-battle.

Then, of course, I did the same thing I would imagine most of you have done a few times, immediately cast to the same spot where you just missed the big one, thinking for some reason that it'll come back and hit the same fly again, when in reality, that fish is hunkered down and won't even attempt to feed for some time. Plus, the fight caused so much commotion, that you scared every other fish in the area as well, so they're hunkered down too. After a few more casts...I walked over to the chairs, defeated, sat down, and started drinking.

*I stood there on the platform in the front of the boat,*
*my head down, awash again in complete and utter defeat.*

# 3 YOU REALLY NEED TO LEARN HOW TO DRINK

I AM AN ABOVE-AVERAGE FLYCASTER. I can read a stream with the best of them. I usually know what bugs to use, at least well enough to take a few fish each time I go out. In saltwater, I'm getting better at casting heavier equipment and slinging big wind-resistant flies. I am learning to "see" better into the water so when the guide is screaming "two o'clock, fifty feet, cast NOW," more times than not, I can actually find the fish I'm supposed to be casting at.

In New Mexico, I have guided many people. I have taught hundreds how to cast. I have participated in seminars and outdoor shows, but when the rubber meets the road, I will never be a "star" fly fisherman, because I have the mental stamina of a hedgehog.

Call it choking, call it too much adrenaline, call it too much caffeine. There have been far too many times when I've been out primarily in saltwater, that I literally lose control of my entire musculature and fall to pieces, collapsing in a twisted mess of fly line and lost dignity. At least, I keep control of my bowels.

To put a positive spin on it, I am a very intense fisherman. How can I describe it? I am very "visually" happy when I make the perfect cast, when I hook and catch the fish I was after. I will express my happiness vocally and with plenty of body language...not in a boastful way at least from my perspective, but I am quite joyful when things are going well. On the other hand, these outward demonstrations have their dark side, especially when things start going to hell. I am my own worst enemy when I let my emotions take over my brain, causing me at times to look like I have some mental or physical disability. My buddy Jer has fished with me for years and says that I am "Donald Duck with a fly rod." Visualize the old Disney cartoons, where Donald throws a temper tantrum. That's me and I can't argue with his assessment. All my fishing buddies including Bob, Mo, and Roger would agree. Mo, on the other hand, is the quietest, stealthiest fisherman I've ever known. There have been occasions where we have been fishing a high mountain stream and I haven't seen or heard from him in a long time. I have stopped fishing and spent an hour trying to find him, thinking he had broken his neck or was dragged off by a gang of prison escapees. I swear he just disappears like he has some kind of Harry Potter-esque invisibility cloak that he made in his garage. Then like magic, he just shows up. It's totally unnerving.

I, on the other hand, am very easy to find. You will hear me laughing, grunting, making exultations, swearing, grumbling, or even uttering incoherent almost Tourette's syndrome words and noises like some alcoholic flyfishing circus chimp. It all depends on how things are going. I could be around two bends in the river in heavy water, but you'll know where I am. God forbid that I get caught in a tree, or throw a giant monkey-fist into the wind, because when that happens, you don't want your kids around if you're trying to teach them the virtues of patience and not using profanity.

David, my saltwater guide/buddy, has probably seen the worst of it. Flyfishing on streams and rivers is one thing, but when the challenge gets tougher as it does with saltwater fishing, instead of confidently meeting it head-on with strong body and mind, I crumble.

The yips probably best describe it. My definition of the yips? The inability to perform well under pressure or adverse conditions especially when the payoff is big. And even worse, when you have an audience that is more than willing to watch you act like a spastic lunatic while trying to perform simple functions.

For instance, a couple of years ago David and I were on West Bay near Panama City, Florida looking for redfish. It was a pretty clear and calm day, no wind to really mess anything up. We were in his boat in less than two feet of water. David was at the back slowly poling us through the mud flats near the sea grass-lined shore looking for schooling or tailing reds. I was in the front on my platform, eight-weight in hand, trying my best to do the same. David told me to look about two hundred yards ahead of the boat at about 11 o'clock. I did, and saw a very large area of what appeared to be discolored water slowly making its way towards us. In hushed but excited tone, David said, "That is a HUGE school of redfish coming right at us. I want you to settle down, make sure you have enough line out and be ready to cast. We're gonna sit here and just wait for them to get to us. And when I tell you to cast, I want you to cast right in front of the school and start stripping in fast."

For most reasonable people, all this wouldn't be a problem. But for me, watching the school get nearer and nearer, it gave me time to think about it, not unlike the guys in the front line of Pickett's charge at Gettysburg. So, as I prepared for battle, my heart rate increased, my blood pressure rose, and my thought process got caught in some kind of neurotic loop, totally overthinking what I needed to do. Time slowed down to an inexorable crawl...the school was now a hundred yards away...two hundred feet...one hundred feet...I heard David saying, "Get ready to cast...get ready..."

Seventy-five feet...fifty feet...

"OK cast now!"

I started flailing like a hyperactive windmill, my rod almost touching the water behind me and I threw out a cast not even close to the school, maybe twenty feet out from the boat, landing in a giant depressing heap of fly line.

David's voice, louder this time with more insistence: "Cast again now! No false casts just get it out there!"

The adrenaline really began to take over. As I was shifting my

Saltwater guide David Mangum and me in front of his flats boat on the Florida panhandle. One of the few people who has seen me at my absolute worst while fly fishing. I'm surprised he agreed to have his picture taken with me!

weight back and forth between my feet, I picked up to cast and it was cut short because I was standing on my line.

Now David was getting really annoyed, shouting, "Goddam it! Pick up your line and cast again! You have one more shot!"

But this time, my line was tangled beneath me, all around my legs and as the biggest school of redfish I've ever seen serenely swam by our boat. I stood in the front, utterly humiliated and defeated.

You want another one? This happened in roughly the same place, maybe a year later. It was late April and we were again looking for tailing reds. As we backed the boat into the water, the bay was covered with a thick layer of fog. It was very warm for that time of year, and there was not even a suggestion of wind, making the entire scene kind of surreal. It looked like we were embarking onto a sea of glass. We headed out into the fog slowly, finally arriving near the flats area where we intended to fish. The fog had lifted some by then and the water had not even a hint of movement. As David poled us closer towards the shore, I swatted away one, then another, then another bug. In about a minute's time, the onslaught began. We started getting devoured by tiny biting bugs, "No-see-ums" as David called them. The night before, he said the bugs have been bad the last couple of days, so I had jeans on with a long-sleeved t-shirt, and brought along enough DEET to have us declared a superfund site. It didn't matter. They got under my shirt, up my pants leg, up my nose, and in my ears. As we crept along towards some tailing redfish we had no chance of even casting at them because every couple of seconds I devolved into bug-swatting contortions, trying to keep these little blood sucking freaks away from my face and eyes. Since it was so calm, every time I raised my hand to get rid of the bugs, the fish would spook and tear off into deeper water. Maybe David had more of a stoic, Zen way of dealing with these little bastards. I sure didn't.

Then it was late morning, the fog had lifted, and we started getting some wind, which blew the bugs away, but also put a chop on the water. Happy that we're no longer being eaten alive, we took off to find a place sheltered from the wind and hopefully find some more tailing redfish. We were about two-thirds of the way across the bay and a very large fish surfaced and rolled about a hundred feet in front and to the left of the boat. David said, "Holy shit, that's a tarpon! They're not supposed to be in this early!"

Immediately our mission changed. David's attention was completely riveted on finding one of these monsters I could cast at. He was really excited. "This is amazing and rare that they're in the bay now," he said. "Your eight-weight is not gonna be enough. I have my twelve-weight with me that you can use. If we get close enough to one, you're gonna have to put the fly in front of its nose so it can see it. If you do that, you'll be sure to get a strike!"

This was my first experience with adult tarpon. I'd caught baby tarpon on my eight-weight before, and it was a gas. The one's I've caught averaged from fifteen to twenty-five pounds, and it was almost like dry flyfishing for huge rainbow trout. When I was down in Belize, we'd pole the boat back into mangrove lagoons and look for them. When we'd see one, I would throw my fly close to them and start stripping back. Sometimes you wouldn't even need to strip it. It would be a big explosive strike, and then the battle was on. After countless acrobatic jumps the fight was over. This was a different game altogether though.

We crept into a large alcove somewhat protected from the wind. We were still out in open water, several hundred yards from the shore in maybe five feet of water. David turned off the motor and we sat in silence, watching and waiting. Sure enough, another one surfaced and rolled. Then another. There were definitely two, perhaps four tarpon close enough that we could hopefully get a decent shot at one of them. David handed me his 12-weight with a big tarpon fly tied on and said, "This is gonna be a pain in the ass to cast. Just do the best you can. I'll try to get us close enough to give you a good shot."

He didn't have to. From nowhere, a big tarpon surfaced less than thirty feet in front of the boat and rolled slowly in the water seductively, almost enticing us to cast at it. And then it just sat there, barely moving. David was flipping out. "This is great! I can't believe he's so close and not going anywhere! This never happens! Just take your time, think about what you have to do, and put the fly in front of its face. Now cast!"

Yeah, right. At that point a handful of Quaaludes wouldn't have taken the edge off. I was literally defecating in my shorts. My heart was racing and my palms were sweaty as I start hyper kinetically whipping the line back and forth, and at the worst possible moment, I let it fly. It sailed far to the right, hitting the fish on the side of the head. I even think it laughed at me as it turned tail and took off. I blew it. Badly.

David had had enough. "Do you know how rare that was? Do you realize you will probably never get another chance to cast at a tarpon that close? Seriously TJ, what the hell is wrong with you? You know how to cast...I've SEEN you cast! I've seen you catch fish! All you had to do was cast that fly twenty-five feet, maybe only twenty feet! You can't cast a fly twenty feet?"

I stood there on the platform in the front of the boat, my head down, awash again in complete and utter defeat, listening at length to David's indictment of my fishing ability, questioning whether or not I had the mental toughness to even fish for bluegills with a can of worms. What could I say? Every word he spat at me was true. I just stood there and took it. He'd had enough for the day, as I had. We rode back into town, attempting small talk, but in my mind I realized what a dork he thought I was at that moment. I can only imagine what he told his guide buddies after he dropped me off.

In retrospect, I've had good days too. David and I can now laugh at the stupid stuff. Well, at least I can laugh about it, but he has a point. The other day he asked me "Do you really want to know what your problem is?"

"I got plenty. Which one?"

"See? Even what you just said! You are way too hard on yourself. You make a bad cast and then you beat yourself up about it, and then it gets worse and worse. I mean, everybody gets pissed at themselves, but you would think you just backed your truck over a bagful of puppies

or something. You gotta let it go, man!"

"Is it that bad?"

"No, it's worse than that... I think you need to take a Xanax before the next time we go fishing!"

My buddy Jer needs to meet David. Maybe someday it'll happen. I told him this story, and he said, "Xanax! That's funny! How many times have I told you that you really need to learn how to drink?"

Yeah, I think we all need to go fishing together.

Can you believe it? I surprisingly got my act together enough to catch this redfish while fishing in West Bay.

# 4 THE SEA WAS ANGRY THAT DAY, MY FRIENDS

*A note to all of you…If something happens and all
your guide can do is yell "Fuck!" repeatedly,
you know you're in trouble.*

THINGS HAPPEN AND THEN THINGS HAPPEN THAT really mess you up, at least temporarily. Years ago, former president Clinton was in Air Force One when the plane hit a pocket of something or other, and it plummeted several thousand feet before the pilot regained control and righted it. I remember Clinton calling it a "character-building experience." After what happened to me and my fishing guide on a rough and windy afternoon off the coast of Marblehead, Massachusetts in August of 2001, I knew exactly what he meant.

Being the host of a successful rock morning show had its perks. It used to have more perks before the FCC and Clear Channel clamped down on what you could and couldn't take advantage of. Right or wrong, people like me are offered many "ups and extras" like trips, food, clothing, vehicles, drugs, women, barnyard animals, you name it. Some we were allowed to accept if we can show there is benefit to our on-air performance, or if we legally and officially agree to promote an advertiser's product and not be secretive about it. For instance, I could've held my head up high and forthrightly accepted a new boat from Jaxon's Marine IF I told everyone on the air that I took it in exchange for doing their commercials for them. But if I sneaked around and did it on the down-low, I'd go to prison.

Beer companies know how to play this game. They are huge advertisers on rock stations, and know what it takes to legally promote their product and make all the people like me happy without breaking the law. I was fortunate enough to get to know Jim Koch, owner of Samuel Adams in Boston. I'm sure you know Jim by his radio ads: "I'm Jim Koch, owner of Samuel Adams/" And I'm sure you've seen him many times on TV as his own pitchman. Jim used to love radio, until an incident a few years back. He was in the studio with two jerk-off DJs in New York city on the day they got in trouble for getting a couple to have sex on the air, on their show, that morning, in the balcony of St. Patrick's Cathedral, resulting in public outrage and an advertising boycott. Jim had nothing to do with this, he just happened to be in the wrong place at the wrong time, and he has personally shied away from having an intimate relationship with radio ever since. Bummer. Because for several years before that, he'd invite fifteen or so of his favorite radio shows out to Boston to do a two-day broadcast, and luckily, I got invited each year. He'd set us up in the courtyard of the brewery under a huge tent and he'd line up a bunch of movie and TV stars, musicians, and various weirdos who would walk from show to show talking with all of us. We'd talk with the likes of Matt Damon, Ben Affleck, Gene Simmons, and Mark Wahlberg. They brought in Johnny Knoxville from "Jackass," comedians I don't remember, adult film stars, and a George W. Bush impersonator who was actually very good. Then Samuel Adams head brew master Walter Schuerle would make the rounds and talk about the love of his life, which would be brewing beer.

Walter is a stout German guy now in his seventies, with thinning white hair and a white beard and he speaks with a thick German accent. He looks kind of like a cross between a fatter Ernest Hemingway and a drunken Teutonic elf. I was fortunate (or unfortunate) to have seen him once, dressed in his own personal lederhosen. How many people outside of Bavaria or maybe Milwaukee have a pair of their own? And to top it off, I am still amazed at how much beer Walter and Jim, for that matter, could put away and still remain coherent.

Walter is actually a shy man. Late in his career, Samuel Adams sent him around the country as their goodwill ambassador, and we'd have him on the air once, maybe twice a year. But he was scared to death of going on the radio, so he would sit in the parking lot and slam a six pack or two at 8am, to give him the courage to talk with us. After that, all was good with the world.

Walter is also a genius. He worked at Sandia National Labs in Albuquerque as an engineer, but his love of beer making brought him and Jim together, and together they made history and a lot of money. But he is most notorious for blowing his garage to smithereens. He was distilling a private batch of schnapps, like 190 proof schnapps in his homemade still. Something went wrong and he nearly took out the entire block. He never told me if he was arrested.

The last I heard he was living in Cozumel, deep sea fishing and enjoying himself. This has absolutely nothing to do with the story I'm about to tell you. I just like Walter and wanted him to be in this book.

Anyway...

Samuel Adams would provide everything; free beer, great dinners, and posh hotel accommodations. An odd twist to this story: This all occurred in late August of 2001, which was less than two weeks before 9-11 happened. In a chilling coincidence, a few of us stayed at the same hotel at the same time where the Boston-to-New York terrorists were staying. And weirdly, I remember the cable TV in this hotel ran an Arab-language TV station and I watched it out of curiosity, not being able to understand a word they were saying. Others in our group saw it too, and we laughed about it. I think about this every once and a while, and it still gives me creeps. It was not unlikely that we walked by these jerks in the hall, obviously not knowing what was about to happen.

For three nights, there was all this wild partying and debauchery going on, and what am I doing? I want to go fishing, so I am trying to find a fishing guide who will take me out for stripers. Not the kind of stripers that are transplanted into western tail waters that die as soon as you reel them in. I wanted to catch real stripers that earn their living near the craggy shores of New England; stripers that are strong and fast because something bigger and stronger and faster wants to eat them. I did some on-line research and finally found a guy based out of Marblehead, Massachusetts who could take me on Saturday morning, after all my broadcast obligations had been met. And by the way, he will remain nameless. You will understand why later on.

It was Friday morning and I was very excited about the next day's adventure. Apparently, they saved the best radio guests for last weekday, as we had Matt Damon, Mark Wahlberg, Gene Simmons from rock band KISS, as well as a charming assortment of weirdoes and pornstars, including Tera Patrick, who was tall, leggy, had long jet black hair and had that nasty porn-star allure. Plus, she smelled great. Her bodyguard, who happened to be her husband, was a very large, tattooed monster of a brute that could have pounded me into a fine organic soup if he chose to. That said, she was charming, engaging, and smart, on and off the air. We actually seemed to be getting along, and when I mentioned to someone about my upcoming flyfishing plans for the next morning she said, "Hey! I fly fish!"

"You do? How did you get into it?"

"Well, I grew up in Montana and everyone I knew fly fished so it seemed like the natural thing to do..."

"So where have you fished?"

We got into a conversation about some of the places we've both fished, and in the back of my mind I'm thinking, "Should I? Should I actually ask her to go with me tomorrow? I mean we get along, and she talks like she's not bullshitting about flyfishing, and I know her husband is right there, and she is a more attractive woman than I would EVER in my life normally have any chance with, and I'd be totally intimidated, yet she almost seems like she WANTS me to ask...But again, her husband is standing right there next to her, and he could break my neck just by looking at me, but then lots of these porn stars have "alternative" lifestyles where the husband really doesn't care what his wife does...Oh what the hell...You only live once and he could come too, not that I'd have any choice in the matter...And bottom line, it's just a fishing trip, and I love my wife so nothing's gonna happen anyway!"

So, the mics went on and we're live on the air, so I brought up what I'm doing the next day and say, "Tera, we were just talking off the air about flyfishing and how you love to do it, so why don't you come with me tomorrow?"

She hesitated for a moment, smiles and says, "Sure, why not?"

"I'm serious! This wasn't just an on-air thing. Do you mean it?"

"I WANT to go. What time do we need to leave?"

"Early...Probably have to meet 4:30AM in my hotel lobby."

"I guess I'll just have to stay up all night...I'll be there!"

So we went into a commercial break, and again, I asked her, "OK, we're off the air now. Do you still want to go?"

"I do! Let me make sure I don't have a conflict."

At this point, I was nearly crapping myself, thinking Tera Patrick is going fishing with me tomorrow! "Let's see. I gotta call the guide and let him know they'll be one more person (two if her husband comes), so he'll need to get her equipment..."

The show had ended so I left our table and ran inside to take a leak while Tera consulted with her husband. When I returned, she and my newsperson, Erica, were ending up a conversation. As I walked up, Tera said, "Bad news, sorry. We have to catch a flight at Logan late morning tomorrow so I can't make it, but I really wanted to. Thanks for asking me." I say it's fine, she gives me a hug, and she and her husband walked off to do whatever porn-stars and their spouses do at 10:30 AM.

I'm not going to say I was crushed, but I was pretty bummed out. Erica walked up to me and says, "Don't feel too bad. We were talking, and she really DID want to go with you, but she couldn't."

"Yeah, it's OK...Would've been fun, though..."

"Although I should tell you, as soon as you walked away, she came up to me and said, 'TJ IS gay, isn't he?'"

"WHAT? She thought I was gay?"

"Yeah buddy, she did...Sorry, man!"

Now THAT hurt! Talk about being completely emasculated...After having a good conversation with her...feeling there was at least an intellectual connection, and at least considering the idea, however farfetched, that there might have even been a slight physical connection... Wrong. She didn't even think I played for her team! NOW I'm totally bummed. A beautiful porn-star that fly fishes didn't think I had a molecule of straightness inside my now shrunken and pulled up-inside testicles.

OK. I had to look at the bright side. Nothing really changed in the past hour. It was still Friday, and I was still going fishing for stripers on Saturday. A little emotional setback but I'm an adult. I can take it-- always look on the bright side of life!

All I had to do is get myself to Marblehead. Friday night, I had a rental car delivered to the hotel, and while everyone else is out partying and drinking and doing unspeakable things to each other, I ordered room service and was in bed by 9PM, so I can make my 6AM date with "my guide."

The next morning, I left before sunrise after getting explicit instructions on how to navigate the macaroni twists and turns of Boston's ancient streets and successfully got out onto the highway. Once I'm out of the city limits, I stopped at a Dunkin' Donuts for a cup of coffee and continued on. If you're not from Boston, you don't realize what a big deal Dunkin' is out there. Boston was its birthplace, and it's held in the same high regard as things like Paul Revere and Ted Williams' frozen severed head. Caffeinated up, I got back on the highway and continued on northward, passing through Salem, and finally reaching Marblehead.

Marblehead is what you would expect from a coastal New England town. It's historical, charming, and gentrified because of its close proximity to Boston. Marblehead's history began when it broke free of Salem and became its own town in 1684. Life there revolved around the sea and it became a major commercial fishery. It also holds the hotly disputed title of being the birthplace of the American navy. Today, sailboats dot the harbor and it's now known as the yachting capital of the world. The centuries-old waterfront retains the history and charm of its past, inhabited by plenty of eighteenth- century buildings, some of which are still residences; others have been transformed into restaurants and gift shops. Farther up and down the coastline was where the million-dollar houses were, the retreats built by Boston's rich folk. I parked in a space near a harbor-front restaurant and met "my guide," and we walked down to his Boston Whaler as the local gulls screamed at us, demanding an early breakfast.

It's already windy, but a very warm morning. There was a chop off the coast, so we motored inward a bit and started fishing where a power plant released its warm water into the bay. It's not the most scenic place in Marblehead, but the fish didn't seem to mind the heavy industry surrounding them. In fact, they were thrilled with the delightful bath water-like outflow. And since we've never fished together before, I think my guide liked to take his newbies there first to see how well they performed. I put on a lime green and white Clouser minnow, and with a sinking line on my eight-weight, started casting towards the rocky outcroppings on shore. I got a strike but not a striper. I hooked and landed a decent bluefish. Then a bigger strike and a bigger bluefish. A third strike, and this time another blue bites through the line and is gone. I've caught bluefish for years surf-fishing off Delaware beaches and the first thing you notice is they do indeed have a row of sharp teeth with the propensity not only to shred your line, but your fingers as well. So, the two questions I had for my guide were, why no wire leaders, and where are the stripers? First, he claimed wire leaders scare the fish, so instead he ties on hard to bite through, heavy monofilament which still occasionally gets shredded. And secondly, the blues like to swim with the stripers, so be patient. I didn't have to be too patient because my next strike is my first of several stripers.

It was clouding up, and the wind was not abating. The sky was a low slate gray threatening to rain, but for some reason, it didn't. Since the fish seemed to be biting, he decided we should venture out into open waters despite the heavy chop, so we did cautiously. We passed out of the harbor and are met with three-foot swells. Not too bad, but now not only did you have to cast well with a sinking line and bigger equipment, you also had to do it while keeping your balance and not falling overboard. I was game. His technique was interesting, logical, and potentially dangerous. Marblehead's and much of New England's coast was lined with sharp, jagged, ancient rocks, which is precisely where the stripers liked to hang out. So, our goal was to get as close to these rocks as possible without smashing into them. Making this difficult is the line of breaking waves that constantly pummeled the shore. My guide crept up as close as he could get on the outside of the break line and kept the motor running in the opposite direction so in essence, we were stationary in the water, directly behind the breaking waves. While he was doing this, it was my job to cast into the rocks, let my fly sink and then strip like hell back towards the boat, all while keeping my balance in less than perfect conditions. It must be working because I immediately got a strike and landed maybe an eight-pound striper. And they keep coming. I hooked another and as it gets close to the boat, I saw a large shadow beneath it, thinking it's a small shark interested in a meal. Turned out it was about a 30-pound bluefish with eyes on my hooked striper. We landed the six-pounder intact and toss him back in.

At this point the seas are getting heavier and we debated whether or not to call it a day. He had one more place he wanted to try and then we'd head for the harbor. It was a tiny jagged island, no bigger than fifty

View from the peninsula, showing the treacherous rocks of Marblehead. These could have been my demise!

feet across and maybe six feet above the crashing surf. It sat a hundred yards off the mainland, which, like the rest of the coast, is also a wall of craggy rocks. Beyond the rocks, a modest house was perched up on the shore, from where a path led down to a small beach. On a clear sunny, calm day, it would be something Thomas Kincaid might have over painted, but today, not so much. Any blue that was left in the water had turned to a dark soot gray, matching the sky.

Our plan was the same. With the motor running, he held the boat on the outside of the break line while I casted in towards the island. It was not getting any easier to cast. The wind was increasing, and the waves appeared to be getting larger. One cast, and then another, then out of the cacophony of noise, I noticed something is missing.

The roar of the motor.

In rough surf, just on the other side of the breakers, in front of a small rocky island, we had no power. Cursing repeatedly, the guide frantically tried to start the motor over and over. It was too late. A large wave hit us broadside, and we lurched beyond the break line into the rocks, knocking me off my seat onto the bottom of the boat. I managed to right myself just as another wave smashed into us, this time throwing the entire boat on top of the small patch of jagged rocks. We were almost completely on top. The bow of the boat had turned around and was facing the incoming waves at a downward pitch. My guide was yelling "Fuck! Fuck!" over and over again.

A note to all of you... If something happens on the water and all the guide can do is yell "Fuck!" repeatedly, you know you're in trouble.

I waited for words of assurance, but none came, just fear tinged with near panic. Stupidly, neither of us was wearing our life jackets, so he barked at me to get them. They were stowed in the compartment in the front of the boat, so I crawled on my hands and knees while we were being repeatedly hit with big waves, retrieved them and returned to my seat in the middle of the boat.

While all of this was happening, a man and a woman came running out of the house on shore and we started waving our arms and shouting for them to call the Coast Guard. There is no way they could have heard us over the crashing surf, but somehow, they got the idea and the woman ran back up to the house.

Sitting there, I looked to the shore where the breakers behind the island are just as ferocious, and contemplated the odds of survival if we jumped into the water and tried to swim to shore. I asked the guide if this would be a wise choice and he goes "Fuck no! We're gonna sit here and wait for the Coast Guard. We have a better chance of getting out of this if we stay with the boat." I figured he knew what he was talking about, at least I hoped he did, so we sat and waited while being battered by the waves.

Remember the death scene in "The Perfect Storm" when the boat finally gets creamed by that giant wave? Off in the distance I noticed that something didn't look right. The level of the ocean on the horizon seemed to have risen. Rolling towards us was a mountain of a wave, considerably larger than what we were being hit with. There is absolutely no way we are not going to be slammed by this. We looked at each other and my guide said very solemnly, "Look, I don't know how this is gonna turn out. We're gonna be hit hard, so what I want you to do is hold on as tight as you can and try your best to stay with the boat."

They say when you're facing your own demise, your life flashes before your eyes. In my case, my mind was almost totally blank. Instinct took over, and I thought of nothing other than survival. Everything was happening in slow motion, and there was an extreme clarity to it. It was probably the only time in my life that I was living completely in the present. At least I had the dignity not to—you know, crap in my pants.

The wave was huge, comparatively speaking. We watched in silence as the water pulled back from the island and the crest began to form over our heads. With a deafening explosive roar, it crashed into us and under us, lifting the boat high into the air and for a moment it was like we were flying. I am not normally a man who believes in miracles, but for some reason, the boat did not list, or tumble, or roll, or break in two, or go end-over-end. We were propelled backward off the island, landing upright in the water about fifty feet beyond it. We sat there in stunned silence for a minute or so, then looked each other directly in the eye, and just like Roy Scheider and Richard Dreyfuss in the last scene of "Jaws," and we started to laugh. We were safe. Not even dead. The boat seemed to have suffered little or no damage and when he tried the engine, it started right up.

Shaken but alive, we began heading back to Marblehead, our spirits buoyed by the fact that are lungs were not filled with sea water. But our journey was not done yet. Apparently, the Coast Guard got the call from the people on shore. Their boat raced towards us and signaled for us to stop. They pulled up aside and asked how we were, if the boat was OK, and then asked the guide what had happened. He explained his strategy for striper fishing, told them about the motor stalling, and the guy in charge had heard enough.

"You know, I should pull your license right now! What the hell do you think you were doing? Do you realize you almost died out there? Only an idiot would have done what you did, especially in rough seas like this. Now we're gonna escort you back into the harbor and after you drop your client off, you're coming with me and we're gonna file a report. You have a lot of explaining to do!"

My guide took it all in, interjecting an occasional "Yes sir" or "No sir," and with a Coast Guard escort, we made it back into the harbor. We unloaded my stuff onto the dock and my guide was walking away when I told him to wait, and I handed him what I owed him for the trip, along with a generous tip. He looked at me confused and said, "After all that, I wasn't expecting anything, but thank you."

I said "Hey, we survived, and you gave me a story I'll be telling to the day I die, and the sad thing is, most people won't believe it!"

We actually hugged, said goodbye, and I haven't seen or heard from him since. I hope he didn't end up in some roach infested Coast Guard brig.

I walked back to my rental car, and it was not until I was behind the wheel and belted that I realized I was shaking. It occurred to me I hadn't had anything to eat since 5am, but I figured I could make it back to the hotel and have a beer and a sandwich or a bowl of chowder or something that people in Boston eat. Of course, I missed my exit and became hopelessly lost. I knew I was somewhere near Harvard, which meant nothing to me. Most cities are laid out in a logical grid or something reasonably understandable, so if you do get lost, you probably stood a decent chance of winging it. Not Boston. Freaking out, I called my Boston friend Suzie, who also wanted to be in this book, (There you go) and she stayed on the phone and talked me back to my destination. Hungry and exhausted, I went to the hotel restaurant and had some late lunch, and then I went back to my room, lay down and actually slept through the night, dreaming the dreams of someone who just dodged a major bullet, thus ending one of the more memorable days of my life.

# 5 HOME WATERS...WELL, KIND OF

*I was geeked...giddy like a little school girl over this.*
*There were trophy trout swimming around in a lake we*
*created, less than ten minutes from the radio station.*

I NOW LIVE ACROSS THE STREET FROM A BEACH where I can pretty much fish anytime I like, weather permitting, which makes me think how incredibly stupid I was in New Mexico that I didn't try to move somewhere that was near or on a river. Twenty-five years and I never pulled the trigger. So, I did the next best thing.

Holly Casman is the manager of the Albuquerque Aquarium, which is part of the city's bio park system, also including the zoo, the botanical gardens, and Tingley Lakes, with a little train connecting them all. Tingley Beach was an area created by the city decades ago as a swimming and fishing area for residents, located pretty much in the city center. It sits next to the Rio Grande bosque where the aquifer is close to the surface. They formed a small narrow lake by pumping the water out of the ground at one end and having it drain back into the river at the other end.

When I moved to town in 1986, Tingley Beach was a couple of steps above a septic tank. Previous administrations had let it deteriorate to the point where it looked like a large overgrown sewer. Those of you who are long-time residents of Albuquerque remember that in my first TV commercial to promote my radio show, I rose out of Tingley with a fishing lure in my mouth, playing up on my last name. What you all don't know is after we shot that scene, I had to put these bacteria-killing drops in my ears and immediately took a hot shower, using disinfectant soap. The water was gross, and that same year, the city decided to do something about it, hatching its plan to totally re-do the lakes, as well as build the Aquarium that Holly now manages. The plan devised by the city and the Army Corps of Engineers was to make a series of small lakes draining into each other, continuing to use the natural aquifer as their water source. The project began in 2004 and the new lakes opened in 2005. Luckily, the water coming out of the ground was a constant 50 degrees, perfect trout water, and Holly and fellow aquarium employee Joe Martinelli realized this and came up with the idea to make the southernmost pond a trophy catch-and-release lake for fly fishermen. Holly then contacted Bob Gerding and me with the idea, and we both approached then Mayor Marty Chavez. Being a fly fisherman too, the mayor enthusiastically agreed, naming me and Bob the official two-man Citizen's Task Force, and the planning began.

Bob and I take absolutely no credit for the science and nuts and bolts of turning the idea into reality. The hard work and subsequent credit goes to Holly, Joe, and her crew. How deep should it be? What should the lakeshore look like? What type of vegetation should be planted? And then, should we charge people to fish? Should there be a fly shop? Should there be seminars? How about fishing lessons? How about bathrooms? This was a really cool endeavor, almost godlike in a sense, creating a work of nature from scratch.

Ultimately, the Tingley Lakes project was a smashing success. Our trophy lake was the upper one in elevation, draining into the meat (catch and keep) lake, draining into a kid's fishing lake, draining into a model boat lake. The swimming lake was last and has yet to be completed. But the city turned an eyesore into a real jewel, and congrats to them for having the foresight and the balls to do it.

I was geeked...giddy like a little school girl over this. There were trophy trout swimming around in a lake we created, less than ten minutes from the radio station. I started taking my fly rod to work with me, and more often than not, I'd be down there for sure once a week, sometimes more depending on the bullshit that was going on at Clear Channel.

Then, a few problems started to surface. The lakes were in an economically challenged neighborhood, and before the transformation, Tingley Beach was a prime area to do business if you dug the meth. In fact, several of the scenes from "Breaking Bad" were filmed in the neighborhoods adjacent to the lakes. And right after it opened, apparently the drug users and dealers didn't get the word that they were no longer welcome. So, the citizen task force called a meeting with the mayor and told him if he wanted his project to be a success, he'd have to get these low-lifes outta the park. Arrests followed, along with strong suggestions by the cops that it would be wiser for them to take their business elsewhere. It was an immediate turn-around, restoring my faith in good over evil. One problem solved. The other two were not as easy.

The next task was to educate the public about catch and release, letting them know they could only use single barbless hooks, no live bait, and no artificial worms--period. Then we needed to teach the unknowing and ignorant how to properly release a hooked trout without dragging it through the dirt and killing it. Volunteers were found, seminars were held, and signs were put up, explicitly explaining the rules, along with pictographs on how to release a trout. Initially, the results were not pretty. It was a long, slow learning curve and a lot of fish were needlessly killed. Lots of people just didn't get the concept of catch and release. Some were even militant about it, and it didn't matter what argument you used with some of these mental midgets. First, I usually tried the most rational I could think of, being money. I explained that these fish, especially the larger ones were very expensive, and if people kept taking them, we wouldn't be able to have the lake anymore.

Didn't work.

"It's stupid! Fish are for catchin' and eatin'!"

"Sure. But do you realize that lots of people derive pleasure from hooking a big trout, fighting the fish, winning the fight, and then gently releasing it back to fight another day?"

"Why would you let go a big fish like that?"

"Look pal, it's not like the fish naturally reproduced in that lake, fought adversity, became the alpha fish in its home water, became wise and crafty, and then you, being the skillful master angler, tricked this veteran fish who has seen it all, into biting your power bait. No, this fish was in a hatchery as little as a week ago and was put in an artificial environment and has none of those qualities that I just described. And keeping that fish does not make you more of a man. In fact, in my eyes, your macho bravado would be diminished. In other words, if you keep one of these fish, you have a very tiny penis."

I never really said that to anyone.

And for some reason, a lot of these morons thought that once you put the fish in the lake, they just magically start to reproduce.

"You know, you're absolutely right! In fact, every time you catch one, another one just pops into existence because of the high tech inter-dimensional replicator that the city put at the bottom of the lake. Each fish has a computer chip implanted beneath its skin, and as soon as the chip senses the fish is out of water... Bang! Another one just materializes, just like Captain Picard on "Star Trek the Next Generation" ordering a cup of "Earl Grey tea, hot."

I didn't ever say that either.

Actually, the first couple of months were great. But as time went on we all began to notice that there were fewer and fewer fish. Then we started discovering illegal equipment hidden in the bushes. Even trotlines were found. Apparently, the neighborhood had figured out what was going on and they were coming down after the park was closed and poaching the crap out of the lake.

What do you do about this? In these challenging economic times, the city had no money to hire a security force to hang out at the lake 24 hours a day when roads had to be repaired and real crime had to be fought. Plus, who was really willing to confront some of these idiots and

Stocking the "magic trout" at Tingley Lakes.

literally risk their lives over a poached fish? The daytime security did their best to catch and verbally punish offenders, occasionally throwing someone out, and nothing was really done to solve the problem. The mayor figured he'd just quietly re-stock, and since I was the media guy, the 94 Rock Morning Show would hold an annual fundraising event down at the park to fund the stocking.

I had some ideas that were not exactly taken seriously:

—Put up hunting stands in the nearby river bosque and have volunteer snipers blast to hell anyone they saw poaching our precious lake.

—Put a sign at the lake saying that each trout had been treated with some kind of lice-killing chemical that made them not only inedible, but deadly poisonous.

—Make a deal with McDonald's and install a couple of free fillet 'o fish coupon dispensers on the lake. Have a sign that said, "Please don't poach our lake. But if you're really hungry and need to take one of our fish to feed you and your wife and kids and your extended family and neighborhood, please take one of these coupons instead, courtesy of McDonald's and the city of Albuquerque."

I actually thought the last idea was a pretty good one! The potential perpetrator does the right thing and gets fed in the process, the city gets credit for an innovative idea, and McDonald's gets kudos for feeding the hungry. Apparently, I was the only one who considered this brilliant. The thinking was, someone would end up stealing all of the coupons, then the dispensers would be torn out and sold for scrap metal, and after all that, the lake would continue to be poached.

Don't get me wrong. The lake was a great idea, still is, and is enjoyed by many law-abiding citizens. And as time went on, it was very interesting to see a man-made lake start to turn into something resembling a natural body of water. In the beginning it was pretty much an artificial PVC-lined pond. But then, lake vegetation showed up, and the flora planted around the lake started to mature. Then the bugs showed up, and there were actually hatches coming off our little lake! But as with all heavily fished areas, another phenomenon occurred; the fish began to get smart and very picky. When the fish were first stocked and after a period of adjustment when they weren't all freaked out, they'd just about bite at anything. But after a few weeks of being bombarded by every fly imaginable, they really started to have a discerning appetite. And to make matters even trickier, the Albuquerque Biopark would feed them fish pellets a couple times a week, so the plan was to get to the lake before their feeding.

But then, people started tying their own "pellet flies" which actually worked pretty well. When you think about it, how different is that than matching the hatch on the San Juan or the Madison? Personally, I couldn't bring myself to fish with one. It just seemed...wrong. But I ended up catching most of my fish on a beetle pattern which looked a whole lot like a kibble of fish chow, so who was I kidding?

# 6 SANTA FE RADIO AND THE PECOS

*We would make it back to the hotel, where our promotion*
*director and her boyfriend always had some chronic weed,*
*and anyone who was still conscious after that*
*would end up in the hotel's hot tub...*

OK, SO MAYBE THE PECOS RIVER COULD BE considered
Albuquerque's home water too, but it's more like Santa Fe's, which
lies about a half hour to the west of the Pecos. I like Santa Fe. The first
time I saw it was back in 1982 on a cross-country trip I was taking with
my brother and my wife (that's two people, not one. What the hell do you
think this is, some kind of hillbilly reality show?) Up until then, none of
us had ever been west of the Mississippi, and it seemed like some exotic
foreign land with strange mud buildings and spicy food and Indians.
One of the first things I noticed was the fragrant smell of the air after
a thunderstorm, full of sage and native essence. I remember driving
into Santa Fe and it not looking real. It looked like a Disney movie set
of what a New Mexican town should look like, with all its adobe and
narrow streets. I remember going to a restaurant and ordering a bowl of
chile (chili, I thought), expecting what you might get in Ohio, and being
a flatlander with flatlander taste buds, it nearly blew the top of my head
off. Of course, after living in New Mexico for 25 years, I've acquired a
taste for the local cuisine. In fact, before I sat down to write this chapter
here in Delaware on a mild but windy September afternoon, I got off
the phone with my friend Cindy Hernandez who is shipping me two
boxes of hot unroasted New Mexican green chile. This proves that you
can move out of New Mexico, but you can't move New Mexico out of
you. It's true.

Every year, usually in late August or early September, we would
do the 94 Rock Morning Show from the plaza in Santa Fe, always on a
Friday. And every year it would turn out to be one of the biggest parties
of the year, until my entire staff stopped drinking, but that's another

story. This would require an overnight stay on Thursday night, so we'd get a client to sponsor the trip, meaning, every time we opened a microphone we'd say, "We're being brought to you by Big Bob's House of Swill. We eat there every day and we love it!" Or something like that. But the thing was, we would stay at the best hotels, eat the best food, drink the best tequila, and didn't have to pay a stinking penny. It was all comped by Big Bob, and he dug it because he was a fan, and he got to hang with us and eat dinner with the team, and we'd have him on the air the next morning and kiss his ass from every angle. We'd bring the morning show crew, plus anywhere from six to eight support people, including two strippers from a local Albuquerque titty bar who I called the "Troutettes." They'd wear cut-off 94 Rock t-shirts and booty shorts, and would mingle with the mostly male crowd and make everyone happy while we were on stage on the bandstand doing the show.

How we ever got that show done was a miracle. I am normally a pretty boring dude. As I related earlier, I go to bed early, get up early, get to work early, and have a disciplined work ethic. Not in Santa Fe. It was one of maybe two times a year when all that good student bullshit was thrown into the dumpster and a good time was to be had at all costs. The other was our annual ski trips, which under penalty of murder, I will not write about.

The evening would start at the hotel bar. Then it would move to the restaurant for the meal that involved fine bottles of wine, or more libations for those who didn't like the grape. Then it was back to the bar in the lobby or out into town for more serious debauchery. We would make it back to the hotel where our promotion director and her boyfriend always had some chronic weed, and anyone who was still conscious after all that would end up in the hotel's hot tub, where more than once we deservedly got thrown out for making too much noise.

In my life, I've been thrown-up on three times. Once was at a carnival when I was sixteen with a new girlfriend. We'd just gotten off the tilt-a-whirl and it projected out of her pretty lips onto my shirt. Next was at a radio promotion and the salesperson whose account it was bought us both shots of Jack to celebrate the great night. He downed his and it came right back up all over my new Chuck Taylors. The third time was a "Troutette" in Santa Fe. I forget the name of the bar, but after being illegally over-served, we walked back to the hotel through the crisp early fall 7000-foot elevated air. We made it to the hotel lobby and with her big bleary stripper eyes, she looked up at me and said, "TJ,

I don't feel so good." I swear to you, I have never seen anyone, male or female, dog or cat, hurl out the volume that she did that night. All over the saltillo tile floor, onto the wall, and unfortunately, onto me. It was certainly not a "happy ending to the night. Amazingly the next morning she was as bright and chipper as ever.

Two hours sleep and it was time to work. Amazingly, these were always some of the best shows we'd do (at least we thought so), which lends itself to the question, "Well why didn't you just do that all the time?" The answer? Because we'd all be dead. Believe me, some of the staff tried and I guarantee you it doesn't work.

Of course, the other reason I liked to do the Santa Fe show was its close proximity to the Pecos River. After we were done and packed up and all the necessary good-byes were said, I'd get in the truck and head east for about 30 minutes into the tiny town of Pecos, New Mexico, which sits at the southernmost tip of the Sangre de Cristo, or Blood of Christ mountains. The Sangre de Cristos are a huge mountain chain... one might say they're the backbone of the Rockies with several "fourteen-ers," peaks over 14,000 feet, when you get up into Colorado. The Pecos drains the ass-end of the chain, travelling southeast through New Mexico, passing through Carlsbad as a much larger river, and eventually emptying into the Rio Grande and the Gulf of Mexico. But above and through the town of Pecos, it is a beautiful small freestone stream flowing through deep pine tree lined canyons and grassy meadows, supporting a healthy population of native brown trout. There are stocker rainbows as well, and some of the private landowners stock their own larger trout, which may or may not stay on the property. Most of the fish are smallish, but on any given day, browns of 15 inches or more can be caught.

But here's the problem. A lot, and I mean a lot of the land on either side of the river is private, and unfortunately it contains some of the best and accessible water on the river. So needless to say, public access is limited to several heavily stocked but even more heavily fished areas. And forget about the catch and release areas. What you need to do is go during the week and take your chances, or, you need to buddy up with one of the private landowners, which is the path I took.

I was fortunate enough to become friends with a certain prominent Albuquerque businessman, whose family has been successful in their chosen field for decades. Let's call him "Igor." Igor's family owns a sweet piece of property in the Pecos area. And no, I absolutely will

NOT divulge the location. They have about a half-mile of the river running directly through it, with a gentlemen's agreement to fish the guy's ranch below theirs. It's enough water to keep you busy for an entire day. The water has always been good with lots of small but native browns making it their home. It's one of those places you go when size doesn't matter. His land is more easily fished than a lot of the Pecos, less vertical, with the river running through meadows and rolling hills instead of the heavily forested steep canyons that the Pecos is famous for. His stretch of the river is very forgiving, with gentle riffles, deeper pools, and one particularly swimming-pool sized really deep run with a picture- perfect riffle feeding it. Of course, this particular pool has an insanely tricky current, making it almost impossible to get a good drift, but providing the perfect home for some of the river's largest trout.

It was the perfect late summer-early fall day in 2009, sunny with temperatures in the 70's. After another successful Santa Fe show, I made the drive to the Pecos and I had great success. Easily a thirty fish afternoon, maybe more. It was time to go home and I was parked near Igor's big pool and I thought, "What the hell, I have to leave in ten minutes, but let's try and coax one of those big ones to strike." I had no luck on the surface there earlier so I just moved on and caught fish elsewhere, thinking I'd save time at the end to try again. I took off my

Contract time at 94 Rock with me, Milt, and Jaxon a LONG time ago. Looks like a fake beard...

hopper with my small prince nymph dropper, replacing it with a large copper john. I put a BB shot about a foot above it and cast it upstream into the riffle where it fell into the deep chasm beneath. Directly below me were two large Volkswagen sized rocks on either side of the pool, looking almost like they were positioned there on purpose as some kind of ancient stone gateway. The fly slowly passed near the upper rock and before it left its late afternoon shadow, the fish struck forcefully and immediately jumped. It was a rainbow, at least 20 inches, the biggest fish I'd ever seen on the Pecos. It frantically ran back and forth, up and down the pool as I did my best to keep it out from under the rocks and the roots near the bank. It jumped a few more desperate jumps and I finally landed it. Of course, I was alone and again had no camera, so I have no proof of any of this.

When the stone fly hatch hits sometime in May, Igor's land, and the rest of the Pecos for that matter, turns into a Roman orgy for the trout, and a drunken bacchanalian flyfishing feast for the rest of us. Imagine bi-plane sized black and orange bugs buzzing through the air, landing on you and the water with the fish recklessly striking at anything large and orange that you put not even that close to them. On days like that your blind grandmother with osteoporosis could get out there and catch a fish. The trick, and it's not easy, is hitting the hatch on the right day. You can be a couple days off on either side and still do well, but if you are there on that perfect day, you will remember it for the rest of your life. Personally, in 25 years, I've only hit it perfectly maybe five times, and each time it gave me stories to pass down to my kids and grandkids, if I had any. I've had instances where I'd stand at the bottom of the same riffle for an hour, loudly flopping down an obscenely big stone fly imitation, and not moving, catching fish after fish, actually getting tired of the action.

What could possibly ruin such a perfect day?

Sometimes I wonder if this stuff only happens to me. I was standing at the bottom of a perfect riffle on a perfect day, on an unnamed stretch of the Pecos that ran close to the main road, with stoneflies materializing out of thin air all around me. I was gleefully pulling in trout after trout, laughing to myself about my perfect luck and how I'm rarely the guy who gets to tell the story. But today was MY turn! Unfortunately, I had decided to come up alone and had no witnesses to my fortunate circumstances, but who cares? I didn't need proof! I was having the time of my life and it was totally unimportant if people believed me or not. Cast after cast resulted in a fish, some of them striking so hard that they leapt completely out of the water and came down vertically to take the bug.

I had just finished landing a large brown and was in mid-cast when a real stone fly flew directly into my face, lodging itself under my left sunglasses lens. Instinctively I fell back, flailing at my face with my right arm, knocking my glasses and the bug somewhere into the river next to me. I fell backwards hard, hitting my head on one of the rocks in the streambed. I knew I had fallen and started thinking that this probably wasn't a good thing, and then I blacked out. The next thing I remember, some guy was standing next to me, asking if I was OK. I blearily looked up at him and then realized I had a dull throbbing pain emanating from the back of my head. I reached back to feel a prominent bump, sat up, and then threw up. After several minutes, I sat up on the riverbank, and he wanted to call the paramedics, but I insisted I was feeling much better and would be OK and assured him I could drive home. Right before he left he said, "I gotta tell ya, I was driving up the road and it looked like you were either crazy or were havin' some kind of epileptic fit! And when you went down, I knew I better stop!"

I profusely thanked him for that, and he drove off, leaving me there to ponder my fate in life and why I couldn't be normal like everyone else.

# 7 CHICKEN DINNERS AND PANHANDLE PORN

*Thinking I was bleeding, I waited for the pain,*
*but none came. What did come was the smell;*
*a sweet sickening rotting sort of smell.*

EVERYONE HAS BAD DAYS. But then there are days that start off good, turn bad, then turn horribly bad, and then take a sharp left turn into a twilight zone of absurdity, complete with evil clowns and calliope music. OK, no clowns or circus music in what's coming next, but if there were, it couldn't have made it any weirder.

I have been coming to the Florida panhandle for longer than a decade. My wife was originally attracted to the village of Seaside, which she read about in one of her magazines. Seaside is a town that was built from the ground up. It is a 100% planned community, all conceptualized on paper and then constructed. The town center, the residences, the restaurants, the non-denominational church, the shops, all pre-conceived, pre-determined where they'd go, and then the town rose from behind the sugar white dunes of the Gulf of Mexico. So perfect was this town that the Jim Carrey movie, "The Truman Show," was filmed there. After having a realtor take us through the town, we decided it wasn't for us. All the houses, while attractive, looked pretty much the same, and all had signs out front saying, for instance, "The Reubens: Ben, Julie, Johnny, Marsha, and Rover." Plus, the fact the entire town was a perpetual tourist attraction, with throngs of people walking up and down the streets, giving you little or no privacy, especially on weekends. No lounging on the front porch in your underwear or any backyard amore in the hot tub with the missus, unless you're into the exhibitionist thing. We decided we'd buy a modest beachy cottage down the road in Destin. We're a two-minute walk to the beach, where the sand is pure white, and the water is a beautiful clear emerald green, very Caribbean for that far north.

Our only complaint is the hordes of spring breakers that descend upon us in March. We figured out years ago that we couldn't fight it, so we either left town the week they invade, or slept with earplugs which we kept in the nightstand next to the bed in case the little bastards got to be too much. I have to keep telling myself that decades ago, I was one of them and was probably more of an asshole than they are. My wife agrees.

In this particular region of Florida, the fishing can be fabulous. Many of the beaches are on barrier islands with a large series of shallow bays behind them. Destin is known for its Gulf fishing for grouper, snapper, jacks, cobia, mackerel, and out in the deep blue water, marlin. Fishing charters occupy the docks in front of the bars and restaurants that encircle Destin Harbor, and each fall the Destin Fishing Rodeo attracts hundreds of entries and thousands of spectators who come down to the harbor in the afternoons of the tournament to gawk at that day's catch. The bays offer great shallow water fishing for sea trout, flounder, redfish, and starting in late spring, tarpon. Choctawhatchee Bay is on the backside of Destin, where very little fly-fishing takes place. West Bay, near Panama City Beach, is where a lot of people take their fly rods. West Bay has vast areas of flats, with many nooks and coves that are supremely fishable, depending on the tides and the wind. The bay is lined with sea grass and the area is full of life, above and below the water. Egrets, osprey, and heron abound, and as you pole through the water, the muddy bottom is in constant motion with crabs scurrying to and from, rays gliding through the shallow water, and vast schools of minnows and mullet completing a nearly perfect ecosystem. Of course, humanity has left its imprint on West Bay as well. You can see the scars of boat motor tracks on the muddy bottom, letting you know that you were not the first person to be there that morning. A large skeleton of a yacht lies washed up on the north shore of the bay, destroyed by Hurricane Ivan in the year of Katrina. It is now a landmark that helps navigate to one of the better areas of flats.

Going after redfish with a fly rod in West Bay is not easy. I have never personally fished for reds in Louisiana, but I'm told there are lots more of 'em and bigger ones, and they don't spook easily. Out here, it ain't like that. There are plenty here as well, not as big though, and skittish as hell. In order not to scare them, we would kill the motor easily a couple of hundred yards from our destination and then slowly pole our way until we were adjacent to the sea grass-lined shore, where the reds will be feeding not unlike bonefish, tail-up and nose down in the water looking for shrimp and crabs. As we would silently creep up on them, trying to get in the best position to make a cast, one slight twitch of the tip of your rod, one nose scratch, one testicular adjustment, and they sped away like they were shot out of a rifle.

I should have realized from the beginning that this trip was not going to go well. It was Easter weekend of 2006, and we had flown in from New Mexico the day before, expecting to arrive late in the afternoon in time for dinner, but the now-assimilated Continental Airlines had other ideas. Our flight out of Albuquerque was cancelled, so we hopped on a Southwest flight, forgetting it was arriving at Houston Hobby instead of George H. W. Bush Airport. We took a cab and missed our connecting flight by ten minutes. Shit. Apparently, the weather sucked to the west, where most of the flights were coming from, and combined with the fact it was a holiday, every flight was oversold, delayed, or cancelled. We got into this obscenely long line at the Continental service desk, and after creeping along for more than two hours, the only thing we could get was standby on a late flight into Mobile, Alabama which was a two-and-a-half-hour drive to Destin. Not wanting to miss the next morning's redfishing trip, we took it. We got to the gate and since we took matters into our own hands and got on that Southwest flight, Continental was unaware that we actually arrived in Houston, despite the fact we were standing in front of them with IDs in hand. After telling our story over and over again to three different people, they finally let us on the plane. Have things changed since 9-11? We rented a car in Mobile, made the drive, got in around 2am where my niece and her family were already there and in bed.

We decided to stick with the original plan which was to meet David our guide, at 5:30 AM, and get to West Bay at sunrise, which of course meant I would only get a couple hours of sleep beforehand. But it's fishing, right? And to quote Warren Zevon, "I'll sleep when I'm dead."

It was an agreeably mild spring morning with no wind. The bay was covered with a light fog, which almost immediately began to dissipate with the sunrise, bringing the sound of birds and splashes from jumping mullet. The air was crisp and cool and we were bathed in a rich amber light from the rising sun. It was beautiful, man...Tom, my niece's husband, was in the back of the boat, spinning rod in hand since this was before he became a fly fisherman. I was in the front with my 8-weight, and David was at the helm. All was right with the world, In fact, I was thinking that all the bullshit we had to endure to get here meant nothing! It was gonna be a great day! It started off well, even before we really started fishing. I blindly made a warm-up cast and immediately got a strike and landed a respectable sea trout. Cool! David started poling us through the rising mist and we saw a couple of redfish tailing in the distance. Dave slowly advanced us towards the feeding fish, and my first real cast of the morning was surprisingly perfect. The fish was not spooked, saw my fly, and attacked it aggressively. My line tightened, realized it was hooked, and bolted out for the open water of the bay. After several desperate runs, the fight was over and I landed about an 8-pounder. A couple more fish followed, and Tom got one on his spinning rod right before lunchtime. It could not possibly have gotten any better than this.

It could not and it did not. This is where it turned into some kind of bizarro David Lynch movie and kept getting weirder and weirder.

We were all full of confidence, talking loudly, busting on each other while we enjoyed our lunch, and didn't really pay much attention to the wind which was steadily increasing. By the time we were through with lunch, the wind was blowing out of the southwest, filling the bay with whitecaps. David decided since the morning was so good, we were going to continue fishing since the reds were in and biting. He fired up the motor and jetted across the bay looking for one of the coves that was protected from the wind. He found a suitable one, and he was right. I got another redfish almost immediately, and then the wind started to shift and blow harder. But there were more fish tailing where we were, so we stayed. We spotted a pod of fish and I made a cast just as a gust of wind caught us in the face. The cast was wide, so I pulled up to make another. I started my back cast as another gust hit us, propelling the fly directly at my body. Not knowing yet that it hit me and thinking it was somewhere behind me, and knowing there were still feeding redfish in front of me, I stupidly tried to re-cast. That ill-conceived action made me acutely aware that the fly, which was an interesting copper colored lightweight "spoon" with a large hook attached, was stuck in my left forearm. The motion of the thwarted back cast only served to implant it ever more deeply into me, past the curve of the hook, into sinuous veiny places where I'd really rather not have it. The realization of what I'd just done hit me, and that's when I became aware of the slow dull throbbing pain and the blood oozing out of my newly created wound. David took one look at what I'd done and said, "Well boys, we're done for the day, and you get a trip to the Doc in the Box!" Meaning, I was going to the urgent care center in Destin, which was about an hour drive from where we launched the boat.

So bleeding, my arm wrapped in a rag, we took off for the boat ramp and after an ass-jarring 20-minute ride through the whitecaps, and a verbal chastisement from David about casting in the wind, we arrived.

The ramp was situated almost under one of the bridges that crossed West Bay. It was a high bridge, maybe 50 feet above the water that spanned a somewhat narrow neck of the bay. David tied us onto the dock as Tom and I stood in the boat while he walked back to get his truck.

Our initial thought was some type of explosion. It was the deafening sound of a bomb going off. Tom and I both flinched and were momentarily stunned. It was then that I felt the wetness on my head dripping down onto my shirt. Thinking I was bleeding, I waited for the

Fly embedded deeply in my arm, right before I was pummeled by chicken guts. Truly a day to remember!

pain, but none came. What did come was the smell; a sweet sickening rotting sort of smell. Then I saw the bones. Chicken bones. And the mashed potatoes. And the green-yellow gravy. And the creamed corn.

From more than 50 feet up, some jackass had thrown an entire bag of half-eaten chicken dinners off the bridge, and by the will of God, I was ground zero. It could not have been a more direct hit if it came from an air force drone on an al Qaeda safe house. The loud noise we heard was the remaining offal, hitting the bottom of the boat, amplified by the echo caused by us being under the bridge. I mean, consider the vectors, and the angles, and the wind speed and direction, and the velocity of the car. Everything had to be absolutely perfect for that to land on my head. Was it fate? Was it karma? Was it blind randomness? I ponder these questions to this day.

David heard the sound and began running back to the boat. When he got close enough to see what happened, being a southern gentleman, he politely turned his back so I couldn't see him laughing, as I stood there, gravy and potatoes dripping down my chest and legs, stinking like a dumpster behind KFC. At that point, what could we do? We all had a good laugh; I apologized ahead of time for bringing my filth into his truck, and sympathized that it would take hours to get the decomposing chicken smell out of his boat. We drove back to Destin, and David dropped Tom and me off at my house, where I immediately jumped into my truck and headed to the closest emergency room. I was now guaranteed not only because of the hook impaled in my arm, but also by the flying chicken debris to be in need of a tetanus shot.

You would think that would be enough drama for one person for one day, but no. I walked into the "Doc in the Box," which was an accurate description of the place. It was a bunker-like building in the middle of town where I signed in, filled out forms, apologized for smelling so bad, and sat down in the small waiting room, with the fly still embedded in my forearm. As I sat, blindly looking at some non-descript magazine waiting my turn, I noticed two women walked in and after signing in, sat across from me, about ten feet away. Not that I was eavesdropping, but the one was there to have some kind of test done, and the other was there for moral support. The one having the test done is blonde, with short hair and glasses, slender, not a beauty but not unattractive either.

Her friend, however, was a study in what could happen to a woman in the Florida Panhandle if things started to go wrong. Now maybe fifteen years ago, she might have been attractive, maybe even hot. But life had not treated her well. She was about 5' 6" with long black hair, wearing black booty shorts and a black tube top. Above the shorts and beneath the tube top rested a splendid roll of fat, almost like her outfit was made to show it off. You know the look. She had skinny legs and arms, but the weight she had put on decided to show itself at that particular location. Her face showed the signs of age and bar fights, where once there might have been down-home beauty. And to complete the look, she was missing one tooth in a particularly conspicuous spot. I went back to pretending to read *Golf Digest*, and their conversation winded down and came to an end.

Again, realize I was sitting there bloody and smelly with dried chicken dinner guts all over me, when I heard, "What yew in fer?"

I looked up and it's her. The one in the black tube top. I lifted up my forearm and showed her the fly and briefly explained what happened and go back to my magazine.

Silence for a minute or two.

Then, "Did that hurt?"

"Well, it hurt a little, but not as much as I thought it would."

"Oh yeah? Yew wanna see what hurt?"

I didn't know how to respond to that so I didn't.

"I'll show yew what hurt." So she got up and walked over across the room and stood directly in front of me, smelling of an overpoweringly cloying cheap rose perfume. Then with her right hand, I thought she was forming the shape of a gun and pointed it at me like she is about to shoot.

"Now that hurt," she said. I had no idea what she was talking about until I realized she was not making the shape of a gun intentionally. She was showing me that three fingers on her hand were missing, with only her thumb and index finger remaining. Below them was a nasty red scar where her missing digits used to reside.

Now, a feeling of revulsion began to creep over me. Not really wanting to engage her in conversation, but being naturally curious, and not wanting to offend her, I replied, "Oh my God, how did that happen?"

Her eyes brightened and she smiled a crooked smile, realizing she had succeeded in engaging me, however briefly, in a conversation: "Ah was cuttin' wood and the chainsaw kicked back and cut off my damned fingers."

I said something like, "Yeah, that must've really hurt," and she walked back across the room and sat down again next to her friend. Then silence for a minute or two.

Then she looked up at me, cocked her head to one side and says, "Ah... know... yew!"

"Really? Because I don't remember us meeting."

"Yeah ah do! Yew was down at the Harbor Docks the other night. Ah saw yew there!"

Now I was trying to remember the last time I was at the Harbor Docks restaurant and bar and did I see anyone looking like her. Unlikely because I was with my wife, and we had family in town. "Sorry, I don't recall seeing you."

Silence, and then she stood up and walked over in front of me again thrusting one of her hips out to one side, and with the best girlish croak she could muster, she said, "Hey! What say yew and me git together and go out for a drink or two and some good times?"

Oh my God. I am being hit on.

I am a reasonably average looking guy, certainly not George Clooney. But especially at that moment, given the condition I was in with the aforementioned blood, stench, and chicken guts, what kind of woman in her right mind would hit on me? And yet, even I, in my current state of decrepitude, was a great catch for this chick?

And "Good times?" Compared to what she was offering me, "Good times" would have been being locked up in a North Vietnamese prison camp, eating rotten cabbage while wallowing in my own waste.

At that exact moment, not knowing what to do or say and being stunned into a nauseated silence, the doctor's door opened and the cute little nurse said, "Mr. Trout, we're ready for you now!"

Thank you, God! I made some excuse about having to leave town later today and walked with the nurse into the doctor's office. The nurse was a twenty-something perky little Christian girl, very friendly with an engaging southern accent. We were talking about my fishing accident when she said, "Sir, I don't mean to get personal, but I am really curious. You know that lady in the black tube top in the waiting room?"

"Believe me, I know who you're talking about."

She hesitated and then blurted out, "Well, was she hitting on you? Because I'm sorry but I couldn't help but overhear what was going on and I thought that it was totally inappropriate behavior on her part!"

I filled her in on the whole story and we laughed. The doctor walked in, numbed me up, took the fly out, gave me a tetanus shot, and I was sent on my way. I walked out the door, and David was sitting there in the waiting room. In all the confusion, I forgot to pay him. It turned out he got there about fifteen minutes after I did, and witnessed the entire courtship incident from the other side of the sliding glass waiting room window. I asked him, "You saw the whole thing and just sat there? Why didn't you come in and save me from my trauma?"

"Hell no, this was too good! I wanted to see how it was going to turn out. And after today, I'm torn between not wanting to fish with you again, and wanting to fish with you more!"

We fish together a lot.

*And they were all trapped in Jer's head, trying to get out...Picture all these personalities seething inside his brain.*

# 8 JER, HORNETS, AND AN UNLUCKY BREAK

JER IS A PIECE OF WORK. If he likes you and you need his help, he would sell his mother if that's what it took. If he doesn't like you, you'd know it pretty quickly. He is really smart…smarter than most people he encounters. Chicks dig him. He's tall, blonde, lanky, and handsome, all in an outdoorsy way. He's been married to Kate forever, so I ain't implying anything.

Jer is insane. Not in a bad way, but there are plenty of demons bouncing around inside his head that need to be appeased. He was my partner on the air at 94 Rock for 10 years, and then after he had enough, he continued to be the voice of all of the characters on the show. If you are familiar with the show, you know what I'm talking about: his characters were **Byron and Mrs. Krunch**. Byron was an agoraphobic hypochondriac who sounded like Woody Allen and lived with his overbearing former porn star mother, who happened to also be the mother of Kaptain Krunch, my traffic guy.

He also played, **Stephan**, my supposed gay lover, who called in with various domestic issues we were having, with me loudly denying that I even knew him. I remember vividly when we came up with the Stephan character. Mo and I went up to Colorado to fish with Jer. I told him my idea for the character; he got this look in his eye and all of his mannerisms and voice inflections immediately became "Stephan," and he literally stayed in character for the entire weekend. I'm not lying. Ask Mo.

His other characters: **Cinderella** was my very Hispanic, drug-dealing next-door neighbor who worked in the evidence locker at the Albuquerque Police Department. **Dave Chuckleson** was a falsetto-talking deadhead hippie, still not over the decade-earlier death of Jerry Garcia. Dave lived with Hank, who is, for lack of a better term, a psychopath. **John Gallipski** was the president of rock programming for Clear Channel Communications. John is a dope-smoking moron and was the perfect figurehead for everything that was, and is, wrong with corporate radio. **Vince** was a typical mental midget listener, except when he droped acid. Then he becomes a financial genius and ended up getting hired by Goldman Sachs. **Cowboy Bo and his little pal Woody** are especially charming. They are a radio ventriloquist act, the joke being, a ventriloquist act can't work on the radio because you can't see the dummy talk. Woody, being the dummy, is a hopeless alcoholic, and has accused cowboy Bo of sexually abusing him while he's sitting on his lap. And then there was **Joe Camel**. Jer IS Joe Camel. Joe is a redneck, chain smoking, heavy drinking, womanizing, foul mouthed, politically outspoken nihilistic…camel…who, after getting fired from the tobacco companies, was always trying to come up with get-rich-quick schemes. Jer got his voice from a guy named Ron, who worked with Jer for a time at Charlie's Sporting Goods in Albuquerque. Ron is a great guy who is nothing like Joe Camel, except for the fact that Jer does his voice, dead-on. And in Albuquerque, Ron accrued a modest amount of celebrity status as the "Real Joe Camel."

This wasn't your typical, run-of-the-mill radio bullshit pap. Some real dysfunction went into these guys. Every one of these characters was blessed with at least one human weakness or foible, and we exploited them to the extreme. They were all platforms for high satire on current events, politics, or whatever was in the news.

And they all were trapped in Jer's head, trying to get out. And that's not even all of 'em. There were several more that were short-lived, didn't work, or we retired because they weren't relevant anymore. Picture all of these personalities seething inside his brain.

The bits were all phone calls to the station by one of his guys. Supposedly they would call in on the request line to talk to me. The way it worked was, Jer would have an idea, or we'd write a script for the next day's show and email it to him. Or, we'd call him early in the morning with an idea, flesh it out off the air, then call him back and do it live on the air, or we'd record it if it had to be "bleeped" because of profanity. Sometimes he'd do bits with three or more characters talking to each other. This was amazing because he would do these by instantly changing voices depending upon who was talking, having a three-way conversation with himself and I would interact and engage with "whomever" was on the phone. A lot of times he'd be doing these at the breakfast table with Kate observing. According to her, during one of these "multi-personality" bits, it was like being in the room with a schizophrenic.

Jer never was fond of Albuquerque, and the last straw was when his vintage 60's Chevy truck got ripped off in front of his house one night. The next morning, he and Rainman (Jason Rainey, my producer), armed to the teeth, went on a tour of the surrounding neighborhoods looking for the truck, intent on forcibly taking it back and dispatching the thief either to law enforcement or directly to hell. But that was it. In 1998 he gave notice, packed up and moved to Salida, Colorado, where he built his dream house with his own hands on three acres next to a sweet stream packed with brown trout. Eventually after making furniture, then buying a roach coach and selling his pulled pork barbecue for a while, he became a fishing guide on the Arkansas River, while continuing to do characters for the show. And now, he's quit guiding and is back to making furniture. Stay tuned for updates.

Jer is a gifted fly caster and a master drift boat captain. As a guide, he has patience to a point. But there IS a limit to his patience. Lots of times when companies held their big business conventions or conclaves in Colorado Springs, they'd offer their participants choices of excursions, usually horseback riding, biking, or flyfishing. If enough of 'em picked flyfishing, they'd put them all on a bus and take off for Salida, and more often than not, Jer would be saddled with teaching a bus full of newbies how to cast and then hopefully, they'd catch a fish. This was not Jer's favorite assignment. Generally, most people would be OK, but there's always one or two on the bus who are just douche-bags.

Jer would line them up on a stretch of grass and give them all quick lessons, and when they could at least get the fly line to go beyond their shoes, he'd take them over to the kiddie area of the river where at least a couple of them might have a chance to actually hook a trout. As it often happens, it's usually the guy with the least amount of casting skill

An old publicity photo of Jer and me at 94 Rock. What a couple of dorks!

has the most amount of lip, as in the situation he related to me:

"Hey man, come here! There ain't no fish in this river!"

"There are plenty of fish here. You just need to get your fly over there and let it drift through..."

"I keep doing that! This river sucks!"

"You're not getting your fly out far enough. Remember how I showed you how to flick your line back and stop your rod right here so..."

"Hey man, you got a spinning rod or something?"

"Look, you can do this. Just calm down and remember to do what I said earlier and..."

"It don't matter! Here! (Thrusting the rod in Jer's face.) You do it! You won't catch nothin' either!"

Now the gauntlet has been thrown, and Jer's integrity has been insulted.

"Really??? Do you really want me to show you there's fish in here?"

"Be my guest! Like I said, you won't catch nothing either!"

At this point Jer had three options: walk away and help someone else. Punch the guy in the face and push him in the river. Or calmly take the rod and start casting. He chose number three. Without saying a word, he grabbed the rod, made a cast thirty feet upstream and on the first drift gets a strike on the tan caddis and lands a nice 15-inch brown.

Jer in command on the Arkansas River in Colorado.

After releasing the fish, he hands the rod back to his now humiliated, but schooled nemesis, and walks away without killing him.

After about an hour, the fun and games were over, and they all filed back onto their bus and head back to their world of spread sheets and bottom lines.

Bob Gerding and Jer taught me how to fly fish. After being on the air in New Mexico for three or four years, I was finally badgered by both of them into giving up my bait slinging ways, and I bought a fly rod. It was Jer who took me out into the parking lot of the radio station and gave me my first fly casting lesson, and then it was the introductory trip to the San Juan River with Bob. On that first trip, I found I was pretty at good casting and getting strikes but not so great at keeping a trout on the line and landing it. I remember it being a very frustrating but learning experience. It got better after that.

When we were still working together on the radio, we'd practice what I called "Graft and Corruption." We would plan radio promotions that outwardly looked legitimate, but were actually ruses to get us to go fishing somewhere on someone else's dime. We were so good at this that no one, especially the advertising clients who footed the bill, knew what we were doing. In our defense, we bent over backwards to "whore" ourselves out for the advertisers, going over and above what they would get elsewhere, so they were happy. The listeners who participated were happy, especially if they won the contest, and most importantly, Jer and I were happy because we got to spend a weekend—or even a week sometimes—with fly rods in our hands.

One of our most creative capers was our "Running on Empty" promotion back in 1995. We got a new car from a dealer who was advertising with us and created a contest where we would fill the tank before we left Albuquerque, as well as filling a gas can. Then the listeners would try to guess the exact number of miles we travelled before we ran out of gas. The closest guess got the car. Great promotion, right? Again, what could possibly go wrong?

Two weeks before our adventure, a hornet somehow got into our bedroom on a Saturday morning, and Marti was screaming for me to dispatch with it. I ran upstairs to see what the commotion was all about. The large hornet was beating itself against one of the three clerestory windows that were above our head board. Instead of getting a fly swatter or a magazine and killing it, I decided to try and spare its life. I ran downstairs and got a piece of Tupperware. My plan was to trap the little bastard against the glass with the container, quickly slide the lid on top, and go out through the sliding glass doors at the foot of the bed, onto our deck and set it free. So, with Marti standing in the doorway to the bathroom, I climbed onto the top of the bed, and with Tupperware in hand, slammed the bowl over the hornet and trapped it on the glass. So far so good. Then, when I lifted up the edge of the bowl to slide the lid under, the hornet recognized this as its chance for freedom. It flew out of the miniscule crack of daylight that I provided, directly at my face. Instinctively I leapt backwards, and I mean LEAPT. I flew through the air and landed badly on my right foot. Searing pain shot through it and directly up my leg causing me to cry out loudly.

This really hurt.

The hornet on the other hand, was ecstatic. I watched in agony as it flew a victory lap around the bedroom ceiling and then departed out the sliding glass door to freedom. You might think that my wife would have been sympathetic to my plight. You would have thought that seeing your spouse crumpled on the floor in the fetal position whimpering would elicit at least a small amount of empathy. Well, think again.

"Why the hell didn't you just kill it??? That was the stupidest thing you have ever done! You could have killed yourself over a hornet! And you could have killed me too, or did you forget I'm allergic to hornets?"

She did, of course, have a point. But still...

"Look, you gotta take me to the emergency room. I think I broke my foot."

"I should make you drive yourself! Can you make it down the stairs or do you need me to help you with that, too?"

Why don't you just shoot me and put me out of my misery?

Not only did the x-rays show I had broken my foot, I broke it in three places. For some reason they decided not to plaster it up and just gave me a walking cast and a pair of crutches and told me to take it easy for at least two weeks, and then they'd take another look at it.

Well, that sucked. I was going on our fishing trip in two weeks, and it was too late to back out now, so I was bound and determined to pull this off, even at the risk of permanently disfiguring myself.

Now armed with my cast, the crutches, and a suitcase full of painkillers, Jer and I headed for the Gunnison, Colorado. We ran out of gas somewhere between Coal Bank and Molas Passes on Route 550 between Durango and Silverton. We called the station and gave them the exact mileage. They announced the winner, and our end of the bargain was fulfilled. The rest was gravy. It was already dark, and I could hobble around OK, so I got out of the car with the gas can and refueled us, giving us enough to get to Ouray, still in Colorado.

Red Mountain Pass between Silverton and Ouray is easier to drive at night for the simple reason that you can't see how treacherous it is. It is a twisty-turny road full of switchbacks with a serious lack of guardrails where they need them the most. I'm talking sheer drops of several hundred feet, possibly more. If you slide over the edge, you have an exactly zero percent chance of survival. Call me a wuss, but heights bother me. Not unlike Independence Pass, this is a white-knuckle drive. I tend to either hug the inside lane or drive directly down the middle of the road depending on traffic. That said, I would rather be the driver than the passenger. But since I had a bum right foot, Jer was at the wheel, and all was good as we hit the town of Ouray. We tanked up and were now getting close enough to Montrose, which would be our base camp. Then we saw the flashing lights behind us, and apparently in our zeal to get to our hotel and a hot meal, we were a little aggressive with the speed limit. The state trooper came up and asked for identification and the car registration. Of course, the car was not registered to us, so he asked, "So what are you doing with the car?"

"Well officer," Jer began, "this here car is part of a radio promotion. You see, we were supposed to run out of gas and a listener had to guess when, and we got the car from a dealer because he got radio advertising out of it, and we're going fishing so..." The more Jer tried to explain, the more ludicrous it was all sounding.

The cop, obviously confused and a little annoyed, looked us up and down and said, "Wait here," and walked back to his patrol car. He got in and in the rear-view mirror we watched him sit there and try to figure out what he was going to do. There was no one at the dealership so he couldn't call them. We didn't have a contact number to give him, so we thought this could break several ways, none of them good. The worst being he shoots us in the head, throws us off Red Mountain Pass, and takes the car. After at least fifteen minutes, he got out of his car and walked up to us and said in an exasperated tone, "Look, I don't know how to write this up. I really don't understand what you're doing with the car, so I'm just gonna let you go. Just take it easy, will, ya?"

With that, he got in his car and drove away. Didn't even give us a warning.

The next morning it was over to Starvin' Arvin's for a breakfast of biscuits and gravy with more food than was necessary for the starting offensive line of the Cleveland Browns. It was a beautiful sunny September day. We boarded a jet boat and were transported as far as we could go up the Gunnison River before entering Black Canyon, disembarked and got into our guide's inflatable raft for the float down. The trip turned out to be rather uneventful. I caught maybe ten small to medium brown trout, and I witnessed something I had never seen before. Jer got skunked. No fish. I think this surprised him so when we got back to camp, we started drinking, resulting in a couple of massive hangovers the next morning. The next day, however, would prove to be one of the more enjoyable memorable days I've had.

It was another beautifully sunny Sunday morning, and on our way back home we decided to do a little exploring. Somewhere on the other side of the mountains from Telluride, we followed a dirt road and came upon a small, nearly perfectly round high-mountain lake, nestled in a small, almost crater-like depression that was lined with pine trees. We parked the car and walked (hobbled) up to take a closer look. The water was absolutely clear and with the bright sunshine, it appeared almost Caribbean-like. There was an abundance of plant life under the surface and then it occurred to us that we had stumbled across a naturally spring-fed pond, with no dam in sight. The colors were so bright and vibrant, it almost looked like a giant outdoor aquarium from the movie "Avatar." Then we noticed movement, and saw that the movement was fish. Countless numbers of brook trout were living here, hiding under the thick vegetative growth, venturing out for a quick meal and then retreating back to their cover.

This was too much to bear. We had both brought our float tubes, and Jer was already heading back to the car to get his while I stood there, figuring out how I was going to do this with a broken foot. After about two seconds of worrying about my problem, I limped back to the car, got my float tube and my fly rod, and managed to transport it back to the lake. I brought a plastic trash bag that I rubber--banded around my wrapped foot, somehow put on my flippers and got situated inside my float tube and we both ventured out into the water. I figured, "What the hell. I'm floating in water. I'll try to fin gently. There's no wind, so I'm good." After pushing off from the shore and after a few tentative kicks, I realized this would be no problem.

We spent the whole day on that lake in perfect solitude, taking brookie after brookie, many in their brilliant orange spawning colors, and mostly all on dry flies. With the sun and the water and the warm temperatures, it was almost like a day at the beach. This was paradise. Everything was the way it should be, and it reinforced why we all fell in love with this sport in the first place.

Left to right: Mo, Alison, Jer, Krunch, and me at Bob Gerding's Outdoor Adventures show.

*Walking to meet me was my long-suffering wife,*
*and as she got closer, I could tell she was quietly weeping.*
*She looked me in the eye and with tears streaming*
*down her face she said, "Please! Can we go home now?"*

# 9 WHETHER OR NOT TO TAKE THE LITTLE WOMAN, PART 1

AS I JUST MENTIONED IN THE PREVIOUS CHAPTER, every once and a while you need to take one of these trips with the Little Woman. Why, you ask? For a number of reasons, but the number one is assuaging the guilt you feel for having some of the best times in your life, and they don't involve your wife or girlfriend. Conversely, if she'd really be honest with you, she'd tell you that she needs to go on at least one or two of these trips too, just to show you that she actually IS interested in your little hobby, even if she isn't. She'll make a game effort to participate, even trying to fish, and possibly she might not even complain (too much) about mosquitos, the weather, the food, the accommodations, or all of the above.

There are two ways to look at this: First, if you really REALLY don't want to take her on one of these junkets, but feel you must, make sure you choose a place that is on the low scale of creature comforts, but not so low that she turns suicidal, crying all the time, and finally demanding to go home. Remember: It needs to be bad, but not TOO bad... Uncomfortable enough so when you go, "Honey, I'm planning another trip, this one into the back country of the Siberian wilderness and I'd love for you to come! Whadya say?"

I guarantee you she will respond in the negative, maybe even feeling sorry for you that you're actually going to put yourself through such torture just so you can fish.

The other way to look at this is if you actually enjoy the company and companionship of your spouse on trips like these, and you would like to plan one that caters to her comfort and well-being, as well as your own desire to fish until you drop from exhaustion. It can be done, and I have actually done it successfully.

But more on that later. Let's get back to the first scenario for a minute. As an example, the following is a true story, and is a perfect example of what NOT to do; although I claim ignorance on this, because I had no idea what we were actually getting into.

It was the summer of 2001 and we were still all blissfully unaware of the terrorist attack that was just months away. I went on a radio station-sponsored trip up into the backwoods of New Mexico above the town of Mora. It was also at a time during a drought when the bears were coming down and getting into people's gardens, fruit trees, and garbage cans. Right before the trip, KOB-TV reported that a 94-year-old woman had been attacked and eaten by a bear that apparently just walked in through her unlocked screen door. Tragic. But what made it worse for us was the dead woman lived less than a mile down the dirt road where we were going to stay. With that on our minds, we made the trip. When we got to that same dirt road, it took us further and further back into a heavily wooded area that had no break in the trees on either side making it somewhat claustrophobic. It had that feeling of being completely wild; somewhere you definitely didn't want your vehicle to break down. At some point even I started wondering if this was some kind of cruel hoax, and that we were going to be killed and eaten by some inbred mountain people, never to be heard from again.

Eventually we came to the sign for the "Lodge," so we turned and were met at the foot of a wooden bridge by the owners of the property. They were nice enough, but certainly did not look like lodge owners. The husband had long, stringy unkempt greasy hair, and his wife looked a little better, but the missing front tooth scared Marti a little. We were told to park on our side of the bridge because they weren't sure if it would hold the weight of a car. OK. Strike two with Marti. They took our bags and told us to watch our step as we crossed over the bridge because there were a few open spaces between the wooden slats. Open spaces? More like 6-inch to one-foot chasms on a bridge that had certainly seen better days. I think this is when Marti started to cry for the first time. The only other way to cross the river which flowed 15 feet below was to slide down the bank on our side, walk through the river, and then climb the steep bank on the other side, using the roots and branches of river foliage as hand-holds. Seeing no other alternative and quietly whimpering, Marti took my hand as we slowly, gingerly walked across the bridge.

As we walked up the path, the lodge looked OK from the outside. It was a large stone and log structure built back in the 1920s as an exclusive hunting club for one of New Mexico's senators. As I said, pretty impressive, so far. We walked through the front door and entered into a very large rectangular dining hall, its walls constructed from giant logs from the beginning of the last century. There was a huge heavy wooden table that sat in the middle of the room, underneath a deer antler chandelier. A large elk head stared at us from one wall, and a very large stuffed mountain lion stood growling at us from a corner table. The room was dimly lit and on further inspection dusty. I asked the owners about the stuffed mountain lion and the wife said, "Yeah, Billy shot and kilt him last year and we ate him."

They ate him?

Being a cat owner, this did not sit well with Marti either, and I was not aware that anyone ate mountain lion. I guess they did. We then followed our host couple back to where the living quarters were, and this is where it got scary. Did I mention the place was built in the '20s? That was probably about the last time it was cleaned and repaired. The walls were black with filth, finger smudges, dirty sink, nauseating toilets, and to top it off, for some reason we had no water at the moment but they were going to try and figure that out. The mattress was a Hilton for bedbugs. And when Marti turned the blankets down to reveal unwashed sheets with pubes glued onto them with decades-old bodily fluid, probably from Calvin Coolidge, she'd seen enough. "I can't stay here!" she sobbed. "This place is a nightmare! Why didn't you tell me it was going to be this awful?"

"Now Sweetheart... First, I didn't know anything about the place and secondly, we can't be rude and just leave. We have advertising clients and contest winners with us, and the trip is supposed to be with "fishing with me," so let's give it one night, and if you still feel the same way tomorrow, then we'll make an excuse and hit the road."

Marti desperately trying to land a trout while Bob Gerding instructs.

At this point, I'm making a mental note to rip the lungs out of the promo person at 94 Rock who set up this disaster without knowing that even the family of Honey Boo Boo would have been offended staying at this dump.

If there's one thing I credit Marti with. It's is a snootful of common sense. Since she was in the advertising sales end of the radio industry, her business rationality kicked in and she agreed to tough it out for one night. So, we kept our clothes in our bags, not wanting to put them inside any of the furniture for fear of what rodentia might lurk inside. The dinner bell rang, so we made our way back to the dining area, at least happy with the knowledge that the dining room had been up kept. The food was decent, unremarkable New Mexican fare, and after we drank enough to face what was ahead of us, we headed back to our dilapidated room to endure the night. Needless to say, I didn't sleep well, and Marti not at all, spending the entire night on the lookout for some loathsome creature to crawl out from under the bed, or worse yet, slither out from inside of the mattress.

The next morning after an early breakfast, the winners and I went out to the "pond" in front of the lodge. It was more than obvious that this artificial body of water had just been put in, probably sometime the day before. It was basically a couple hundred foot long, somewhat narrow hole in the ground, lined with thick black PVC, and it was too early for any aquatic flora or fauna to have started accumulating. The owners had at least bought lots of oversized rainbows that again were probably dumped in just as we were pulling up. An occasional fish could be had, but I think it was mostly luck.

Probably, the fish struck at the fly out of rage fed by shame, humiliated that after growing up in a fish hatchery, they were assigned to spend the rest of their born days in this living hell. Marti finally made it down to the pond with no visible signs of trauma, and actually caught a couple of fish herself. But now, the owners of the lodge had a special treat in store for me. They knew I wanted to do some stream fishing, and they insisted the same small creek that ran through the property was full of browns and brookies. I took my rod and vest and threw it in the back of their rusting Ford Econoline van. Right before we were about to leave, Billy whistled and four hound dogs came running towards us and jumped into the van as well. I asked "So are you taking the dogs for a ride?"

"Nope. They're coming with you."

"Why do I need the dogs to go fishing?"

"Well, as you recollect, we've been havin' a bear problem up here lately, so they're gonna stay with you while you fish."

"OK, so if a bear comes around, they'll start barking, which will give me more time to head back here?"

"Kind of. What would probably happen is the bear will try to kill and eat the dogs before it comes after you, so yeah, you will have a head start to make it back here before the bear decides to get you."

Comforting words. Surprisingly, this did not deter me from fishing. I figured I'd rather be mauled to death by bears than succumb to some hideous disease left behind by a syphilitic hunter that last slept in my bed. I pressed on, surrounded by dogs, and proceeded to fish my way back to the lodge, which took about two hours. The stream was extremely tight and overgrown, maybe fifteen feet across at its widest and about a foot at its narrowest. I spent most of my time roll-casting and using my newly acquired bow and arrow cast, where you hold the fly in one hand, pull it back to your cheek, aim, and then like in archery let it fly forward. It's a surprisingly accurate and useful way to fish when you have no other alternative. And all-in-all, it wasn't a bad day. Billy was correct that the stream was full of little browns and brookies, and I caught plenty before trudging up through the woods and reappearing at the lodge behind the stock pond.

Walking to meet me was my long-suffering wife, and as she got closer, I could tell she was quietly weeping. She looked me in the eye and with tears streaming down her face she said, "Please! Can we go home now?"

I knew there was no need for discussion. We were leaving. We would make some excuse about her having one of her horrible migraine headaches and head out, leaving everyone else to fend for themselves. Apparently, the last straw occurred in the rancid bathroom next to our rancid bedroom. As she was sitting down on the rancid toilet that was just fixed by our somewhat rancid host, a large mother mouse that had just given birth recently went ambling by, dragging four of its offspring who were clamped onto Mom's engorged teats. It was just too much for her to take.

We packed our bags, made our excuses, and hit the road. She stopped crying by the time we hit I-25, and I was feeling so bad, that

I took her to Harry's Roadhouse, one of her favorite New Mexican restaurants on the outskirts of Santa Fe. And after several glasses of wine, she was even almost to the point of laughing about the whole ordeal. Almost.

# 10 WHETHER OR NOT TO TAKE THE LITTLE WOMAN, PART 2

*...she KNEW that she had just experienced
the almost perfect trip, so she happily resigned herself
to nearly a week of hanging out with sweaty men
and eating bug spray.*

I'VE JUST DESCRIBED TO YOU THE WORST POSSIBLE
trip to take the wife or girlfriend on, excluding ones involving death, violent crimes, or severed limbs. There ARE ways to do this where you get what you want, meaning, a whole lot of quality fishing, and she's happy too. For instance, consider the following.

Somehow both of us actually found two consecutive weeks that we could turn into a pretty darned good vacation. I hadn't had a good "exotic" fishing trip for a couple of years, meaning something substantial out of the state of New Mexico, so I was really desperate to get on a river, somewhere. So...how do I incorporate THAT into a trip of a lifetime for her that she doesn't even realize IS a fishing trip? And how do I do it all without the use of a Vulcan mind meld or prescription drugs?

First, you'll probably need a little cash. This is what I did, but you can follow your own path. Realize, I was making quite a bit of money at the time, and I'd never fished in British Columbia before.

It was the middle of August in 2005. We flew into San Francisco on a foggy Saturday morning, making the approach and landing fairly interesting. As we were at the car rental place, the fog lifted, and we drove over the San Francisco-Oakland Bay Bridge in full mid-morning sun, heading north. Knowing that we were both big fans of the fermented grape, I got us a room at a Napa bed and breakfast, and we spent the next day and a half touring wineries and eating and drinking. We'd walk hand-in-hand through the streets of Napa and Sonoma, going in clothing stores and knickknack shops, with me smiling all the time, being supportive, all along knowing that MY time would soon be upon us and it would be her turn to trudge gamely up a riverbank wearing ill-fitting waders with boots that didn't fit her narrow feet, and sit for hours in the back of a drift boat with a book. I shopped, and walked, and did wine tastings, and spent too much money on dinners, but don't get me wrong--it was fine. For most chicks, that would have been enough, but no, the first week had only begun.

Early Monday morning, we got back in the little SUV we rented and first headed west, crossing over the Coastal Range, and descending into Bodega Bay, the little seaside town where they filmed Alfred Hitchcock's "The Birds." We found a little seaside café right where the Russian River empties into the Pacific, and while the seals were sunning themselves on the rocks watching us watching them, we had lunch. Then it was back in the car as we hit California's famous Highway 1, the scenic curvaceous two-laned road that hugs the coast. This part sounds romantic, and sure, the views were great, and we got to see a lot of little seaside villages along the way, but all of those goddamned Winnebagos were enough to make you want to mount a howitzer on the top of your car and blast them into another dimension; making matters worse were the ones that were towing cars, or even worse, towing SUVs.

Look, you may own one and really enjoy your monstrosity on wheels, but the rest of us don't! In fact, if you're towing another vehicle, we all should be legally allowed to either run you off the road, or slash your tires when we see you at a rest stop. I can't tell you how many times we were in a line of cars climbing or descending a switchback, with one of you idiots in the lead, making life miserable for the rest of us. Am I pissing you off? Good! You all deserve to die fiery painful deaths. Alaska has the perfect law regarding this: If you have five or more cars following you on a road, you are REQUIRED to pull over so they can pass you or you will get a ticket. Common sense, my friends.

But I digress, again.

So farther up north, we connected with US 101, which took us through the Mendocino County, the largest pot growing region in California, and probably the U.S., and with a trunk full of A-1 Kryptoweed (not) we made it to the Oregon border right around dinnertime where we got a cheap hotel room and had dinner at a local seafood joint. The following day we were back on the road. US 101 through Oregon is even more spectacular that California's Highway 1. Beautiful huge sand dunes, cliffs descending into awesomely rustic beaches, all with the outside temperature hovering in the mid 50's in the end of July. Made it through Oregon with another brief stop in Tillamook to buy some cheese, and then onto another painfully charming bed and breakfast in Gig Harbor, outside of Tacoma, Washington. The next morning, we continued north and took the ferry from Port Angeles over to Victoria Island.

I'll mention two things in passing about the ferry ride. Number one, most people today have GPS, so this doesn't really apply anymore, but if you're in a hurry because you're going to, like, miss a ferry or something, NEVER trust MapQuest. Following their directions precisely, we turned off the main road to the ferry terminal and ended up dead-ending on a residential street where we could actually see the ferry loading. Cursing bitterly, I did a U-turn and sped out, luckily making it in time to be the last car they let on the boat. Secondly, while on the ferry, just as we crossed over into Canadian waters, we were escorted for the second half of a trip by a herd of otters, swimming in a V-formation. Again, interminably charming. The wife loved it. We stayed at a "boutique" hotel in the city of Victoria, which is British Columbia's provincial capital. I'll hand the Canadians one thing: They really know how to keep their cities. Victoria was spotlessly clean; no litter, flowers growing all over the town, beautiful parks, with First Nation and lumberjack art prominently displayed everywhere. We spent two days going to art galleries, more shops, and I DID have the best Peking duck I've ever had in a little Chinese joint.

By this time the Little Woman is thanking God Almighty that she married a man who was so in tune to her needs and desires.

But there's even more before the fishing.

Next stop, Vancouver. Two and a half days' worth. Vancouver is a huge, modern, cosmopolitan city, again, clean as can be, surrounded by some of the most breathtaking scenery on the west coast, with towering mountains to the north and east, and beautiful bays and inlets to the west. We did big city stuff like go to the art museum, ride the subways, and eat incredible sushi. And then, that was it. What more could a woman have wanted? It was now time to go into the middle of nowhere for five full days of fishing, and she KNEW that she had just experienced the almost perfect trip, so she happily resigned herself to nearly a week of hanging out with sweaty men and eating bug spray.

I wanted to find a place that was near enough to Vancouver but far enough away from civilization. And still smarting from the experience of the trip to Mora, I wanted to be sure that the place I chose was clean, had good food, and comfortable accommodations. So, I went on-line and found the Pitt River Lodge, a place that none of my flyfishing buddies had ever heard or read about. Turns out, it was probably one of the better choices I've made, considering no one knew a thing about it.

To get to the ferry (Canadians love their ferries) that would take us up to approximately where the lodge was, we drove northeast out of Vancouver for about two hours, following the Fraser River, putting us right smack in the middle of where the Cascades meets British Columbia's Coastal Range, so yeah, it was pretty scenic with towering peaks, mostly covered with thick pine forest. We parked the car at the bottom end of Pitt Lake, which is one of two, almost fiord-like lakes in the area. Pitt Lake has the distinction of being the largest freshwater tidal lake in North America, and one of only two in the entire world. The ferry would take us from the bottom of Pitt Lake all the way up to the top, where the Pitt River entered in. It was a long boat ride, although again, quite scenic as the lake was lined with vertical walls of green descending from high above. At our destination, we were met by Pitt River Lodge owner, Danny Gerak, who loaded our gear into his truck and took us the remaining half hour deep into the forest to where the lodge was situated.

Similar to Mora, the lodge was built from large hewn logs from the forest surrounding it, yet, this place was perfect. Clean, well-equipped, even with working plumbing and plenty of photos on the walls of satisfied customers holding big fish. The food was fabulous, and the beds were comfortable.

The area is interesting, full of legend, logging, and lore. The area where the lodge is located was once in the logging town of Alvin, which was abandoned by the 1950's, and bulldozed in the 1980's. As we were being driven in, we saw the crumbling remains of logging infrastructure including abandoned buildings, and heavy equipment left to decay. The area is still logged today, but the slopes are so vertical, you could even call what they do "extreme" logging.

HOWEVER, if you're after adventure and intrigue, you can go up into the hills and look for "Slumach's Gold." Legend has it that back in the late 1800's, old man Slumach found a bunch of gold above the town in the Pitt Range. Murder and intrigue followed, along with tantalizing clues as to where the gold might be. Several have tried to follow in Slumach's footsteps and most have died, but not without allegedly finding just enough gold to keep the legend alive. Truth be told, no one really knows if the gold really exists or if it's all bullshit. If you want the whole story, go to the Pitt River Lodge website—it's pretty interesting.

If you get tired of fishing, you could ask the Gerack's to point you in the right direction to start your own private prospecting search. I decided not to. But you could try. They probably wouldn't tell you anyway because you'd end up getting maimed or killed in the rough terrain and then your family would try to sue them for damages.

So, back to fishing and the trip. It was one of those times when you plan and book a fishing trip, and everything is what the website says is. And our hosts, Danny and his wife Lee, could not have been more gracious. I had not yet ventured out back to take a look at the river, and was hoping it too was as spectacular as they said it was.

It was.

The Pitt River is a glacially-fed stream, which gives the water that brilliant, turquoise blue color. In some areas it was unspeakably beautiful, with the color of the water framed by the backdrop of green forested cliffs and white peaks in the background. The headwaters are somewhere on the backside of Whistler Ski Area, and the water runs cold and strong. Except for the side eddies and sloughs, wading can be, shall we say, technical. The guides use their rubber rafts as transportation only, taking us from spot to spot where we'd get out and wade. The river has runs of King, Coho, and especially Sockeye salmon. When we were there, the kings were just about done, and the sockeyes were

A nice bull trout caught on the Pitt River in British Columbia, an hour or so before the 'big chase.'

starting up strong. There is a big sockeye hatchery nearby, so thousands of fingerlings are dumped into the river each year. I ran into a couple of local sockeye fisherman who were complaining bitterly that all the sockeyes they were catching were the same size and looked exactly alike. I just smiled and listened, thinking, "OK guys, so you'd rather go back to the days when there were NO sockeyes in the river because of damming and commercial overfishing? You are catching big, fresh out of the ocean great tasting salmon and you're complaining? Go fish the Cuyahoga River in Cleveland, and THEN talk to me!"

Morons.

The Pitt also has healthy populations of rainbow trout, and cut-throats, which they consider junk fish. But it is mostly known for its large numbers of big bull trout, which I had never caught before. These are large, kind of blue-ish fish and fight like their name implies. Much like a brown trout, they're bullish, don't jump, shake their heads a lot, and hang on the bottom until they tire. My biggest one of the trip was probably eight pounds. I think that's the picture I included in this book.

Four days of fishing, in a remote location, on a beautiful river full of trout and salmon. The first three, Marti went with me, and brought along a book as she always does when she gets either frustrated with not being able to fly fish that well, or bored from watching me catch fish after fish. At one point her head DID perk up when on a back channel, a seal decided to do the backstroke through the run I was fishing. Our guide immediately said, "We're done here. Nothing's gonna bite here after that." We continued downstream in the raft to other equally pro-ductive areas.

It was my last day, and Marti decided that I needed to have one day alone with just me and the guide, so she stayed at the lodge while we headed out. I had experienced three totally satisfying days of catching mostly bull trout, plenty of brightly colored rainbows, a few sockeye, and some trashy cutthroats. We had just finished fishing a huge back-water whirlpool lined with huge boulders set against steep slopes dark green with pine trees. I maybe pulled three or four unmemorable fish out of the eddy, so we moved downstream to a point right before the river began to really widen. There was a pretty powerful chute above us which flattened out into a gentle riffle. I was using my six-weight, with a weighted olive and black wooly bugger, anticipating more bull trout or a rainbow. I cast upstream at about a 45-degree angle and let the bugger drift below me with the current, and began stripping it in as it reached the bottom of the run. After maybe three or four strips I got a solid "thud" of a strike. Thinking it was another bull trout, I set the hook against what felt like a car bumper. My line shot upstream into the middle of the riffle, and then the fish jumped, almost fully breaching the surface.

It was huge.

"Holy shit!" I yelled to the guide. "What is that?"

"You just hooked one the late kings that are still in the river. Don't lose it!"

Yeah, don't lose it, he said! This fish was probably 50 pounds and I was SEVERELY underpowered with my 6-weight. When the fish jumped, it probably saw the two of us standing on the bank with our jaws dropped below our knees, which scared it. So, as soon as it hit the water it shot out like a bullet downstream. The line was tearing from my reel and in no time at all I had not just reached my backing, I reached the end of my backing, so I was fighting this guy using the bend in my rod, hoping the line wouldn't snap off my metal spool.

We gave chase. Both of us took off running downstream on the bank, frantically trying to catch up to it and in the process not lose it. I would reel as I ran, only to have him take what I brought in and get me back to nothing. Realize that we were in logging country so every 200 feet or so would be a twisted log jam on the bank that we somehow had to traverse. My guide would climb up on the gnarled mass of tree parts, and I would hand my rod to him, and then run to the downstream side where he'd hand it back, and the chase would continue. After successfully overcoming the first jam, I took my rod and realizing this was not the place to make a stand and fight, I again started sprinting downstream with my guide behind me and the King actually keeping pace ahead. Next is why someone my age should NOT race down a riverbank without looking where he's going. My left foot caught an exposed root sending me rocketing face first though the air, landing on my outstretched arms as my rod flew in front of me.

Miraculously, I was not dead, but I was both full of adrenaline and abject dejection, thinking I had just blown it. I got up, apparently with no sprains or breaks and began to follow my rod which was skittering along the bank in front of me. I had not lost the fish! I picked it up, felt resistance, and continued the chase. Up ahead there was another tangled mess of dead trees. I climbed on top this time with my rod, and my guide sprinted around to the other and took it with the fish still attached. We finally came to an area in the river with a wide sand bar, and the woods had pulled back a ways, so we decided that this is where we would try and land it. The fish was finally tiring and giving line back. I was tiring as well, actually exhausted at this point, fearing my left ventricle was about to explode. The salmon no longer ran downstream but was running perpendicular to me as the river had widened considerably. I finally got him to within about twenty feet of the shore when he decided he had one more run in him and took off across the river, all the way to the other bank, and decided to hide under a twist of logs on the other side. He stopped, and I applied more pressure.

Nothing.

My heart sank, realizing he had won the battle by wrapping my line around one of the logs he was hiding under. Completely spent, out of breath, and sweating profusely, I broke off the fly, reeled in the line and sat on the bank, head down for several minutes. My guide came up to me and said, "Dude, that was awesome! That was one of the most amazing fights I've ever seen! Don't feel too bad about losing the fish, because you now have a story you can tell for the rest of your life!"

True. And I DO tell the story. But in quiet solitary moments, I think about that fight and what I might have done better; how it would have been different if I had a heavier rod, and I play out all the "what-ifs" in my head, sometimes to the point of compulsion. I even wondered if it eventually made it all the way upstream to spawn with my encounter being its only annoying distraction on its journey. I certainly hope it did. Then, after spawning, the big brute died. They all do. That's nature for ya.

# 11 BIMINI, THE SCAM OF A LIFETIME

*"Back in those days," he said, "boats would come in through the cut in the reef at night, and under the cover of darkness, they would drop thousands of these containers, which were full of cocaine, into the water."*

I MIGHT HAVE ALREADY TOLD YOU that the great thing about having the radio gig was the ability to do a lot of groovy stuff that you wouldn't normally get to do. I pulled off a few of these trips during my tenure at 94 Rock, all marginally above board. The one that was the absolute best that probably pissed off more people at the station than any of the others was my week-long stay on a dive boat, floating in the azure blue waters off the coast of Bimini in 2007. To legitimize the deal, I broadcasted live from the island, telling tales of my daily adventures, and putting some colorful locals on the air, trying to make it at least somewhat interesting to the New Mexico audience and hoping the listeners would be vicariously living through me. At the same time, I tried to raise money and awareness for the Albuquerque Aquarium, by making the show somewhat of a Radiothon, giving out a phone number that people could call and donate to the Albuquerque Bioparks. So Rainman, my producer, put some steel drum and calypso music behind me to give it a real island feel, and off I went but not without a few internal problems.

Berated by the station sales manager at the time, who saw through my thinly disguised ruse and called a complete waste of broadcasting time by one or two of my on-air co-workers, I summarily dismissed their protestations and behind-my-back grumblings, chalking it all up to sour grapes and proceeded to have the time of my life.

Here's how it worked: Instead of paying a professional fish broker to get new aquatic life for their tanks, the Albuquerque aquarium rented a dive boat from the Shedd Aquarium in Chicago, and sold spaces to local New Mexican divers who would do the collecting work for them, all under the instruction of my friend and Albuquerque Aquarium Manager, Holly Casman and her crew. When Holly approached me with the idea of going and supporting the aquarium, I had to think about it for all of two seconds. Let's see, I get to live on a boat in a tropical paradise for a week that was stocked with beer and wine, eat meals prepared by the on-board chef, play in the water, and get to fly fish on some of the most beautiful sand flats I'd ever seen. And all I have to do is broadcast from a seaside bar built right on the beach and talk about how great the local aquarium is? Yeah. Like I'm NOT gonna do this!

Which leads to the question: Where is Bimini?

Not unlike New Mexico and Delaware, which are now my other part-time home states, no one really knows where Bimini is. Bimini is actually three tiny islands, barely more than pinpoints on a map. They are part of the Bahamas, the closest Bahamian islands to the U.S., laying short 53-miles directly east from Miami over the Gulf Stream. They have the dubious distinction of being located at the westernmost corner of the Bermuda Triangle, attracting scores of crystal-wielding weirdos and other nut-jobs.

Years ago, Bimini was also a crucial stopover point for the drug trade. One of the above-mentioned "colorful locals" who will remain nameless is a very prominent person on the islands, holding a position of power and wealth. He told me that during the '80s everyone living there to a person was somehow involved in the transport and distribution of cocaine. I was getting a history of Bimini and was in this guy's office. He pointed to a strange parcel-shaped object on one of his shelves and asked me, "Do you know what that is?" I had no idea. He took it down from his shelf and handed it to me. It was a light brown fiberglass parcel the shape and size of a small loaf of bread that had been torn into and its contents removed. On the outside of it was a number and someone's name.

"Back in those days," he said, "the small planes would fly in at night, and under the cover of darkness, they would drop thousands of these containers which were full of cocaine into the water. Then, the person whose name was on the bag was responsible for going out in the water and collecting all of his numbered bags and bringing them back to shore to be cut, re-packaged, and then re-shipped."

"Is it still going on?"

"That doesn't happen here anymore, but during those days, there was a lot of money being made, and every native on the island seemed very happy to be gainfully employed."

And long before that, during the days of prohibition, Bimini was an important location for rum runners. So, apparently, the more things change, they remain the same.

The same individual who educated me on the cocaine trade also had dealings with weird shit that happened in the "Bermuda Triangle," as well as weird dealings with weirdos who were attracted to all that weird shit. This person swore to me that he had a "lost time" experience, involving a strange trip through time and space with no suitable explanation. He was out on his boat one morning, not sure what kind of boat it was, and then instantaneously it was late in the afternoon, and he was five miles north of where he had last been. I asked him if he was drinking or doing hallucinogens, and he said no.

He also occasionally would be hired by all the new age, crystal-carrying post-hippie wack-jobs that would come to Bimini to conjure up their dead cat or whatever else they do. On one particular morning a group of women of that persuasion knocked on his door and insisted that he take them on his boat to a particular point that jutted out into the ocean. He asked if he could at least get a cup of coffee first, and they told him there wasn't time. He was told they had to leave now, or it would be too late. Since they were willing to pay him well for the task, he agreed, gathered them up in his van, went to the marina, and off they went right before sunrise. Each woman had a large, oblong, what looked to be amethyst crystal in her possession, all at least the size of a cucumber, no batteries included. On the boat ride over he asked why they were going to that particular spot, and they informed our buddy that they were going to "call in the dolphins."

OK. No problem.

They reached the point just as the sun was inching over the horizon. He anchored the boat near a beach next to the point, and they all waded ashore, crystals in hand. They climbed up on top of the coral rock outcropping, shoulder to shoulder, staring out over the water at the rising sun. Without warning, the woman who appeared to be the ringleader raised her crystal over her head and started making what he could only describe as police siren noises. Then the rest joined in, crystals raised, caterwauling in a bizarre cacophony of almost unbearable sound. Just as the guide was about to ask them, please for the love of God, stop, the first dolphin appeared. Then another, and another. As they continued to wail, more and more showed up until there were dozens of them in the water beneath that rocky point, seemingly mesmerized by these women and their lunatic antics. Then without warning again, the women stopped and stood there in silence. The dolphins must have figured the show was over, and since none of the women seemed to have any dead fish to throw at them, they all slowly swam off. The ringleader turned and smiled at our friend and said, "Take us home."

He swears this is true, too.

The waters surrounding the islands are considered some of the best deep sea fishing spots in the world, attracting the likes of Ernest Hemingway. He used to hang out on the island, staying at the "Compleat Angler Hotel" back in the '30s and was said to have written *To Have and Have Not* while a guest at the hotel. Tragically, the hotel and bar burned to the ground in 2006, destroying a priceless cache of Hemingway photos and memorabilia, as well as taking the life of the owner. The ruins are still there today, and I am damned glad that I got to drink a few bottles of Kalik beer at the bar before the fire, and got to see the original signed photo of Hemingway with Carlos Gutiérrez, the inspiration for his book, *The Old Man and the Sea*.

Today, Bimini is a destination for lots of yacht-owing Miami weekenders who make the channel crossing in a few hours and spend their time fishing, diving, drinking, and having sex. The waters around Bimini are absolutely beautiful, attracting divers and snorkelers. Adding

The ruins of the burned-out Compleat Angler Hotel, one of Ernest Hemmingway's hang-outs back in the day. The fire destroyed priceless Hemingway photos and memorabilia, and took the life of the owner.

to that is the large number of shipwrecks which attract a huge array of fish. One of the wrecks I had the pleasure of visiting was the *SS Sapona*, a ship that was actually made of concrete and built during World War One. It was kind of creepy because its top half was exposed above the water looking like a ghost ship out of some horror movie. Underwater though, it was spectacular. I have never in my life seen such a large concentration of colorful reef fish that lived in and around the moldering submerged hull.

I knew that before we left Miami for Bimini, we'd be spending some time in Little Havana. At that time in New Mexico, I was working out with Massi, my pint-sized female Cuban trainer, who grew up in Little Havana, so I had her teach me several completely inappropriate and obscene Cuban-Spanish phrases that were guaranteed under the proper conditions, to get me shot or at least into a knife fight. Even more importantly, I got the name of a couple of great Cuban restaurants that we did go to. So now am I not only prepared to insult the local Cuban community, I am also prepared to eat well.

I flew into Miami a day early and caught a cab to the boat, which was literally five minutes away from the airport on the Miami River. The boat was by no means glamorous or fancy. It was a working dive boat that had seen many hours on the water, and was docked at an industrial ramshackle boatyard in a rundown part of town, miles from the ocean. I met Holly, Captain John or "Cappy" as I called him, and his first mate, and then stowed my crap in my cabin, which like everyone else's, was below deck. The cabins were very small, with tiny bunk beds and a communal john/shower down the hall. It was a boat toilet, meaning, you had to flip the timer switch before you flushed and let the pressure build up before it blasted the remnants of last night's repast out of the bowl and into its bilge tanks.

*Looking like a ghost ship, the WWI-era wreck of the SS Sapona. Its above-water decaying hull belies a virtual wonderland of reef fish below.*

"Cappy," was the captain of the dive boat, and had spent decades taking divers on excursions throughout the islands. He looked the part as well: Curly graying hair with an overfull beard and thick glasses, he was a cantankerous yet goodhearted character, who made no bones about it being HIS boat. Although we got along, I got to know his cantankerous side more than the other. I think he was confused by my presence on the boat. I wasn't there to collect fish. I had a fly rod and snorkel gear, and he or his first mate had the task of shuttling me with the boat's rubber dinghy into Mackey's Sand Bar at 7am to do the show that started at 8am Eastern Time, and then, they had to pick me back up at noon. Bottom line, I was a pain in his ass, and he was not shy about letting me know it.

Cappy carried a large firearm on board, and when I asked him why, he said quite simply, "Pirates." In his time travelling around the Caribbean, the drug trade was still alive and well, as was the occasional commandeering of boats that were suspected of having a stash on board. There was also the problem of stowaways. He told us the tale of a Nicaraguan stowaway who was in the cargo hold for three days before one of the divers finally noticed him when he crept back to his hiding place after using the boat john. Cappy went below deck, gun drawn, pulled the guy out, who offered no resistance, and restrained him in an empty bunk room. The man turned out to be polite, even gentle. He told his story of trying to escape the abject poverty of his native country by sneaking into the U.S. and making some money for his family. Sympathetic to his cause, but bound to do what was lawful, Cappy took a detour to the closest port, dropped him off with the local authorities, and continued on with his dive trip. He had no idea what the local law did with him.

So that night, we went to a cheap Cuban restaurant right across from the dog track and had some of the best seafood I've ever had for not much more than a McDonald's combo meal. Then we went to the liquor store with the task of stocking the boat with beer and wine for the entire week. Just so the City of Albuquerque doesn't get the wrong idea, the money for the booze was NOT from city funds and neither was the trip for that matter. I don't want them to get their civic panties in a wad. Even so, we didn't buy $150 bottles of Opus One or bizarre Belgian beers brewed by castrated monks. It was pretty much Bud and Coors Light, and whatever cheap wine I could find that wasn't totally repulsive.

The next day the rest of the people arrived, including former mayor of Albuquerque, Marty Chavez. Holly felt it appropriate that the mayor and I bunk together, and we spent many a peaceful night spooning, rocked to sleep by the gentle lapping of the tropical waves against the boat.

Not really.

After meeting all the participants and getting their gear stowed away, we all went out for another fine Cuban meal and then returned early to prepare for the overnight crossing to Bimini. Cappy sat us all down in the main room where we'd share meals and free time in the coming week, and read us the safety rules and regulations concerning the boat. The marine forecast was calling for 6- to 9-foot swells for the entire crossing, so we were told that once we hit the open ocean outside the relative safety of the Miami River, we'd all have to go to our bunks and remain there until we were in Bimini. Cappy ominously told us if any of us fell overboard during the crossing, we were pretty much dead, never to be found, con-sidering it would be the middle of the night and we were going to expe-rience rough seas. With that sobering informa-tion, we all gathered on deck around 7pm, as we departed the boatyard and made our way down the Miami River.

The trip to open wa-ter took a considerable amount of time as we were travelling slowly through a very urban area, giving us a unique, rarely seen perspective of the city. We triggered draw bridge after draw bridge, and the seedy neighborhoods gradually gave way to high-rise con-

Wow! Look at Holly Casman, Albuquerque Aquarium Manag-er sporting that bikini, and friend Mike Kelleher, Aquarist at the New England Aquarium, on the dive boat in Bimini.

dos and opulence as we approached downtown Miami and then Miami Beach, where the river emptied into north Biscayne Bay. Near the mouth of the river was a strangely unexpected sight. Docked on our left was an evil looking stealth submarine flying a French flag, looking almost like an elongated spaceship. In these post 9-11 days, we could only speculate what the hell it was doing there. And French? Maybe they were delivering fresh croissants to LeBron James.

Speaking of LeBron James...

There is some real money in Miami. Cappy related the story about when Cleveland expat LeBron left the Cavaliers to "Take his talents to South Beach." Cappy knew the realtor LeBron did business with. Apparently on their first meeting, LeBron asked the realtor to show him the "most expensive house in Miami." The realtor smiled and replied, "You can't afford it."

This has nothing to do with the story, but it's nice to see that even LeBron James gets humbled every once in a while.

Not that I still harbor any ill will towards him, or what he did to Cleveland.

The boat continued on towards the open waters of the Atlantic, South Beach to our left and Fisher Island to our right, which, by the way, has the highest per capita income of anywhere in the United States. Sorry, LeBron. You can't afford Fisher Island. As the lights of the city

My real reason for coming to Bimini. My ten-pound bonefish caught on my last day of fishing.

came on and started to become smaller and smaller on the ever-shrinking horizon, the wind picked up and the seas started to get noticeably rougher. Cappy barked that all of us needed to get below deck and into our bunks for the passage, which will take us east for another 46 miles, directly across the Gulf Stream and get us into Bimini very early the next morning.

It was rough. There was no getting around it. It wasn't "puke your guts out the entire way," rough, but more like a roller coaster ride. The boat would climb up to the top of a swell and then speed down the other side into the trench between the waves and then do it all over again. And this went on for several hours. It really wasn't that bad, once you got past the uneasy feeling that the big killer wave was out there, just one or two waves away that would send us all to a deep dark briny hell. I actually fell asleep and was awakened hours later by the sound of the water lazily lapping against the side of the boat inside the safety and calm of one of Bimini's protected bays. The sun was rising over the water, and it was a beautiful clear summer morning; I had to get up to make it through customs and then get to work.

Before I got to the islands, I talked to Frank Cooney, Jr., the guy who runs Mackey's Sand Bar, and he agreed to let me do the Morning Show from his place. Mackey's was literally a "sand" bar. The place had a sand floor, since it was built on a beach, and was on a rocky outcropping on the southernmost point of the northern island near Alice Town. Each morning the dingy would get me to the bar, I set up my equipment, had a cup of coffee, watched the sun rise, watched the fishing and dive boats leave the local marina, and more often than not, watched the same guy flyfishing for bonefish on the sand flat that was directly to my right. It was awesome. Frank would show up around the same time, usually after being up most of the night, and he'd tell me about the drunks from the night before, and the women who decided it was the perfect night to dance on the bar without a shirt on. Again, awesome.

Some of the women who liked to frequent Frank's bar worked at the shark lab, set up by a marine biologist from the University of Miami. I had one of the charming young ladies on my show as a guest one morning, who told tales of shark encounters and all the scary stuff they did. Most of it was not really scary, but we were talking about sharks, right? So, who am I to get all the facts straight and exaggerate from time to time? Anyway, she invited me back to the lab for a tour, which I immediately took her up on, and showed up that afternoon. The building was a small bungalow painted sea blue surrounded by palm trees, located about a hundred feet from the open water. There was a large lagoon in back where they kept their boats and equipment. I stood on the dock watching two immature barracuda pick off small bait fish one by one as I waited for Kristine to come out. Not only did she greet me, but she brought all of her female bikini-clad, 20-something graduate student co-workers with her, all attractive, tanned, and in my mind, willing. Then, I met the two guys that were also living there. That's right. Two guys, ten women, living in a tropical paradise, all young, sweaty, and full of pheromones, and all they had to do was go out on the boat once a day and count lemon sharks. And in my mind, these were the two luckiest males on earth, as I began to imagine twosomes, threesomes, tag teams, you name it. This was about the time I went into a deep depression, thinking I had completely blown my entire life. When I was in school, I was not even aware that a place like this existed, or that I could have possibly had the opportunity to work there! Why didn't I major in marine biology? Why didn't I go to the University of Miami? Why didn't someone in Cleveland tell me there was more to life than being a disc-jockey and a loser Browns fan?

Damn.

One of the things I made sure I did was to inform Frank about the importance of me doing as much fishing as possible while in Bimini. He was good enough to hook me up with one of the local fishing guides called "Bonefish Ebbie." Apparently, all the guides use "Bonefish" as their nicknames, adding an island charm to the whole thing, as there was a "Bonefish Willie," "Bonefish Samuel," and "Bonefish Joseph," and probably others who I hadn't met.

Frank drove me to the marina to meet Ebbie after my Wednesday show and he was waiting there with his fairly up-to-date flats boat. A small, slightly built, very dark man with a thick island accent, Ebbie greeted me with a big smile as we shook hands and got my gear onto the boat. We had to travel around the southern point of the island where Mackey's was and then go north and fish the mud flats and sand flats on the eastern side of the island. That side of the island is pretty much jungle. Mangroves lined the shore and the bottom is covered with sea grass. The mud flats were teeming with life. Crabs and shrimp scurried along the bottom while sharks, barracudas, and rays patrolled their territory above. Large, beautiful red starfish punctuated the sandy bottom areas between the vegetation.

When I'm flats fishing in or near the tropics, there's always a period of adjustment in order for me to see the fish. And even after that, I'm still not the best at spotting them, unless they're in a big school. So there's a lot of, "11-o'clock, fifty feet, cast now!" going on, and more often than not, I am relying on my guide to be my eyes. Luckily, I'm getting better at it, and the water in Bimini was so clear, it was easier for me to actually spot fish on my own. We got to the mud flats first, and luckily it didn't take me long to spot and hook my first bonefish. After my second or third fish, a curious barracuda began to accompany our boat. As Ebbie would pole us through the flats, it would patiently follow and stop when we stopped, keeping at a distance of about fifty feet. I found this quite unusual and Ebbie said, "He is waiting to make a meal of the next fish you catch." We saw a pair of bones slowly swimming from right to left, and I made my cast and the closer of the two took my fly and started to run. Almost instantly, the barracuda took off like a torpedo, racing at a vector to intercept my fleeing fish. It was over in less than a second. My line went immediately limp, and I had no fish, not even a part of a fish, and no fly either. Thinking this might have satisfied it, we tied on another shrimp pattern and continued poling up the shore, looking for more bonefish. Unfortunately, the barracuda returned again to follow. Another cast, another fish, and another barracuda assault, and another lost fly. That was enough. Ebbie powered up the motor and we took off for the sand flats farther up north.

What came next is one of those instances where you almost feel bad writing about it especially if you, the reader, are sitting at your cubicle at work, or in some dingy room with a bare light bulb over your head, or it's the dead of winter and you're suicidal because of a vitamin D deficiency caused by a lack of sunlight. We came to a point on the island and had to make a hard left to follow the shore, so I couldn't see what lay ahead. As we made the point and turned the corner, I found myself in heaven. A vista of turquoise blue water appeared, stretching as far as the eye could see. It was a sand flat bigger than any I'd seen. Its beauty bordered on surreal, like something someone had painted and you commented, "That's bullshit! Reality could never look like that!"

Well, my friends, it did. The water hues were in gradients of blue, bright blue, and even violet as it approached the horizon. The sand underneath was as white as diamonds, with large orange starfish or other sea creatures scattered on the bottom. An occasional ray or shark were on patrol, and even more importantly, were the darker areas in the distance that were moving; huge schools of bonefish entering and leaving the flats, looking for a meal before the sharks noticed them. We would key onto a school and Ebbie would race the boat ahead of where they were traveling, and then we'd sit and wait for it to get in casting range. His advice was always the same: "Make sure you get your cast into the middle of the school because there are jacks on the edges, and they'll get your fly before the bonefish see it."

Needless to say, I caught a lot of jacks that day, which was OK with Ebbie because he and his family loved to eat them, so we kept every jack I caught until he had enough in his cooler. On my good casts, I also caught my fill of bonefish. We followed the same school for at least an hour, with each of my casts resulting in a fish.

When we got tired of doing that, we took the boat around the rest of the island where there was a passage into the interior. After passing through mangrove channels and other unnamed routes, we emerged at an open bay with the backside of Alice Town to our left, and a new area where they were building a new resort. This new development was ill-planned and when they decided to dredge a deep- water inlet for the new marina before doing any hydrological studies, they broke through to the island's only freshwater aquifer, inundating it with saltwater, thereby ruining the islands water supply, probably forever. So now the island's drinking water has to be shipped in. Brilliant. What they hadn't ruined (yet) was the flats area that backed up to where the construction was going on. As we poled closer to the shore, Ebbie noticed two per-mits the size of large Thanksgiving turkey platters feeding up against the baby mangroves. I made two or three 60- to 70-foot casts before I spazzed out and knocked by sunglasses off my head swatting at some kind of flying vermin. Of course, that action spooked the fish and we spent the next ten minutes looking at the bottom through the sea grass before miraculously finding them. Dumb-ass.

We poled further down to a point when Ebbie yelled "Quickly! Thir-ty feet at ten o'clock...cast now!" It was probably the best way to get me to do anything in a flats boat. I had no time to think or prepare. I raised my rod and fired off a blind cast, hoping I was at least close to where he was pointing. As soon as my fly hit the water, I instantly got a rod-bending strike. It was the biggest bonefish I'd ever hooked, and I didn't even see it. It wasted no time in blasting out towards open water, with my line burning off my reel, getting into my backing in a flash. Ebbie was visibly excited. "You don't want to lose this one, Mon!" he yelled in island speak. I frantically tried to get the fish back onto my fly line as Ebbie poled in the direction the fish was running. After twenty minutes, and several runs to the end of my backing, it finally tired, and Ebbie boated what we estimated a ten-pounder--my biggest, and one of the biggest Ebbie had ever boated. He could have been lying to make me feel better, but at least that's what he told me.

At some point I looked over at Ebbie and said, "I'm sure you heard this before, but I gotta tell you anyway. You DO realize that you're living in paradise, don't you?" He just grinned a big grin and nodded in affirmation. I hope he does. When you're born and raised in one of the most beautiful places on earth, maybe it gets old too. Maybe it's just another day in the same place with the same scenery and all the same troubles. At that point, I found myself longing for a simple life on his island, not working too hard, making enough cash to feed my family when some American tourist like me throws down a couple of Franklins to go fishing. I think I could manage to do that. I sure would miss my wife!

*A couple of my secret places on the Pecos happen to be right above or below fenced private waters, where I have caught and released several trophy-sized trout, courtesy of the adjacent property owner.*

# 12 PRIVATE PARTS

I HAVE SPENT MOST OF MY ADULT FLY FISHING LIFE on the rivers and lakes in the Rockies, mostly New Mexico and Colorado. I am not a trespasser. As everybody intimately involved in the flyfishing world will tell you, before you get your ass pumped full of birdshot, common sense would tell you to ask permission first before entering private land. Or, if after mistakenly entering private land on foot you are confronted with an irate landowner, apologize profusely and get off his property before he fills your ass with birdshot. I get it. Who would want a bunch of people like us walking around on their lower forty while they're out in the gazebo with a bottle of wine having a nooner with the old lady? This is common sense stuff. This got me to asking, what is legal and illegal when it comes to river usage in America? To find out, I went to three different sources. I checked out the website, rivers.org which was very helpful. Then I asked Bob Gerding, and I asked Dick Gerding, Bob's identical twin brother who lives in Farmington, New Mexico and is an attorney. Dick has litigated river access cases, and is intimately involved in preserving and promoting the San Juan River in northern New Mexico.

First to the website: I asked the question, "Who owns the rivers in the U.S.," and here's what I found, and I am quoting from the website: "The U.S. Supreme Court has held that the bed and banks under all rivers, lakes, and streams that are navigable, are owned by the states, held in trust for the public. The public trust ownership extends up to the ordinary high-water line (or ordinary high-water mark) encompassing what is commonly referred to as the submerged and submersible land, as opposed to the upland."

If I'm reading this correctly, according to the feds, if we access any navigable river above or below private land, we can legally fish through private land if we stay between the high-water marks on either side if we don't venture beyond those high-water marks. So far so good.

Now, what defines a "navigable river?" That is where it gets goofy. There are several definitions, including those from the Rivers and Harbors Act of 1899, the Clean Water Act, and the Commerce Clause in the U.S. constitution. Quoting rivers.org again: "None of these definitions...is the same definition federal courts use to determine navigability... This has caused much confusion, such as the common misconception that only a few particularly large rivers are legally navigable. The fact is that even rivers and streams that can be navigated only by small watercraft and logs are still navigable for title purposes..."

It still looks good for most of us, right? OK, how small of a watercraft do you mean?

More from the website: "Federal courts have held that even those rivers that are navigable only by small, non-motorized watercraft are still navigable for title purposes."

Looking better and better! We're talking canoes, kayaks, and yes, drift boats. Meaning, if you can float through it, it's legal to wade through it, right?

More questions and answers from rivers.org. "Do shallows, rapids, and other obstacles make a river non-navigable?" The answer? "No. The courts make no requirements that a river be uniformly deep, or flat, or that navigation be practical going upstream as well as downstream...the presence of...even numerous rapids and waterfalls, does not disqualify a river."

Yippie! And it even gets better in the eyes of the feds. Even if the property owner's deed reads "to the middle of a river" or "surrounds and includes the river," according to the federal government, it doesn't matter. Federal law says the states own the riverbed and banks of all rivers which are defined as navigable.

Bob Gerding says there is historical precedent that makes rivers free. He notes, "Think about the settlement of the West when there were no roads. The rivers were the highways of the 1800s. All things moved on the rivers including trade goods, people, etc. So, no land owner could limit access on a river."

Rivers.org goes a step further: "Rivers....have been public since ancient times in all civilized societies...in colonial America they were held for the public by the king of England. "

Then what's the problem? Federal law says navigable rivers are public and owned by the states. Period.

Not so fast, bucko.

You might recall that America fought that Civil War thing, which of course involved the abolition of slavery, but also was fought over "states' rights." For instance, what happens if the feds say you can't stand naked on a street corner, and South Dakota says its citizens consider standing naked on street corner part of their rich historical tradition. In fact, they have "Standing Naked on a Street Corner Day" every August 23, along with parades and face painting, so the feds can cram it.

What happens then? It depends on the political party in power, on how important the feds think stopping the standing naked thing is, and probably most importantly, what the expense of enforcing such a federal law in court might be.

With our particular dilemma, two things come into play. First, most landowners have passionate feelings about their private property remaining private, which includes their God-given right to a nasty disposition towards anyone who might wander over their property line.

Second, realize that several states have laws contradicting federal law, believing the current law is outdated and impedes on property owner's personal freedom. This creates the perfect climate for long, drawn-out, expensive court battles that might take years and more money than most of us care to part with.

Landowner Lou Rixham adroitly shows what can happen if you fish on private land without permission.

is, if you see this is about to happen, break off the fish before you hit the rapids. But how many people are actually willing to do this? If landowners would think about it, they would allow boats to temporarily anchor while fighting fish, not only because of potential fish-kill, but because you have fishermen dragging fish several hundred yards downstream, though rapids, and out of your property, you could lose the fish to another holding area out of your stretch of the river anyway. Again, this is common sense stuff.

OK, back to the original point. If you want to have the opportunity to legally fish public and private navigable waters, head north to Montana, which has the most liberal river access laws in the country. There, you can proudly and with confidence enter Ted Turner's vast empire and fish the entire length of his navigable river, provided you stayed between the high-water marks. But don't trespass to gain access to his property because you will be thrown in jail like a common meth cooker. Meaning, you have to find a public access point above or below to enter in. You better do it soon though, because the issue is still a hotly contested one, and who knows how long it will remain legal.

In conclusion, if you wanted to challenge your state's laws and purposely trespass on someone's "private" stretch of river and then take it to court...if you have gobs of time and mountains of money, and your case makes it all the way to the Federal Appeals Court, even to the Supreme Court, you'd most likely win. Really.

There are ways to do this, and rivers.org has some of the necessary forms and information that you'll need to fight the good fight. But now you need to ask yourself some pretty important questions: Is it worth the time, effort, and money? Is it worth alienating all your neighbor landowners who will, at the very least, shun you at the local Walmart? Is it worth possibly alienating the county sheriff, who happens to be good friends with all the local landowners, who will make it a point to notice the burned-out turn signal on your truck, or notice that cigarette in your ashtray smells kinda "skunky?" Is it worth turning into one of those guys who is "on a mission," who gets written up at work or loses his job because his performance is faltering? Is it worth being one of those guys who ignores his wife or girlfriend to the point where they find some big biker guy on the side because you ain't gettin' it done? Is it worth all that?

Yes, it is.

I encourage every single one of you get out there and stick it to

State laws can be interesting. Dick Gerding tried and won a case involving a landowner who thwarted access to his stretch of the San Juan River in New Mexico by running a cable across it so no drift boats could pass. Dick won the case because the San Juan is a tributary of the Colorado River, therefore is navigable. But he also won the case because the cable-wielding plaintiff might have owned the riverbed, but he didn't own the water that travelled through his land. More on that in a second.

On the other hand, in New Mexico and Colorado, it is perfectly legal to run a cable or fence across your river on your property line, if your river is not considered navigable. Those of you who have fished the Pecos River in northern New Mexico know what I'm talking about. This happens a lot when land owners take it upon themselves to stock their stretch of paradise with lunker trout and don't want their investment poached away. However, as many savvy fishermen know, just because you stock big fish in one part of the river doesn't mean they're gonna stay there. A couple of my secret places on the Pecos happen to be right above or below fenced private waters, where I have caught and released several trophy-sized trout, courtesy of the adjacent property owner. Thanks, man. You made my day.

Dick Gerding won his case because New Mexico state law, and Colorado for that matter, says although private landowners do not own the water, they do own the riverbed. This means you can't wade through somebody's land because your feet are touching the bottom of the river and therefore you are trespassing. But, since the water in the river is nature's gift to all of us and owned by no one person, you can legally pay a guide to drift you through it. However, if you are drifting through someone's land and hook a fish, you can't anchor to fight it because the anchor will be firmly planted on the landowner's real estate, and you will be trespassing. Any fishing guide will tell you that this clause in the law is short-sighted and boneheaded. It has severe unintended consequences that result in unintentional and unnecessary fish-kill. I can't count how many times this has happened to me and Mo while drifting the Arkansas River near Salida, Colorado with my buddy Jer. With Jer at the helm, one of us hooks a fish. Since we're on private property we can't stop so we have to keep going. More often than not, especially on a wild river like the Arkansas, we hit a bunch of rapids, meaning if the fish hasn't been landed, it skis along behind the raft and can possibly drown. (Yes, fish can drown.) Of course, the rule of thumb the man! While you're spending all your waking time and money, I'll be kicking back on my porch with a beer waiting to hear an update from the heat of the battle. And when you succeed, I'll give you a big pat on the back and maybe even down the road, I might wade onto Farmer John's property and make a cast or two, in recognition of your hard-fought victory. You go, boy!

# 13 THE BRAZOS RIVER RANCH— HIGH ALTITUDE BLISS

*"When Mo gets freaked out, he does this weird thing with his eyes. His eyeballs start darting back and forth and he gets a quizzical, almost constipated look on his face."*

DOUCHEBAG MACKENZIE. ONE OF THE MANY characters I have met along the way during my fly-fishing career. He is a fine fly-fisherman and great cook, and I met him one fall at the Brazos River Ranch in about the most remote corner of northern New Mexico that you could imagine. A stocky Scotsman somewhere in his 30's with unruly red hair, he served as the lodge cook for the time we were there. He had a great wit, especially with a little 80-proof encouragement. I vaguely recall how the nickname "Douchebag" came into being. It is assuredly not his baptismal name. But its genesis occurred in the lodge kitchen/dining room after a hard day's fishing and a few beers. He was describing some boneheaded incident involving a woman earlier in his life and ended the tale by lamenting loudly, "What a fucking douchebag I was!" That elicited explosions of laughter from all of us, and someone said "Douchebag Mackenzie! That kind of rolls off your tongue!" We all enthusiastically agreed, and it stuck, at least for the entire time we were there. It might have had something to do with the altitude and alcohol since we were at high altitude and not shy about drinking too much. And why did I bring Mackenzie up? No particular reason. He was just one of the enjoyably crazy pieces that contributed to another great fishing trip! Hopefully he still has a sense of humor.

I don't normally gush all over the page when I talk about places I've fished. However, this place... In all my travels and I've travelled a lot, fishing the Brazos River Ranch was hands down one of the best fishing experiences I've ever had. The accommodations and facilities were simple yet more than adequate. We stayed in trucked-in log cabins that slept two, arranged in a large circle around a grass meadow with a large fire pit. The lodge, which served as the kitchen, dining room, and public area, sat on the far end. There was one shower and bathroom for all to share which was next to the lodge. The food was plentiful and good, but not something you'd find at a Michelin-ranked restaurant.

The lodge is situated on the headwaters of the Brazos River, on top of a 10,000-foot plateau, high above the town of Chama. The river, or more appropriately, the creek, takes a jagged route south where Brazos Falls, New Mexico's highest waterfall, plunges a spectacular 1300 feet off a cliff. It continues below, eventually joining the Chama River flowing south and eventually entering the Rio Grande. Depending on the winter's snowpack, the falls sometimes runs dry, but it never has at the lodge, in recent memory anyway.

The setting for fishing was perfect. To get to the river from the lodge you had to drive for about a mile on a graveled but rutted switchback road. The Brazos runs through a high mountain meadow, mostly devoid of fly-eating trees. The hills surrounding the meadow were covered in an ancient pine forest, some possibly never cut before. There are groves of aspen thriving where there's enough sunshine, but it's mostly pine, in some areas so thick that it's perpetual dusk under the canopy. The river is maybe 100 feet from bank to bank at its widest, and it's easily wadable and walkable. This is not a driftable river and doesn't need to be. The wildlife is spectacular. The ranch doubles as a hunting lodge as the area hosts one of the largest elk herds in the state. It was not uncommon to acquire elk or deer as temporary companions as you trudged upstream.

One of those archetypal moments happened to me one fall as I was fishing the ranch with my nephew, Jim. It was a cool sunny autumnal morning as we slowly walked upstream from riffle to riffle when we heard a loud thundering noise to our right. We both turned to look at the same time towards the tree-covered hillside when a huge bull elk followed by his harem of cows crashed through the trees and stampeded across the river, not more than fifty yards in front of us. The ground shook as they passed by. We stood there in awe, knowing we'd witnessed something special up close, something wildlife photographers would give their right nut to witness. Then all was silent except for the sound of the river flowing by. I don't remember who spoke first, but I think the words "Holy Shit!" may have been uttered.

Most importantly, the fishing was remarkable. Not many people have fished it, and only small numbers were allowed access at a given time. Large rainbows, wild browns, and New Mexican Cutts live in its waters and surprisingly, it boasts one of the best naturally reproducing brook trout fisheries in the west. I was fortunate enough to catch a large Brookie that missed the state record mark by a half-inch. I can't prove it because as always, no pic was taken, but Jim was there and will swear it's the truth if enough money passes hands.

The only negative is the length of the fishing season. Maybe, and I mean MAYBE it is fishable three months out of the year. July is a good time to start, when the spring run-off is finally over. In September, fishing is still superb, but the weather is less reliable. That's also when the elk are in a romantic mood, which brings the hunters in. At the end of the month, the snows begin as winter sets in early at high-altitude, making the only road in and out impassable.

Getting there is half the fun, and can be quite a challenge, especially if rain was in the forecast. Mo accompanied me one year in mid-August on a particularly arduous drive in. Driving through northern New Mexico is always a trip, literally and figuratively. As you drive beyond Santa Fe, passing through Española travelling north on U.S. 285, you cross into a different world in a different time. You pass through wide expanses of high desert, dotted with tiny villages, inhabited by descendants of the first Spanish incursion into the New World. I am told this area is so isolated, that many of its people still speak in a Spanish dialect from the seventeenth century. The story goes that recently, a member of Spanish royalty was took a tour of this area, and when he spoke with some of the people, he thought they were making fun of him because of the archaic, stilted Spanish dialect they were using. Talk about being isolated for over 300 years...

It is also said that some of these areas are so ignored by the rest of the state that they're considered "lawless," and still part of the Old West. Visitors are told to consider that fact in their choice of activities. All I can say is, I've heard stories. That said, I've always been treated well, except for that one time at the Dairy Queen in the village of Chama, but that ain't worth talking about.

There is only one road into the ranch, and you had better have four-wheel drive. Mo and I took a left turn off U.S. 285 onto a fairly well-maintained graveled road a few miles past the town of Tres Piedras, and began our journey northwestward towards the ranch. It had just rained so we knew we might run into trouble further in when the road turned into a rocky rutted mess. We had already travelled more than two hours from Albuquerque, and had 37 more miles to go on this road. However, as we were warned, this next 37 miles could also take another 2 hours depending on how bad it was ahead. The sun was out and we circled around the backside of San Antonito Mountain, which was a huge grass-covered extinct volcano where cattle were grazing contentedly on its slopes. It marked the southeastern end of the San Juan Mountains, the large mountain chain where the headwaters of much of New Mexico's water originated. We were in high desert grassland, filled with pronghorns and mule deer, although we saw none that day. As we drove further the road began to rise and started following a small, yet fishable stream. The grassland gave way to sage and live oak, and then as we gained more altitude, to pine and aspen. And that's when the road turned into a rut-covered muddy mess, with deep pools of rainwater every quarter-mile or so. I shifted down into Low 4 and continued on. Coming in the opposite direction was a mud-caked Ford Fiesta, driven by a young hippie-chick, with her man-bunned boyfriend sitting in the passenger seat. She was stressed. Her hands had a vicelike grip on the steering wheel and as we pulled to a stop abreast of each other she asked how much farther it was to the main road, and was the road passable. They had already been stuck once in deep muddy ruts so I assured her she had already driven through the worst. Her boyfriend was silent, probably too buzzed to speak. I hoped he at least got out of the car to help. She inched back onto the road as Mo and I wondered why in the hell they were on this road to begin with. Then a couple miles ahead after driving through a sloppy mess, and amazed that the Fiesta wasn't still stuck in one of the mud pools; we saw a turn-off with a solitary picnic table near the stream. So much for a pleasant outing. The road continued to climb and we crept along as best we could. After nearly two hours, my altimeter said we'd reached 9600 feet, which meant we were getting close. Up ahead the road forked to the left where there was an unreadable wooden sign nailed to a tree. I knew we had to take a left but I wasn't sure if this was the turn, so we kept going straight. Bad idea. The wind picked up and clouds were rolling in again, promising another thunderstorm as the road narrowed even more and entered the darkest, thickest primeval pine forest I have ever seen. It appeared it had never seen a saw or an ax, ever. The trees were huge and very tall, and so close together, I could hardly imagine how wildlife could traverse it. And it got dark. Not only from the approaching storm, but also from the meager amount of light that forced itself between the tree limbs. It was like being in some witch's enchanted forest and honestly, it was unsettling. If we had a problem and we got lost, they MIGHT find our gnawed-upon skeletons decades later, or never.

When Mo gets freaked out, he does this weird thing with his eyes. His eyeballs start darting back and forth and he gets a quizzical, almost constipated, look on his face. This is compounded by the fact that he stands about 6'2" with a large bald head, scraggly hair and beard, and weighs maybe 130. If James Taylor and Ichabod Crane had a baby, there he is. I took one look at him and knew we could get into some serious trouble. I figured we had better turn around soon before either the second storm hit or the flying monkeys started dive-bombing the truck. As this realization hit me, we came over a berm and I slammed on the brakes because at the bottom the road, which had pretty much become a trail, had completely washed out, and a huge pond stood in front of us. I put the truck in park, we both got out, took one look at the water and both concluded there was no way in hell we would chance driving through it. There was barely room for a three-point turn, so as Mo directed me, I slowly inched the truck back and forth until we were facing in the opposite direction, and just as the new storm presented itself with an ominous low rumble of thunder, we started back towards the fork. This time I took it and in less than five minutes parked in front of the lodge just as the skies opened up. We ran inside where Bo, the owner and our host greeted us. I told him what happened and complained half-jokingly about the sign and he said, "Yeah, I really have to put something better up there. And you know, it's good you turned around because that road literally turns into a trail and then disappears altogether. You could have been in deep shit!"

Great. Good to know for next time.

After Mackenzie's breakfast and before we left the lodge the next morning, we talked to Bo and Mackenzie about what flies we'd need. Bo said "Don't even bother below the surface," and handed each of us a couple oversized, gaudy, leggy, black rubber Chernobyl ants with bright pink foam parachutes on top. "These usually do the trick," he said. "If you really feel the need to fish under, just throw on anything." Being somewhat skeptical, we politely took the giant ants and headed out.

There is nothing like fishing waters that have rarely seen human traffic. A place where the fish are dumb as hell, and will strike at anything that resembles a meal unless it was cast at them like a caveman. Don't get me wrong; there is much pleasure gained by catching finicky fish in challenging water. The satisfaction of fooling a big learned trout with the perfect cast is certainly hard to beat. However, rarely do you find waters like these without having to travel thousands of miles and spend a crapload of money doing it. Those were the conditions that awaited us as we drove down the hill to the Brazos the next morning. Bob Gerding and Milt had joined us the night before, along with a couple other guys Bob brought with him for some kind of business perk, so there were six of us and plenty of river to spread out on. We paired up, all chose a particular area, and the fun began.

The only thing that kept this from being a perfect day on the river were the persistent lines of squalls that moved through several times, but that's why Jesus created lightweight breathable raingear. There was one cave...OK... more like a deep rock overhang on the river that doubled as a rain shelter that we accessed at least a few times. Despite the frequent interruptions, it was one of those days that every place that you'd expect a fish to be, there indeed was one. Every rock, every deep pool, every riffle, every undercut bank at a bend in the river was populated by a large, healthy fish.

Mo was somewhere downstream doing something, I imagine fishing, or contemplating the
universe and our pathetic existence, which he often does. As mentioned somewhere else in this book, Mo is the slowest, most anal, meticulous, methodical fishing partner I've ever had. Most so-called fly-fishing experts tell you to take a cast or two, and if nothing happens, move up and repeat, and so on. Apparently, Mo missed that lesson somewhere. He will spend upwards of a half hour in one specific area, covering each square inch of water with surgical precision. The same expert would say that he most likely lined every fish in that particular riffle or hole and he was just pretty much jerking off. Not so, my friends. With extreme patience and perseverance, and supposedly against all common sense, he would win out. I've seen him pull in more than one monster trout out of the same area after not moving from the same position. Is it luck? Is it skill? Is he a fish-whisperer? Or do the trout get so annoyed at seeing the same damned fly over and over again that they lash out in anger? Beats the hell out of me.

I was maybe a quarter-mile above him in at the bottom of a straight-line riffle that stretched in front of me for maybe fifty yards. I had my Chernobyl ant tied on, and figured I'd start low and work the left undercut bank first and then work my way to the middle. I put my first cast in the high grass next to the bank, which I like to do, gave my line a little twitch and the fly plopped down directly next to the bank. Immediately a large dark shape darted out and took my fly with abandon. It was a large brown, and was apparently confused by being hooked. It tried to retreat back to its holding area under the bank, but feeling the pressure I was applying, it shot out into the river and sped past me downstream. I followed, not like Brad Pitt in the movie, but retreated from the riffle about fifty feet, careful not to freak out any other fish that might be holding there. After a few minutes it tired and I managed to net the 22-inch beauty and release it unharmed. My first cast of the day and success. I walked back to where I was and this time, cast about ten feet off the left bank. Another immediate strike and an immediate jump. This time, it was a healthy rainbow, maybe 16 inches. I also worked it downstream as well, and it was in the net after a short fight. Then, back to my original position. I cast this time to the middle of the stream. Another immediate strike and another healthy rainbow, maybe 18 inches. That was three casts and three fish. This was getting weird. Was I good, lucky, or did they just dump a truckload of big trout into the river a few days ago? In total during the first 45 minutes or so, I made exactly ten casts resulting in ten fish, the last one being another 20" brown under the bank about fifty feet in front of the first one. Now I know what you're thinking: I'm either full of shit or I'm bragging about my piscatorial expertise. Fair enough. But you gotta trust me on this one.

I figured that was enough success for a while. I left the stream, sat down on the far bank and lit a cigar, thinking I had just died and entered some kind of trout heaven. I got up and walked downstream to see if Mo had moved an inch or two from where I'd left him. As I was walking towards him, it was almost in slow-motion. I saw him cast, watched the fly hit the water just above the right side of a large rock, and as the fly drifted over the sweet spot, a dimple formed around it as a rainbow slurped it down. He set the hook and it made an athletically awesome vertical jump. Mo might have too, but I was watching the fish. Then in perfect Mo form, he gently engaged in a not-too-lengthy battle and brought the fish to bay; another healthy 18-incher. It was his fourth fish.

And that was the story of the rest of our day, except as we walked higher up the river, we started catching Brookies and an occasional cut-throat. When the rains came, it didn't seem to matter to the fish, but it started mattering to us, so we continued to seek shelter. At around 4 PM we all met back at the trucks. We all had been isolated from each other, so this was the first occasion to see how everyone did. As we were enjoying cigars and fine libacious beverages, Bob asked everyone, "So how many fish do you think you caught?" The guesses ranged from the high teens to the mid-thirties. Bob turned to Milt who had not answered and said, "Milt, how many?" He reached down into his vest pocket and pulled out a bright red clicking fish counter and beaming happily said, "Uhh, let me check... 33!"

Milt is a fine fly-fisherman. He is also a very successful businessman, very good with numbers, and is a great decision maker. If there was one decision that Milt would regret, at least for the remainder of this trip, it would be the fateful decision to bring that fish counter along with him. Bob said nothing for a second, and then he slowly started smiling and got this glint in his eye, the glint of a wolf about to pounce on unsuspecting prey. Milt, at that instant, knew he was doomed.

"Thirty-three you say? That's mighty fine clicker you got there! You sure it wasn't 34 or even 32? Maybe you tripped on a rock and clicked it by accident!"

Milt's face turned beet red, and he gamely laughed along, enduring Bob's unmerciful and hilarious onslaught.

"You know," Bob continued, "back in the old days before they made clickers like that, I used a pocketknife to notch a slit in my right forearm so I could keep track. Man, by the end of some days, I was a bloody mess!"

We all laughed, including Milt, got in the trucks and went back to our respective cabins. That night after Mackenzie's dinner of rib-eyes and baked beans, we went out and sat around a blazing fire, and as the bourbon flowed, Bob held court. Having fished all over the world, he told tales of his adventures, finishing each anecdote with, "And I didn't have a goddamn clicker on that trip either!"

# 14 DICK CHENEY

*All three of us looked up into the sky and as we watched,
the helicopters broke formation and literally
surrounded us...*

FLY FISHING OR SPORT FISHING IN GENERAL, is not political, at least in theory. You might be a screaming liberal or a tea party conservative, but you may find yourselves standing side by side on a fine Rocky Mountain trout stream, blissfully engaged in an activity that you both actually agree is a good thing. In fact, fishing may be one of the few things that bring each side together at least on one issue: the effort to protect and restore our national waters and the beautiful lands they flow through and touch. Remarkable environmental accomplishments—from dam removal to habitat restoration—have occurred because fishermen, of even radically differing political views, have found common ground. I could go on and state the obvious that... Gee, maybe if we can agree on THAT, maybe we could take it a step further and... Ahhh, screw it. That's just crazy talk.

I have never met Dick Cheney. I don't know much about the man except for what I've seen in the media and what people who know him have told me. What I do know is he is an avid outdoorsman and fly fisherman, and if you've ever fished the Snake River and surrounding waters near Jackson Hole, Wyoming, everyone had their own personal tale of the former vice president, who owns a home there and considers those his home waters. Unbeknownst to Mr. Cheney, our paths crossed on a cloudy, somewhat rainy day on the Snake River back in the middle of the George W. Bush presidency.

Jackson Hole is one of the most beautiful places on earth. The Grand Tetons' awesomely jagged peaks rise as a granite border between Wyoming and the Snake River to the east, and Idaho and the south fork of the Snake to the west. One could argue that within two hours of the town lie the best flyfishing waters in the continental United States, which include all the famous southeastern Montana rivers, and Yellowstone National Park beckoning to the north.

Jackson Hole is rich, touristy, and expensive. Normal people can't afford to live there. I keep getting a real estate brochure from one of these new river developments who are under the insane delusion that I might be interested in buying one of their mini-river ranches for the price of the entire town of Salida, Colorado. Even post-bubble recessionista prices on these places are still stratospherically high and make me feel like I'm a failure in life because I apparently have not achieved enough financial success to one day see my moving truck backing up to one of these babies. Jackson Hole is where the super-rich build their second homes and the rest of the town struggles to make a living as their supporting cast. Depending on the day if you're into it, you might see the likes of Mr. Cheney, or Sting, or Sandra Bullock during your visit. I could never live there because the winters are bitter cold and I am an avowed sissy when it comes to keeping warm. Despite everything I just wrote, I like Jackson Hole. The town is western, artsy, has plenty of good restaurants, and its natural beauty and great fishing keeps me coming back.

My run-in with Dick Cheney happened on a family trip with our good friends from Cleveland, Al and Karen, and Al's New York City sister, Judy, in 2006. Karen has the voice of an angel and sings with the Cleveland Symphony Orchestra chorus, and at times gets to hob-nob with the cultural elite. She was hobnobbing at one such function and won her bid at a silent auction for a week's stay at a house in Alta, Wyoming, which is on the other side of the Tetons from Jackson Hole. So off we all went.

The July weather was less than perfect with some sunny days interspersed with fog, clouds and storms. While the girls were mapping out their plans for shopping, galleries, and restaurants, Al and I walked down to a fine and very well-known flyfishing shop and outfitter in town to book a day on the Snake with one of their guides. The owner and I had a few friends in common, so we kind of hit it off, and somehow the subject of Dick Cheney is brought up. He said, "Oh yeah, we take him out all the time. The funny thing is, you can't just take Dick Cheney, the Vice President of the United States out on a float trip. You need three boats. One for Dick and his guide, another for his doctor and all the medical equipment he brings along, and the other for his secret service agents."

Apparently, the Secret Service will do a re-con of the area where he's going to be fishing beforehand, then they all get in their boats and the armada takes off downstream. I forgot to ask how decent of a fly fisherman he is.

Al and I showed up early on the morning we booked for the trip. It was cold, dark, foggy, and damp. It rained pretty good the night before, so we're thinking the Snake was pretty much blown out. It was no surprise when we got to the shop and our guide confirmed our suspicions. Ever the optimist and not wanting to miss a day's work, he suggested we put in a little further upstream and fish some of the feeder streams and spring creeks, using the Snake as a highway to get to them. Our time is limited since this is not a true "fishing" vacation, and we're already up, so we agreed. After our half-hour or so drive, we found the river is a turgid, bloated brown mess. But the sky cleared and it turned into a beautiful sunny morning. As promised, we drifted from feeder stream to feeder stream which fortunately for us were running clear. We met with some success generally using dry-droppers, with Al getting the trophy fish of the day, a nice 18-inch cutt that he coaxed from beneath an undercut bank. We sat down for lunch and for a while just took in the stunning beauty of where we were. I don't know about you, but when I'm fishing, I get so intent at the task at hand, I rarely look up. At times my concentration is such that I could be in inner city Detroit and not realize it. During lunch, and maybe when I take a leak, are two times when I actually look around and appreciate why we come to places like this.

Lunch was over and clouds were building and the wind was picking up again. We got back in the boat and decided that the rest of the day was probably a bust, so our guide started our return down the Snake heading towards the put-out. We were still a couple of miles above the airport and there were no other boats on the water, so we figured everyone else either decided not to go out or gave up early. We still had a ways to go so our guide, with his camo-ed drift boat is rowing downstream at a steady pace. We noticed a faint aircraft noise and looking up into the slate gray sky, we saw three helicopters flying in formation that appeared to be coming in our general direction. Not thinking much about it, we kept drifting down the river. As they got closer, we realized these are military attack helicopters, and as they continued to approach us, they started to slow down. NOW they have our attention. All three of us looked up into the sky and as we watched, the helicopters broke formation and literally surrounded us with their noses all pointing towards our little drift boat. With noses turned towards us, they hovered in the air and drifted downstream with us, perfectly keeping pace. At this point we started nervously chattering:

"What the hell is going on?"

"I don't know! Any of you have a criminal record?"

"Yeah, they probably think we're terrorists or something!"

"You're probably right! In fact, right now, they're probably taking our pictures and listening to every word we're saying!"

"Hey, let's mess with 'em! You know how to speak Farsi?"

This went on for about five minutes and apparently the military decided they had enough of us and flew away towards the Tetons on our right, leaving us relieved and curious as to what just happened. We continued drifting downstream, laughing and wisecracking about it all, when it happened. Up from behind a line of foothills a couple of miles toward the mountains, the helicopters slowly rose vertically, almost in slow motion, like a scene out of a Rocky Mountain "Apocalypse Now," and then in attack formation started flying directly at us at full speed. We sat in our boat stunned, unable to speak as they bore down upon us, rotors shrieking, the noise almost deafening as they got closer and closer, flying at treetop level right...at...us. We are surely going to die. And then at the very last second, just when every part of the fine lunch I had just consumed had wadded up in a projectile-shaped ball in my lower colon ready for launch, all three pulled up and sped away to the south, and whether it was in my mind or I really heard it, I thought I heard laughing and strains from "Ride of the Valkyries" coming out of the back of one of those helicopters. We all sat there, in silence, looking at each other, wondering again, what had just happened and what kind of god would allow it to occur, when we realized we were almost to the airport. And there, taking off from the Jackson runway, was Air Force 2.

Damn you Dick Cheney!

Apparently, the vice president was about to take off and the helicopters were dispatched to check us out. Granted, we were in the vicinity of the airport, and were the only boat on the river, and if you really think about it, how did they know our fly rods weren't actually hybridized shoulder-mounted surface to air missile launchers? How did they know that our guide was not part of an al Qaeda sleeper cell that had been sent to Jackson Hole to take out the vice president? I mean, he DID have one of those cover-the head face masks on that the terrorists wear.

The vacation was over, and we got back to Albuquerque safely. And, doing what I do for a living, I related this story as best as I could on the 94 Rock Morning Show. And after the show was over, I got an email from a certain individual who works with the military there in town, who is very well-versed on "things of this nature." He wrote: "You said you were joking about them watching you, about them taking your picture and listening to every word you were saying? Well, let me tell you. When they were drifting down the river with you, they WERE taking all of your pictures, putting them in a computer and sending them back to see if you matched any terror suspects. And they WERE listening to and recording your voices to see if those matched as well. And yeah, if they found it necessary, they were ready to blow you guys right out of the water!"

That's just great.

So now somewhere in some secret location, probably 30 stories underground, there are pictures and recordings of three douche-bag fly fishers from a late afternoon in July on the Snake River. I emailed the guy back and said, "OK. That's all well and good, but why did they go away and then fly back at us like they were gonna kill us?"

"Oh, they were just fuckin' with you—don't worry about it!"

*After the third fish, here they all came, streaming
out of their buildings, fishing rods in hand,
like a scene out of "Cocoon 4" or better yet, "The Walking
Dead," and began flailing the water, blindly
and desperately...*

# 15 OLD PEOPLE AND FALSE ALBACORE

LET'S TALK ABOUT FALSE ALBACORE, a fairly down-trodden fish in most people's estimation, except for me and several of my fishing buddies and others who are in the know. David, my Florida guide buddy had the same experience on the same day and told me that this might have been a once-in-a-lifetime thing, never to be this good again. I was on the beach on the Florida panhandle. It was a beautiful sunny day in the beginning of 2012, with temperatures in the low 70s. A little windy, but for a day in mid-January, it was freakin' paradise. The surf was big and confused—not one of those days when the breakers come in like they're listening to a metronome. These waves were schizophrenic, breaking willy-nilly at all imaginable angles, and sonically, it was thunderous. And the false albacore were going crazy.

Before I get too into the scene, let me set the stage. False alba-core, often mistakenly called a bonito, are the smallest member of the tuna family. That said, the largest one caught on record weighed in at 36 pounds. Generally, they average around 25 to 30 inches, perfect size for a fly rod or light tackle. There are millions of these guys around, probably because they don't taste so good—very oily and bloody and are used as bait for billfish, sharks, or cut up in bite-sized chunks and used to catch grouper and other more desirable fish. However, in some third-world countries, they are canned, dried, salted, and prepared in various other ways. So, they can be eaten, but you should bleed them, and then cut away the blood line and the dark flesh before cooking, and even then, it ain't worth the effort. Although, I've heard from people who love them as dinner fare. Not me.

That said, pound for pound, the false albacore is one of the stron-gest fish I've ever had the pleasure of fighting. Period. Once hooked, be ready for a series of searing runs, reaching line-ripping speeds of 40 miles per hour. They fight much like a bonefish, but in my opinion, are a stronger fish. And unlike bonefish, where you usually will tie on a shrimp pattern, you will be fishing streamers and tiny minnow patterns for false albacore.

And to top it all off, they're "pretty" according to my wife. And I must say, as far as fish go, they are attractive, not in a weird way, but sleek silver, obviously tuna-like with dark green stripes on their backs and a series of spots below their gills. The reason I bring this up, is for the few of you who swear up and down that flyfishing for carp is your version of nirvana. And you know, that's fine—whatever turns your crank. And yeah, I know they're big, heavy, and fight like hell, but for God's sake, look at them! Unsavory is a kind word to describe them... more like a big scaled, rubber lipped, beady eyed, smelly slime-ball, that deserves more than any other to be called a bottom-feeder. And let's be honest. Which fish would you like to have your picture taken with or have taxidermied and put up on your wall behind your desk at work? Be honest.

Now where was I? Oh yeah. Nice day, windy, rough surf. Watching these false albacore feed in the surf was like watching water ballet. Depending upon light conditions, when a wave broke in the crystal-clear water, it opened up a window where you can watch all the action. I marveled at their fluid, efficient, almost choreographed hunt, as they rode the waves solitary, sometimes in pairs, or sometimes in schools, chasing the confused and disoriented baitfish, at times nearly beaching themselves on the white sandy beach. It was beautiful, man.

How do you go about catching one of these on such a day with the conditions I just described? NOT with a fly rod. That's right. Blasphemy for some of you, but seriously, come on! This is what I hate about fly-fishing purists. Sure, you can take your fly rod out there on the beach, in heavy surf with the wind in your face, and yeah, you can try and cast your fly into those pounding waves, and yeah, after your wind-altered mediocre cast, you can try to control your line that tumbles back to where you stand and watch helplessly as it gets wrapped all around your feet before you even get a chance to strip it. You go right ahead and knock yourself out, dumb-ass.

There's a feeling among most of us, at least a little, that we should ALWAYS be using a fly rod. In fact, to different degrees, we all feel a little guilty if we don't. Well, I am here right now to absolve every one of us for using fishing gear that matches the circumstances. If you can't make the cast and if you can't control your line, you ain't gonna catch any fish. It makes common sense. Now don't get me wrong; I've caught many fish in the surf with my fly rod, but on this particular day, I broke out the spinning gear with a fairly heavy silver spoon that looked like the minnows the false albacore were chasing. If you're worried about the lack of skill level required to catch one of these in the surf, don't be. Just like with a fly rod, you still have to be quick, accurate and timely with your cast, and somewhat psychic to determine which way the fish will turn. If it turns out you ARE somewhat psychic and you get your spoon (or fly on a day with better conditions) near the fish, and it sees it, the fish WILL strike, and when it does, get ready for a long a drawn-out battle.

My first cast was a little to the right and behind the fish, so I reeled in as fast as I could and waited to see my next fish, which took about fifteen seconds. My next cast landed perfectly in front of the fish. I hesitated for about a second and started to retrieve, not as quickly as you would imagine because the surf was already helping it. The line tightened, the fish hesitated, and then realizing it was hooked, turned and took off on a screaming tear away from me, heading out into the Gulf of Mexico towards Cuba, line burning off my reel as I palmed it, trying to slow it down. It then headed west, down the beach as I, and the mob of beachgoer spectators that I had acquired, followed. Fifteen exhausting minutes later, I beached a tired, yet unharmed 28-inch false albacore to the delight and applause of my new friends. I disgorged the hook from

Marti and David with her false albacore, a very 'pretty' fish—according to her!

its jaw, walked it back into the water, held it above its tail and gently moved it back and forth in the water until it got its strength back and then released it. Two more fish followed, and then it happened.

All this time, I had a strange feeling that I was being watched, not just by the people on the beach with me, but by some strange presence. It was almost like the time in the northern New Mexican wilderness that all the hairs on the back of my neck and arms stood up while I was fishing a stream, but I saw and heard nothing. Figuring some primal instinct kicked in that told me I was being stalked by a mountain lion or bear, I retreated to my truck.

OK, it wasn't that bad, but I turned around and there they all were. Unbeknownst to me, I was being watched from balconies in the condos that line the part of the beach where I was fishing; condos filled with "Snowbirds," down for the winter from Canada, Minnesota, North Dakota, Michigan, and then even more from Canada. This confirmed that everything I'd heard and read about Florida was true. With the exception of Miami Beach and the red-necky inland areas, the Florida coast is a giant waiting room for death. Thousands of these oldsters either stream down or already live here...and die here! I swear that during January and February, the paramedics came screaming down the street at least one or two times a day.

There they were, cocktails in hand, either overly-tanned or pale to the point of zombie-fication, all watching me intently, and you could hear the excited cackling and mumbling rising up from the condos, as they debated amongst themselves whether or not to grab their Zebco's and give it a try. After the third fish, here they all came, streaming out of their buildings, fishing rods in hand, like a scene out of "Cocoon 4" or better yet, "The Walking Dead," and they all began flailing the water blindly and desperately, not seeing the fish, and not knowing what the hell they were doing or even fishing for. The questions then began, which I answered politely and patiently. Then after several minutes of no one catching anything, except one more for me, they all sullenly shuffled, crept, and crawled back into their buildings, into their elevators and back out onto their balconies. I had enough. It had been a good day in a beautiful setting.

I told David my story, and as always, he verbally abused me for not using my fly rod, even though I explained to him the rough and windy conditions.

"Why didn't you use the fly rod and just concentrate on the ones near the beach and out of the waves?"

"You weren't there, man…I did what I thought I had to do."

"If they're still out there tomorrow, take the fly rod and try that, you big pussy."

Thanks for the encouragement.

Now, if you're going to use your fly rod on the beach, I wouldn't bring anything less than an 8-weight with either a floating or slow-sink line. But here's the problem: on calmer days it seems the fishing isn't as good because high surf brings them in since the baitfish get disoriented in big surf. So on more fly-fishing-friendly days, lots of times the fish just aren't there. But if they are, the same rules apply. You have to get the fly where the fish can see it and hope it swims in the direction you're stripping. Lots of times I've seen false albacore nearly beach themselves in pursuit of their meal, and when they're in that close it's obviously an easier cast. I've literally had them swim within ten feet of me with no apparent fear or care about what I was trying to do. On dead-calm days they occasionally come in close to shore looking for food. If you're at a beach that doesn't have a steep drop-off, you can wade out and sight fish for singular or small schools of them.

The tactics are different from a boat out in the Gulf. My Florida guide and taskmaster David has taken me out several times after false albacore. There are two simple tactics. Either watch for the birds or watch for the fish. When you see a bunch of seagulls dive-bombing the water, that means the baitfish are there, and the false albacore are attacking from below as the birds gorge themselves from above. With a small minnow pattern, cast in anywhere near the boiling mass of carnage, start stripping and you WILL get a strike. Or, if there are no birds, look for water boils and make your way over to them. They're pretty obvious as these guys are voracious feeders that uninhibitedly and enthusiastically rip into the baitfish right near the surface, making it easy for you to get a cast right into the middle of it all. Again, because of the pound-for-pound strength of these fish, I would not recommend using anything much under an 8-weight, and no sinking line is required since they are not only at the surface, some are literally leaping out of the water in pursuit of their prey. However, you have to be prepared for anything, including equipment failure.

Cruising just off the beach, we saw another boil several hundred yards away, so David turned the boat towards it and as soon as we got in range, I started casting. I got an immediate hook-up and the fish took off like a bullet towards the horizon. It had just taken me to my backing when my reel started wobbling wildly and the spool flew out and dropped to the bottom of the boat at the worst possible time. David frantically grabbed the reel, and I grabbed on to the line with my free hand as he tried in vain to get the spool back on the reel. Ain't happening. It was busted. For the next fifteen minutes I had the pleasure of fighting and actually landing a live, yet another false albacore without the use of rod or reel. I literally pulled it in hand-over-hand. Exhausting.

After the fish was landed, David just shook his head and said, "What is it about you? You have more weird shit happen than anyone else I've fished with."

Believe me, I know.

A false albacore near the beach in Destin, Florida.

# 16 YOU NEED A PERMIT FOR THAT (MY FIRST PERMIT, THAT IS...)

*Permit are the big tease of the shallow water tropics.*
*You see them; they wag their tails seductively in your face.*
*They might even turn and wink in your direction*
*if they had eyelids to wink with.*

THIS IS THE STORY ABOUT HOW I ENDED UP catching my first permit and how surprisingly easy it was, but I'll get to that in a minute.

Maybe I'm paranoid, but if you've ever fished in a foreign country, Mexico as an example, an incident like this eventually happens: it's either early in the morning before they take you out, or you're back at the trucks or the lodge after a day's fishing. You and the other clients and the rest of the guides are milling around, and the guides are speaking either rapid staccato Spanish or even Mayan amongst themselves, and you wonder what they're saying. You especially wonder when your guide glances back at you and goes back to talking to the other guides who then start to snicker. I mean, Tacon, who was my guide on this particular trip, was a good-enough guy, but you have to wonder if the communications don't go something like this.

"So how was the dumb-ass you were with today?"

"Aw, man, what a worthless piece of shit he is! I say three o'clock, forty feet, and he's one o'clock, twenty! How about your guy?"

Then, in my case...

"Yeah, just as stupid. My demented arthritic grandma could cast better than this asshole! And to make matters worse, he was like fucking Donald Duck up there in the boat! I see a fish and he goes 'Where? Where? I can't see it!' And then he sees it, and he gets all excited and starts false-casting like some kind of spastic, and then he wraps his line around his foot and his cast just drops five feet in front of him!" (This is the point where the guide glances back at me and they all start to laugh.) "And then, he gets really pissed off and his face turns really red;

he starts swearing really loud, so any other fish that were even close are long gone. What a douche-bag!"

Damn.

But then I put myself in their shoes. Of course, they're talking about me, and every other chump who's on the trip! Hell, if I spoke a language that no one else could understand, I'd do the same thing if I were in their shoes. What power you wield when you can look some big dumb obnoxious redneck moron who just made your day miserable, right in the eye and say with a big smile on your face, "Hey Dickhead, guess what? I just did your mom and she really dug it!" And of course, the client, not knowing what the hell you just said, smiles back and laughs too, and then all the guides start laughing, and they know that you and your mom have just been insulted and there's not a damned thing you can do about it.

But back to my virgin permit experience.

This was one of those trips that WAS wife-friendly, because it involved compromises and beaches. The agreement was, we were going flats fishing in Mexico, but we would spend the first two days in Cancún and do all those beachy, shopping things that chicks dig, and then on to fishing, but not rustic fishing. We would stay somewhere that was nice, clean, all-inclusive, and not hideous. Fair enough.

It was March of 2001, and we arrived in Cancún in a torrential downpour where you hope the pilot was not just out of flight school as he was landing the plane just as the storm hit, with bolts of lightning illuminating our descent onto the runway. After picking up our wet luggage which sat on the nearly underwater tarmac for 15 minutes before they brought it in, we got to the hotel, the skies cleared and the next two days were perfect, as was our entire stay. The little woman was happy, so I was happy.

The morning of our departure was sunny and tropical. We boarded a single engine prop plane at a small airport on the edge of Cancún and headed south. The scenery from above was awe inspiring. As we took off, the island of Cozumel was to our left and the Yucatán coast to our right. We passed over Playa del Carmen and other small coastal villages. If you looked inland, it was nothing but a green wall of jungle that hid ancient Mayan ruins such as Chichen Itza and Coba. Down the coast further was the Mayan ruin of Tulúm, which you've probably seen on TV commercials for Mexican tourism; a large temple on a cliff overlooking a small beach on the crystalline blue waters of the Caribbean, where the Jeff Bridges movie, "Against All Odds" was filmed. It's more beautiful than any TV ad can portray.

From Tulúm, the signs of human life dramatically drop off as the jungle creeps closer towards the beaches. Our trip took us over Ascensión Bay and pretty much where the bay meets Espiritú Santo Bay, we landed on a small sandy airstrip on the barrier island where we would be staying. Back then, this place was in the middle of nowhere, just north of the Belizean border. This is where the little woman started getting nervous, because it appeared that we have been dropped off in an episode of "Survivor" with no TV crew to take care of us. Then we heard the sound of a truck approaching from the south to take us to the lodge. There are two lodges on the island; one was located on the northern end, and further south, was the one where we chose to stay because the amenities looked a bit nicer.

The truck unloaded supplies off the plane and took us and the cache of food, alcohol, and toilet paper first to the northern lodge, and then we continued down the dirt road for another twenty minutes, arriving at our home for the next several days sometime midafternoon. Finally, there was a visible sign of relief on my wife's face. The lodge itself was modest, clean, whitewashed stucco with a thatched roof. It has a large airy dining room where all meals are served, and acts as a gathering place for the day's upcoming adventures and the only place on the island for nightly libations. It is surrounded by coconut palms, under which are charming "casitas" where the guests stay. Ours was perfect. The same whitewashed stucco on the outside and a dark mahogany interior with high palm-thatched ceilings and a big bed with mosquito netting. The front faced the ocean which provides a constant cooling breeze and the hypnotic sounds of the surf. I am now a hero in Marti's eyes. This place is perfect! And the beach is right there! Let's walk down and see what that looks... Oh no!

Every beach has a tide line where flotsam and jetsam wash up, and it usually consists of mostly seaweed and occasionally dead sea-life and a little human trash. This was horrible. If you've ever been to one of the Yucatán resorts, you know how beautiful their beaches are; white coral sand that literally looks like powdered sugar. Picture a beautiful beach like that, littered with florescent light bulbs, shoes, hypodermic needles, plastic of all shapes and sizes, clothing, furniture, you name it. This made me sick. I walked back to the lodge to ask why it was like this. I was told that all the cruise ships dump their waste off-shore and the currents bring it right to their beach. It happens so often that they were spending all of their time cleaning their beach, so they just gave up. What they were told is Mexico doesn't have the infrastructure to handle cruise ship crap, so the ships just dump it. Of course, I would bet that the ships dump it anyway so they don't have to pay waste disposal fees. If you give a rat's ass about this, you might want to ask your cruise company what they do with theirs before you sign on. Just sayin.' I told the guy at the lodge that I'd bet the guests would be willing to pay a little more if they'd fix the problem. I haven't been back for years, so I don't know if it's been dealt with. I certainly hope it has. That said, I would go back there in a heartbeat if the opportunity presents itself because this place is special.

We were on the eastern edge of the Sian Ka'an biosphere reserve, a UNESCO world heritage site, and the largest protected area in the Mexican Caribbean, comprising approximately 1.3 million acres of paradise. Quite frankly, it's one of the most awesome places I have ever been in my fishing travels. The reserve is home to over 100 mammal species and over 330 bird species. It is the nesting ground for many wading birds and endangered sea turtles. We'd launch our boat on the leeward side of the island, which tended to either excite or disturb the saltwater crocs that lived nearby who would hiss and slap their tails on the water at us. At some point on our boat ride to the fishing flats, we'd routinely come across a flock of wading pink flamingos that would either placidly watch us or take flight as we boated by. Curious sea turtles would come up and check us out.

The reserve also has 23 known archaeological sites, some dating back 2300 years, a few of which we visited on our way to or from fishing. And, our island has the ruins of an ancient Mayan temple and village on it, which were being excavated while we were staying there. Luckily, they were within walking distance from where we stayed, and archaeologists were busy working there. The ruins were a walled area with a temple and the foundations of several stone buildings.

My most profound moment there?

We walked over to explore the site and were allowed to climb the steppe pyramid temple. At the top was a small square room with a doorway in front and windows looking out the back towards the water. As we stepped in, there was a noticeable change in temperature, much cooler than the outside tropical heat. It was then we noticed it. In the middle of the room was a large fresh pile of...crap, defecation, fecal matter.

Thinking it was from some large jungle animal, maybe even a jaguar, I mentioned it to one of the archaeologists after we climbed down the temple. He goes, "No, that's human shit—the day workers like to go up there and use it as their john because it's so nice and cool. I really gotta tell them to cut it out and use the porta johns."

Heavy, man.

Then, away from the site and down the beach from us were the re-mains of a 1500-year-old Mayan break wall which was submerged just below the waterline. After a full day of fishing the flats, I would walk down with my fly rod at sunset before dinner, stand on this ages-old edifice and cast into the sea, and wonder how many ancient Mayans had also fished off this same wall countless centuries ago.

That was heavy too, for real, man.

We were sharing the lodge with a couple of old Belgian fishermen with bad attitudes. Supposedly one of these guys holds a bunch of world records for different types of saltwater fish caught on a fly rod. At least that was their story, not that fishermen lie or anything. They were pret-ty much nasty, curmudgeonly blowhards. For instance, after the first day's fishing, all the guides and clients kind of gathered around out-

My first permit ever, on my first cast, after a long fight in the mangrove channels. The old Belgians were not amused.

side under the trees to talk about their day. Fortunately, I had a good one, catching about a dozen bonefish. Our Belgian friends caught none. They didn't take too well to my good news. They muttered something guttural in my direction and then tore into their guide as to why they weren't so lucky. And, it got worse after my permit experience.

We were also sharing the place with an entire extended family from Ireland who were there celebrating the grandfather's birthday. Now these people I liked! Grandpa fished but most of the family did not. But it didn't matter because they were all there for the fun. The non-fishing family members took flyfishing lessons and gamely tried to land some fish, but their primary purpose was to hang out in paradise, eat, and yes, drink plenty of alcohol. And the Irish know how to drink. None of them turned obnoxious…maybe the conversation got a little louder and the jokes got a little raunchier, but you could tell this family dug each other and they must have sensed my Irish heritage because they pretty much adopted us, all while the Belgians kept sullenly to themselves at a separate table, probably plotting our demise.

So back to the permit.

Permit are notorious for telling you to kiss their fishy asses. It's like they can read your mind and know why you're looking at them intently and know you mean to cause them alarm and grief. They know, man.

I equate catching a permit to an old Cheech and Chong bit and I apologize to the guys for bad paraphrasing.

"Hey man, did you eat any of those pot brownies?"

"Yeah man, I almost ate *one!*"

On a good day, you can go out and catch a bunch of bonefish. Jacks are too easy. They must dig the pain because it's almost like they beg you to be hooked. But with permit, most of us might almost catch, like, one. Permit are the big tease of the shallow water tropics. You see them; they wag their tails seductively in your face. They might even turn and wink in your direction if they had eyelids to wink with. You cast your 9-foot rod at them with a colorful French-tickler of a crab imitation, and then you get summarily shut down or coyly ignored.

Little bitches.

But today would be different.

The morning broke sunny but windy. It was about a forty-five-minute boat ride over the open bay into a brisk south wind, which whipped up about a three-foot chop that compressed each vertebrae every time the boat hit bottom. My chiropractor was very happy. Once Tacon and I reached the flats on the other side, we started poling into and through the sinuous channels lined with mangroves. These channels kept forking and splitting and getting narrower, ultimately leading us so far into the mangroves that we might have found the skeletal remains of some poor bastard who got hopelessly lost and then devoured by hungry seabirds and crabs.

As we turned a corner to follow another smaller fork, the two large permits were swimming side by side away from us, and as soon as our presence was detected, they shot up the closest channel to the left. We held back for a minute, and then followed, very slowly, both of us barely breathing. As we rounded another corner, what we saw was amazing. We had turned into another, yet narrower channel, maybe fifteen feet across at its widest, which dead-ended about 150 feet ahead of us. At the dead end, there was one last small fork heading off to the left, far too small for our boat, which dwindled as the mangroves closed in around it. The two permits were literally patrolling this channel, swimming up and down its length searching for food. The water was shallow enough that you could see their large wakes as they approached, and when they got to within about thirty feet of our position, they would turn completely around and go back to the top. Then, here they'd come again! We watched, unbelieving, as they repeated this three times, and as they turned to go back to the far end, we formulated our plan. I was to cast my McCrab to a point right above where they did their last turnaround and wait for them to come back. The cast hit the water and the fly sank to the hard-packed muddy bottom. They reached the top, their wakes subsided, and then nothing. Thirty seconds later like clockwork the dance began again, and they started swimming towards us at a leisurely pace, apparently with no clue that we were sitting there.

Tacon, loudly whispering from the back of the boat, "Wait...wait... wait...wait. Now streeep slowwwly...leeetle slow streeeps!" The fish were nearly upon us as I started moving the fly, inching it back towards their turnaround point. Then I felt resistance and my line stiffened and sweet Jesus God almighty! Line screamed from my reel after I set the hook, and the permit rocketed back up to the top of the channel. Then as quickly as the fight began, the line went limp. With my body and brain still rocked with adrenaline, I started to go through the five stages of grief...denial, anger, bargaining, depression, and I never got to acceptance. I started to reel the line in when I realized it was wound around one of the small mangroves. So Tacon poled us up the channel and that's when we noticed the splashing and commotion behind the mangrove. Apparently, the fish was still hooked. As we approached to untangle the line, the permit literally shot out of its cover, back down the channel in the direction we had just come, ripping off a piece of the mangrove with it and nearly snapping my line and the rod in two and severing my right index finger as the fly line flew off the reel. Miraculously, it had untangled itself and nearly uprooted the mangrove as the fish bolted down our channel towards open water. Close to a half-hour later, after almost taking all of my backing twice, the fish was finally tiring, but sat stubbornly about thirty feet away from the boat, refusing to budge. Tacon had enough. He abandoned ship, waded over to it and after a couple of lame attempts, we finally landed a 20-pound permit. I was exhausted, but ecstatic. My first permit on my first cast. Yippie!

After that, we decided enough was enough. It wasn't gonna get any better. We boated back to the lodge, had a beer or two, informed the Belgians what had just happened and watched a look of disdain and disgust spread over their faces. Life was good.

# 17 EVIL CLOWNS

*In full clown regalia they exit; fat ones, tall ones, skinny ones, all wearing garishly polka-dotted fishing waders, all wearing bright red clown shoe wading boots.*

BY THE TIME YOU READ THIS, I imagine the "Evil Clown" fad will have died a slow, painful death. If you recall, all over the world, well, mostly in the U.S., idiots have been dressing up like clowns and lurking around neighborhoods, shopping areas, parks, and unnerving the general public. There was no real law against it, so it was difficult, if not impossible to arrest these sociopathic numbskulls. However, what happened is what often happens in situations such as these. People took it upon themselves to deal with this odd phenomenon and started beating the living shit out of these morons and remarkably, the problem seemed to go away. Nothing like a little vigilante justice to cure an unenforceable situation. That's not always the right solution, but in this case, it seemed to be what was necessary.

Why am I bringing this up in a fishing book? Because it was Jer's, Mo's and my idea, and we had it nearly a decade before these cretins in white-face usurped it with bad intent. I'll get to the clowns in a minute.

The San Juan River, flowing out of Navajo Reservoir in the Four Corners area of northwestern New Mexico is one of my favorite all-time fly-fishing rivers in the country. It's not your typical "Rocky Mountain High" scene...surrounded by towering 14-er's with pine and aspen forests providing a paradisiacal backdrop. Not even close. This is a dammed-up, high-desert river that flows in a canyon flanked by desert sandstone cliffs. It gets desert hot in the summer and desert cold in the winter. Most days the wind blows upriver, sometimes at speeds making the drift boat guides' lives a living hell. But here's the thing. The dam is constructed so the water from Navajo Reservoir flows into the river from the bottom, meaning, it's cold. Like 42 degrees cold, all year. And as we all know, trout like cold water, and they really like the cold water in the San Juan. Because after the dam was built, and the water turned cold, an amazing entomological ecosystem formed, providing the trout with more bugs that they could possibly feast on, and the hatches continue all year round, even in the dead of winter. These year-round hatches caused the fish to grow quite large and content, and some grew to scary sizes. I have a friend who put scuba gear on and dived into the famous Texas Hole, the best and deepest riffle on the river. He said and I quote, "I saw trout down there so big they fuckin' scared me!" Bottom line? The upper four miles of the river is one of the best, most productive trout rivers I have ever fished. I often say it's like the Snake or the Madison, if you crammed those rivers down to size, and squished all the riffles and runs closer together. It's a short drift trip, it's easily wadable, and everybody knows it, and there lies the problem. There are days when fishing on this river is nearly impossible because of the number of people and drift boats for that matter. Now don't get me wrong. I'm all about the guides, and their ability to make as much money as they can. All I'm saying is, you don't go to the San Juan River for a wilderness experience, or to have some solitary 'back to nature' time. You go to the San Juan because you want to catch large trout, and damn the scenery and damn the seclusion because it ain't there!

On any given Saturday when the weather is good and your favorite NFL team isn't playing, legions of fly-fishers travel to the river, and at times, especially at Texas Hole, you are shoulder-to-shoulder with other anglers. And at certain times of the day, there are so many boats there as well, you could walk across the river on them. I have often referred to the San Juan in these conditions at the Disneyland of Flyfishing. Yet, I still love the river. So back to the clowns. Mo, Jer, and I might have been a little drunk at the time, or maybe a little high on Colorado weed, or maybe neither! This is a fantasy of ours. Its genesis was fishing the San Juan River at full capacity, barely room to move let alone cast. It is a response to the dunderheaded knuckleheads who have no sense of proper fishing etiquette. This is a reaction to the annoyance and anger one feels when someone decides to sidle right up to you, giving you no space. This is a reaction to the San Juan Creep, meaning the slow but sure movement of fellow anglers toward you when they see that you are catching fish and they aren't. This is a response to the drift boats that do the same thing. Etiquette, man. Just some common courtesy would be nice. But sadly, in the times we're living in, common courtesy and a little empathy seem to have flown out the window, and created a bunch of selfish, unthinking douche bags. So, here's to all the space takers and the creepers and the 'what about me?' people.

Picture this: It's a fine sunny morning, perhaps around 10-10:30, just about the time when Texas Hole is full of drift boats and anglers are stacked shoulder-to-shoulder, wherever they can find a place to cast their flies into the wide, swirling trout-packed eddy of joy. The Texas Hole parking lot is packed, and many more anglers are getting into their waders and boots, and rigging their lines in anticipation of joining the bloody fray down on the river, wherever they might be able to squeeze in. The sound is faint at first, coming from the direction of the road up above. It's a familiar, yet out of place sound, and as it gets closer, it becomes recognizable. It is Calliope music, getting louder and louder as it approaches the road leading down to the parking lot. Soon it is nearly deafening...and on the final switchback leading down to the parking lot, a candy-striped VW Beetle appears...careening down the path... barely staying upright as the tires emit a high-pitched squeal and now, the calliope music, thundering from the giant bullhorn bolted to the top of the car, is absolutely deafening. At this point, all of the anglers stop what they're doing and turn towards the noise and the freak show coming down the hill. The car is jam packed full of...well, still too far away to tell who or what is in the Beetle...but sticking out through the open windows on either side are at least a dozen multi-colored fly rods, making the car look like some kind of crazy porcupine on acid. The car enters the parking lot...makes two complete circles around the parked cars and pulls into one of the few available parking spaces at nearly full speed.

And then, they start coming. There must be at least a dozen clowns packed into the Beetle. In full clown regalia they exit; fat ones, tall ones, skinny ones, all wearing garishly polka-dotted fishing waders, all wearing bright red clown shoe wading boots. Some with orange fright wigs, some rainbow colored, all with white-faced clown make-up, and big round red clown noses. All are wearing similarly colored oversized fishing vests, with pockets big enough to hold seltzer bottles, rubber snakes, bicycle horns, along with any fishing accoutrement they might need. The driver, another clown wearing similar fishing garb, but with an old-timey chauffeur's hat, turns off the car but leaves the calliope music blasting, steps out, pulls his waders down, bends over, and moons the now stunned fishermen in the lot. Each of his ass cheeks are both adorned with a rendition of a clown flipping off whoever chooses to look.

The clowns begin unloading their fly rods, and those are multi colored, some striped, some Day-Glo pastels and primaries, each rod has
bulbous horn attached to the end below the reel...and all then stand in a
circle and begin casting in a semi choreographed, yet chaotic display....
and if you listen carefully, you'll hear instead of the clicking whining
sound most fly reels make when line is let out, all of theirs let out a
ding ding ding ding ding, like one of those little counter bells at the
deli. Suddenly the calliope music stops, then silence, and then a loud
blaring horn like one right before the second half starts at a basketball
game calls the clowns to attention. They line up single file, fly rods over
their right shoulders, and they start marching towards the Texas Hole
water. But not before one of the confused anglers walks up to one of the
clowns who might be the leader, but who really knows, and before he
can finish his sentence of "What the fuck is going on h..." he is punched
in the face and then descended upon by the rest of the clowns with
oversized nerf baseball bats and beaten into submission. All then fall
back in line, light up oversized Dominican cigars, and continue their
march toward the water...

As the horrified spectators watch, another vehicle, comes barrel-
ing down the hill. This one a rusted-out Ford Fairlane station wagon,
packed with more clowns, maybe twenty this time, rods again, protrud-
ing from every window. This one is towing a garishly bright white drift
boat covered with large pink and purple polka dots. Again, calliopes
blaring, twice around the parking lot and then down to the boat put-in.
The driver of the station wagon is also the drift boat captain, dressed
in full Jonny Depp pirate garb, but with a fake peg leg and a hugely
oversized stuffed parrot sewn onto his left shoulder. Somehow, they
get the boat into the water and squeeze every one of the 20 clowns
into the boat, which is devoid of seats except for the captain's... all the
clowns standing at attention with their rods at their sides, as the captain eases the boat into the water and heads upstream. Of course, the
boat is equipped with a state-of-the-art sound system, which continues
to blare circus music from its four mounted bullhorns that face in each
direction mounted on a tall wooden mast in the middle of the boat.

As the boat heads towards the top of Texas Hole, the confused,
some horrified, some angry, anglers watch. The wading clowns have
teamed up, and spread themselves evenly in the river, all standing
about thigh deep. And as the boat passes, they all removed their fright
wigs, and place them over their hearts, and I mean their red water-filled

beating heart that is glued to the outside of their fishing vests, that they control with a little hand pump in their pockets. They stand silent-ly as the boat overly crammed with the other clowns, rows upstream. When the garishly styled drift boat arrives at its destination at the top of Texas Hole, it stops moving, the deafening calliope music is silenced, and it sits there, in total silence, waiting. The clowns on board, just like the ones lining the shore, stand completely still, heads bowed, not mak-ing a peep. Then again, the eardrum-busting basketball horn sounds forth, and in near synchronization, they all begin frantically casting.

To the dismay of the observing anglers, all the clowns hook fish. Of course, when all the trout go to make runs, the reels start their ca-cophony of constant dinging, and then when a fish is landed, each rod is equipped with a black bulbous horn at the base of its handle so as they land fish after fish, all hear the bells with the constant farting nois-es of clown horns. Some anglers decide to approach the clowns, which proves to be a very bad idea, resulting in severe beatings, de-wadering and de-pantsing, and then buggering utilizing the own angler's Sage 5-weight. Defeated and humiliated, the remaining anglers hasten back to their trucks and cars, as the clowns jeer them and flip them off as they retreat. Once the stream has been cleared of all but clowndom, the music gets turned off, they, all reel in, put the boat back on the trailer, get back in their cars, and drive up out of the parking lot and disappear down the canyon road. And later that evening, anglers sitting in the Sportsman Lounge enjoying a green chile cheeseburger and a beer or two, will never really know if, sitting at the table next to them, are four of the same clowns who abused them hours before, out of make-up and clown garb, blending in with everyone else. End of story.

I want to film this. I want to enter it into the Fly-Fishing Film Tour. I want it to win awards. And it will, because every single solitary fly-fisher I know has experienced what I was talking about. And in their heart of hearts, would pay good money to actually witness this hap-pening, and actually watch the no-etiquette cretinous douchebags get taken out by a bunch of clowns. I KNOW it. By the way, anyone wants to volunteer to help or be a clown or an extra, or even better, completely fund the project, let me know. It'll be fun.

*Chartreuse cow dung flew out in all directions,
not unlike what happens when a meteor hits
your neighbor's tool shed.*

# 18 CHARLIE MULCOCK'S OASIS PARADISE

CHARLIE MULCOCK IS A CHARACTER. For you old-timers, he could have been a stand-in for Festus on the old TV series "Gunsmoke," or perfectly fit in as one of the prospectors on "Deadwood." Back when I met him, he was one of those guys from southern New Mexico that defined what it was to be a cowboy. An average-built man with a scraggly white beard that is perpetually stained by a line of tobacco spit. He walks with a little hitch in his step, never asked him why, and probably don't need to know. You could imagine some kind of incident involving calf roping or bull-neutering. He always wears the uniform; cowboy hat, cowboy boots, old wrangler jeans, a western shirt, and speaks with the drawl of a man who has spent most of his life down on the ranch.

His ranch is outside of Mayhill, New Mexico, barely a town, that sits on the eastern slope of the Sacramento Mountains in Otero County. This area of the state is by and large, arid high desert scrub, and the farther east you go from the mountains, the land becomes more and more of a moonscape.

Contrary to what you might think, Charlie's ranch is spectacular. His family bought the land in 1902, and it's primarily a working cattle ranch. You might ask how anyone could make a living running cattle and growing alfalfa in such an inhospitable place. Quite simply, his ranch is a miracle, springing forth out of the desert, with "springing" being the operative word. The Rio Penasco runs right through his property. You can stand in the middle of his land, looking west to the barren foothills miles away, and see a green patch on the hillside. That is where the river's genesis is. It literally flows directly out of the hillside and tumbles down into the valley. Charlie's ancestors were smart enough to know a good thing when they saw it and staked their future right there.

The Rio Peñasco is a spring creek. Its water temperature is a constant 59 degrees. It never freezes over in the winter, and in the over 100 years the family has owned the property, it has never run dry. It empties out into the Pecos near Artesia, New Mexico, sixty miles to the east. The Penasco's path is a strange one, flowing both beneath and above the ground. It will just disappear into a rabbit hole, only to re-surface miles away. Weird. The river runs deep and cold through Charlie's property. Up top, it is not a wading river, although there are places you can enter if you really wanted to, but the water is so crystal clear, you would scare every trout within a mile. Like many spring creeks, it has heavy vegetative growth in the water, making it difficult to use light tippet. Many of the hooked fish will swim for cover under these water forests, and 5x or 6x tippet won't do the trick if you have to pull your fish out from under the salad mix.

As I said, his property is a miracle of nature. There are two separate sections to the river. Up top, the river meanders through meadows of grass and alfalfa, where he grazes his cattle. The first time I stayed there, I only fished up top, not knowing what awaited me downstream. The next time I came with my fishing buddy Roger, Charlie said to me, "You *are* planning on going into the canyon, aren't you?"

I replied, "What canyon?"

He cocked his head, spat on the ground, and gave me one of those looks Charlie gives city slickers that ain't too bright and said, "The canyon on the east end of my property! Last time you missed the best part! Don't know why you didn't go there. Thought you might not want to make that long hike down and dirty your new jeans or somethin'!"

Charlie Mulcock in his oasis paradise. He told us to treat his fish gently...Unfortunately we failed, looking more like an episode of "Fishing with the Three Stooges."

Great. I could have started whining and said nobody told me about any canyon, and that I've made many hikes tougher than that one, and actually I'd be more afraid of putting a hole in my new waders, but I kept my mouth shut and agreed to check it out.

This, my friends, was where his land turned miraculous.

We drove our truck to the edge of the canyon and hiked down what actually was a pretty steep path to the bottom. When we got there, we were almost speechless. It was a totally different world with a completely different climate. It was beautiful, almost like being in the tropics. Imagine descending from a hot, brown, and dry, typical southern New Mexican desert, into a cooler, humid, lush, almost jungle-like environment, with trees and birds and grass, and that same beautiful stream meandering right down the middle, full of the same big trout. Not only did the stream flow through, it was punctuated by five waterfalls, some fifty feet high, plunging into clear blue-green pools, as the river travelled from the first to the next. I would not have been surprised at all if we saw parrots flying over our heads and perching in the trees. I swear to you, you would never ever think you were still in New Mexico.

This brings me to my buddy Roger, who has accompanied me on far too many of these trips. Roger is a financial advisor, and I met him because one of his clients was former Atlanta Falcons wide receiver and University of New Mexico Lobo, Terrence Mathis. Roger called me out of the blue one day and asked me if I wanted to have Terrence on the air the next morning, which I readily agreed to. Roger and Terrence showed up the next morning, and a new bromance was born, especially when I found out Roger was a fly fisherman. He and Terrence continued to come in, even after Mathis retired and got into NASCAR, becoming the first black man not only involved, but actually accepted by all those Talladega rednecks. (No offense if you're a big NASCAR fan. Even if you are, I imagine you would agree that NASCAR is a major bastion of redneckery.)

Roger looks like he could be the brother of the deceased actor, Bruno Kirby. He loves baseball and is a big St. Louis Cardinals fan. He is one of the most gregarious, chat-you-up people that you will meet. He will have a conversation with anyone at any time, whether or not the person he chooses to engage wants to actually have a conversation. This becomes even more evident after he's had a couple of beers. That's probably why we get along because I, generally, am very reserved and sometimes even shy to the point of being rude (not on purpose), if I feel uncomfortable in my surroundings. You could say we balance each other out. Roger is also a big tobacco chewer, always keeping a spit cup in his or my truck, depending on who's driving. In my vehicle, this is evident by the red-brown "Missed-the-cup-stains" that run down from my cup-holder on to my now permanently dyed carpet. We had quite the weekend at the Mulcock Ranch in 2007, involving cattle, cow pies, and Three Stooges-like on-stream antics.

Roger is considered a hero in the eyes of the cattle on Charlie's ranch. It was a late-afternoon day in May, and we had just pulled into the ranch, planning to fish the evening hatches on the top side of the property. We were staying in Cloudcroft, which was about a half hour away on the western slopes of the Sacramentos. We chose to stay there because I bent over for someone and got rooms comped at the Lodge at Cloudcroft which is a charming old Victorian hotel complete with a decent restaurant, bar, and lady ghost, not that I ever saw her. We arrived at Mulcock's, being well-rested and fed, said hi to Charlie, broke out our gear, donned our waders and headed through the gate down to the river. We had just started fishing and were upstream about a hundred yards when Roger yelled, "TJ come here! There's a cow in the water and it can't get out!"

I ran upstream and caught up to Roger, looked in the water, and there was the cow, lying on its side, struggling to get to its feet, and making distressed cow sounds. Never confronted by anything like this before, I was at a loss for what to do. The cow was obviously in trouble, having a hard time keeping its head above water. Its eyes were rolling back into its head and was on the verge of exhaustion and drowning. As I said earlier, the river was narrow and deep. I mean over-your-head deep, and there was no gradual drop-off. If you fell in, you were up to your neck immediately, and this poor cow had found one of the deepest holes in the river. Roger said, "I'm going back to get Charlie. You stay here and help the cow."

"Help the cow? What the hell am I supposed to do? Go in and give it mouth-to-mouth?"

"Well. just stay with the cow so we know where it is when we come back."

Roger sprinted back downstream to the gate and all the way to Charlie's house, which was less than a quarter mile from there. I stood and watched the poor animal, thinking it might die before they made it back. After about ten minutes, I saw Charlie's truck come rumbling through the gate. They arrived, and Charlie doesn't seem excited in the least. In fact, it's obvious he's more pissed off than anything. "Damn dumb animal," he muttered, and walked back to his truck and took a long length of link chain out of the bed. With chain in hand, he walked over to the river, jumped in, and somehow got the chain around the neck of the cow. He got out, soaking wet and smelling of frightened cow, and attached the end of the chain to the back of his pick-up. Jumping in the cab, he started the engine, and started to slowly drive away. The chain tightened around the cow's neck and started pulling it out of the water. The beast looked like it was being slowly decapitated, with its eyes bulging out of their sockets as it continued to shriek in the way only a drowning, getting strangled cow could shriek. As I watched this spectacle, I was absolutely sure it would lose its head or have its neck broken. I think the cow finally figured out what was happening because as it got further up the bank, its legs tried to further it along by attempting to climb up and right itself. Finally, Charlie got it completely out onto the bank. The cow laid there for a minute or two, panting loudly. Then after several minutes to rest and gain its composure, it stood up on its own and started to walk away.

Charlie thanked Roger profusely for helping him out, got in his truck and went back to the house. Roger was beaming with pride. I truly believe this was a defining moment in not only the cow's life, but Roger's as well. At the very least, he now had a story he could tell his grandkids about that fateful day on the Rio Peñasco. It's funny, because the two of us resumed fishing, and I have no recollection at all if we even caught anything.

Any respect and admiration Charlie might have had for Roger, and me for that matter was demolished the next day. Before we left for the canyon, Charlie told us to please be gentle with his fish, not to play them too long and release them in the best possible way. We assured him in kinder words than these; we weren't freakin' amateurs, this wasn't our first rodeo, and we hated people who didn't know what to do with a fish after they caught it. Apparently, we convinced him we weren't rubes, so he told us how to get to the canyon and said he might join us later that afternoon, which was fine and groovy with us.

I already described this magical area. We started fishing as low as we could. The stream there was very narrow, in some places three feet across. The canyon walls were close-in too. It was maybe a hundred feet from side to side where we were. Big trees were thriving along either side and the riverbank was covered in thick green grass, and some of it was deceptively marshy. A large bird population made its home in the trees, and they were wary of our intrusion into their private paradise. We hadn't been shat upon yet, but the thought of it certainly crossed our minds. Somehow, several head of cattle had made it down into the canyon as well, although none were in sight as of yet. It was going to be a warm day, but the sunshine was dappled by the trees, making it a cool and pleasant morning.

The river was known for its trico hatches, so Roger slapped one on and began casting. On his third or fourth cast a large head appeared below his fly and gently sucked it in like it was a natural. Roger's line tightened and we both knew he had a trophy on. It was a very big brown trout, surprising since all of the fish we caught up top were rainbows. With the river so small where we were, the fish had little room to run, so it kept hunkering down under the bank and Roger did his best to pull it out time after time. Finally, the fish seemed ready and I offered to grab and release the fish. Roger handed me his camera and said, "There ain't no way I'm not gonna get a picture of this one!" I quickly moved to where the fish was, and not really watching where I was walking, I didn't notice the brand new steaming-warm cow patty that had just been deposited by one of our bovine friends, possibly even the one Roger saved. I grabbed hold of his line and immediately slipped, both my feet flying up in front of me, causing me to land hard, directly on top of the cow pie. Chartreuse cow dung flew out in all directions, not unlike what happens when a meteor hits your neighbor's tool shed. I was covered; Roger had splatter on his face, and since I had hold of Roger's line, my unfortunate quick descent caused the trico to become disgorged, and off swam one of the biggest brown trout I'd seen in New Mexico with no photographic evidence for Roger.

He was beside himself. "That was the biggest fucking fish I have ever caught, and all I got is cow shit all over me!"

I'd blown it, and I felt terrible.

"Look," I pleaded. "I'll be your witness. I'll tell everyone how you hooked it and that it was easily 23, maybe 24 inches."

"A lot of good that'll do. Everyone knows you're a big bullshitter."

He was right. I literally sat down in the middle of the river and cleaned off as much crap as I could. Roger threw some river water on his face, and we continued upstream with Roger muttering something under his breath about my close relationship with my mother. It has been over a decade, and every time we fish, he reminds me what a dork I was.

But, it was his turn next.

We had a great morning and early afternoon, catching and releasing many fish. We had no idea that these waterfalls existed and when we came upon them, it was like being in Hawaii. The falls changed the climate in the canyon again. As they fell into their plunge pools the spray raised the humidity, causing ferns and other almost tropical plants to come forth. Yet, the water was still 59 degrees, and the trout loved these pools. The falls and their pools were connected by short stretches of river. We'd fish one, and then hike up to the top of the falls, fish the stretch of river leading up to the next, and then fish the next pool. While Roger was downstream, I was fishing below a spectacular waterfall that probably dropped at least twenty feet into a clear, blue-green pool. After watching the water for a few minutes, I noticed there were a couple currents coming off this particular set of falls, one of which took a right-handed path and followed along the right bank of the pool and back down into the stream. I was standing above a small riffle where the pool met the river as I watched several large fish lazily feeding. I put on a small Parachute Adams with a red parachute, and an even smaller prince nymph below, and cast right in front of the falls. so my flies would eventual-ly hug the right bank.

The first couple of casts missed the mark, but the next one landed where it needed to, following the current with a perfect drift. Just as it got to the right bank, I saw a shadow dart out from underneath and watched my Adams disappear. It was a large rainbow, maybe twenty inches, and an acrobat. After several athletic jumps in the pool, it decided to take off downstream toward

Rog and me at Bob Gerding's Outdoor Adventures Hunting and Fishing Show in Albuquerque.

Roger. I got the fish to stop about halfway between the two of us, and happened to look up to see Charlie had arrived and was watching the battle. The fish proved very difficult to land, so Roger ran upstream, and unhooked the fish. As he stood up with the fish in both hands, he began to walk quickly through the river towards me and Charlie and as he got to us, lost his footing. The fish flew up into the air as did Roger, and both landed loudly in the water with an explosive splash, accompanied by Roger doing a perfect face-plant. The fish fared much better, swimming away as it hit the water.

All of this after we promised Charlie we wouldn't abuse his fish.

Charlie stood there for a minute, not saying anything, and then turned his back. We had no idea what was going to happen. Was he going to kill us? Was he going to charge us for the fish? Was he going to throw us off his land, never allowing us to come back?

Then we noticed he was shaking. He was shaking because he was laughing hysterically at the slapstick buffoonery that had just occurred. He turned back, all red-faced, a few tears still running down his face, and said to Roger, "I turned around because a gentleman does not laugh in another man's face!" And then he walked away, still snickering to himself. And not unlike Roger, every time we run into him, he mentions that day and how we fished like a couple of jackasses.

# 19 NOT FOR THE KIDS

*Roll the title and the opening credits!*

MY BEST IDEA FOR A FLY FISHING PORNO FLICK has the working title, "A River Runs Through Her."

Opening scene: It's a long shot upstream, showing the beautiful river and all the gorgeous scenery on a beautiful sunny morning. Far ahead, there is a figure standing in the middle of the river, backlit by the warm yellow light of the sun. As the camera pans in, we notice it's a woman with long black hair wearing a black cowboy hat, hip boot waders attached with a wading belt at the hip and nothing else. She is unbelievably sexy. The camera shows her making perfect casts with a fly rod in slow-motion. As she continues to cast, the camera slowly pans past her and goes over to the willow-lined riverbank where a particular section of willow bushes are moving at a frenetic pace. The camera moves through the willows to see my buddy Mo, with his waders around his ankles, intently watching this beautiful woman as he takes care of himself.

Roll the title and the opening credits!

The premise: my buddy Bill runs a fishing lodge that trains and hires beautiful hookers as guides. Mo, of course, is the front desk guy and handyman at the lodge. Each scene is with a different chick and her client in different and fascinating combinations of amore.

This is a no-lose project! And, if you're the type of person who would actually want to make a film like this, I generously give you the idea for free! All I ask is credit at the beginning or end saying, "Inspired from an idea by TJ Trout."

OK. I ask one more thing: Adult superstar Tera Patrick should be cast as the head fishing guide, featured in the opening scene I just described.

I'd make it myself, but I already have enough karma to work off.

*We heard howler monkeys in the distance, and we heard sounds that we had no clue what they were. Are we being watched? Are we being stalked? Are we being paranoid?*

# 20 BELIZE AND THE GUATEMALAN NAZIS

APPARENTLY ONE PARTICULAR SUBJECT RUNS
through the book, because either it's important to me, or it's an issue that we fly-fishers constantly need to deal with. It' whether or not to take your wife or girlfriend along on your fishing trip. Clearly, it changes the whole aspect of the trip, having to mix hard core fishing with the beaching, dining, shopping, and other non-fishing activities. And then there's Belize. A third-world country in many aspects. Belize City immediately strikes you as a place you really don't want to spend much time in. You fly in, get your gear and your luggage, and be sure to handle your own bags by the way. Get as quickly as you can to a taxi or to whoever is holding the sign in the lobby to pick you up, and get the hell out of their and to your destination. No offense to native Belizeans, but Belize City could be the set of some dystopian futuristic movie where society has crumbled and this is all that's left. The zombies aren't here yet, but the zombie virus is lurking somewhere in the rain forest, carried by howler monkeys. They fling their feces at you, hit you in the face, and boom, you're a zombie. In fact, I might write the screenplay.

My first trip to Belize was set up by the radio station. It was a contest where a winner and a guest travelled with us to our tropical destination, and they got to fish with TJ Trout. That really didn't happen, but at least they got to go on the trip... Now, sometimes when you do contests like this, you can get stuck with complete and total assholes. It's happened to me on a few occasions, and by the end of the excursion, you are ready to wrap them in the anchor rope and drown them in the river. We were lucky this trip. The winner was a delightful young single mother who chose to take her 12-year-old son as her guest. As it worked out, they barely fished, certainly did not fly-fish, so the lodge took them separately, fished a little, did some sightseeing, and found a few deserted cays where they could have some isolated beach time. We, on the other hand, fished.

Since this trip was arranged, and not planned by me, we didn't stay at one of the offshore cays like Turneffe, or Caulker, or a number of others. We stayed at the Belize River Lodge, which was not surprisingly on the Belize River about a half hour drive outside of Belize City. It was certainly not an isolated area of the river, as there were other lodges and residences along the river. To its credit, although close-in to the city, the rain forest was right there, so you had the parrots and could hear the howler monkeys bellowing in the trees lining the river. It was very green. Jungle green as you might expect. The lodge itself was rustic, yet charming, with all the amenities to make a travelling female companion happy. The owner could not have been more gracious, the food was good, and there was alcohol. Perfect. However, this was not a place like those on the cays, where you could walk outside your cabana and look for tailing bones in the flats stretching in front of you. Nope. Getting to the flats and any real fly-fishing required a fairly long boat ride through close-in mangrove channels, backwaters, and then it all opened up with the so-familiar turquoise blue Caribbean stretching out in front of us, shimmering under the bright sunlight, the horizon dotted with various sized cays. Okay, so that was maybe one or two days. The other days it rained. Or threatened rain. But we did what we could.

One of my most memorable moments of that trip was Marti's big miss. It was a gray day that threatened rain, and then did rain and stopped. And started again. Our guide decided we would stay closer to home and fish some of the mangrove channels. The wind was howling and even the boat ride to the channel that required a couple stretches of open water turned into an experience I equated to driving on a pot-hole-ridden Cleveland street with bad shocks...Each wave sent a percussive jolt up both of our spines, as we held on to the side of the boat, not to fly out. Marti, at the time, was wearing a two-piece swimsuit since it was still hot, and there was a hint the weather might break that afternoon. We hit a wave at a particularly precarious angle, causing us both to lift off our seats, and to her dismay, and the delight of the guide, Marti comes crashing down, lands on the bottom of the boat, directly onto the plastic hook that fastened here bikini top, snapping it in two. On the rebound bounce, off comes her top, flying towards the guide, hitting him on the forehead, as Marti sits there, on the bottom of the boat, stunned, and topless. The guide, although certainly enjoying the free booby show, is quite the gentleman, and gives us some high-test monofilament line that I used to tie her top back on her.

It was not going to be her day. But at least what happened next gave us another story to tell. I was catching nothing... The water was wrong for my fly rod, the wind was brutal at times, so I was casting the banks with some kind of Rapala-like lure, as was Marti... She somehow managed a cast right to the edge of the mangroves about fifty feet from where we were, and nearly before she started reeling back in, BAM. A sizeable fish—didn't know what it was yet—slammed her lure with abandon, realized it was hooked, and torpedoed downstream towards open water while Marti hung on. I yelled to the guide, 'What the hell is that?' and he yells back "Crevalle Jack! She's in for a big fight, boss." The battle was valiant, well-fought, and worthy of re-telling, especially after a few drinks. The jack ran, tired, ran some more, came in, went back out, and finally after 45 minutes of back and forth, and yes, I timed it, it decided to end it. The jack rolled on the line and spat the now nearly destroyed Rapala back at us, and the line went limp, which made me wonder for a minute, who was playing who in this battle. Did the fish get lucky or did it just finally say to itself, enough is enough? Those who know more than me tell me that fish have pea-sized brains, and are incapable of any thought much more than basic instinct. I tend to doubt that. Marti was exhausted, angry, profoundly disappointed and near tears after such a worthy fight. And, I knew better than to try and console her at that moment. There was no way I was going to fling plat-itudes at her, like, "Oh Honey! Sometimes you win, sometimes the fish wins." Or, "You really should be proud of yourself! That was a great fight!" Or, "Just think of the conversation tonight around the dinner table you can have with the other guests!"

But I did it anyway. And that's another lesson for you all. Don't try to console the inconsolable until a sufficient amount of time has passed that the recipient of your consolation has had enough time to sufficiently process what just happened and rationalize to themselves that in the grand scheme of things, that it really didn't matter. But that takes anywhere from a few minutes to a few months, depending on the fish, the battle, and other circumstances—like the weather, the wind, and if they're wearing a broken swimsuit, with a half-hour boat ride back to the lodge through a heavy chop.

By the next day Marti was good enough to want to go out again, but after I promised her that we'd have our guide find us one of those small, undeveloped beachy cays offshore where I promised her a day on a deserted beach with lunch and white wine. The weather was supposed to break by tomorrow so we'd try it then. Plus of course, the said cay was surrounded by a fairly sizeable area of sand flats that I could wade out and sight fish for tailing bones while she luxuriated on the beach.

But today...not as windy, but cloudy, with an occasional drizzle. The guide suggested that we actually go inland instead of out to the flats because of the unpredictable weather. So, we agreed.

Only three times in my life have I ever been in a wilderness situation where it actually gave me pause, or even a slight trepidation. Dread might be too strong of a word, but only three times have I thought, well, we are now officially in 'wild' country. Where if we got lost or something went amiss, we would be in deep shit, and quickly. One was actually northern New Mexico in the dense woods near the Brazos River Ranch, which I discuss in another chapter. Another was up in the wilds of Alaska near Bristol Bay, where there was no way in or out except for the float planes landing on the river. And third was here, in Belize. We launched right after breakfast. It was early and the parrots were beginning to fly around and make noise. Occasionally in the distance you could hear the howler monkeys. By the way, if you've never heard a howler monkey, the name is fitting... They are the largest of the New World primates, other than us, and their deafening frequent and almost unearthly howls make you think you're in a forest filled with large, predacious, flying, banshee predators who are out for human flesh. I guess the locals are used to them. They can be a tad unnerving. So instead of going away from the sound, we go towards it. We're boating inland on the Belize River, past any riverside housing or structures, past any real human habitation, past any civilization. Just as I'm starting to wonder if I needed a malaria shot, our guide turns the boat left towards the southern bank of the river. All I see is jungle foliage, nothing more. Then as we get closer, I notice what looks like maybe an indentation in the riverbank? Turns out it is a very small very tight tributary, which barely shows itself to anyone passing by, nearly unpassable because of a twisted canopy of foliage that all but blocks the entrance. Rico tells us to keep our heads down, and he pushes away to greenery as we enter into this sinuous watery passageway.

The waterway, don't know if it's worthy of calling a stream, might be six feet wide. The jungle appears to be trying to take it back for itself. We motor slowly along. It is perpetual dusk where we are. The light is green, like the surroundings. The air is still and it is quite humid. And the rainforest is full of noise and life. Birds of all types flit above our heads including all the magnificent parrots. We heard howler monkeys in the distance, and we heard sounds that we had no clue what they were. Are we being watched? Are we being stalked? Are we being paranoid? I sensed that Marti is somewhat on-edge, and I can't blame her because I was too. All we can do is trust Rico, and hope he doesn't belong to some cult of cannibals, where we'll be dismembered, and barbecued, never to be seen again. The water we're in is stained a permanent tea green, yet has clarity. I saw little life in the water other than occasional juvenile fish trying to get out of our way. The creek, I guess I'll call it, meanders on through the rain forest, and after going what seems like several miles—but it's hard to tell because of the crooked path--the perpetual green dusk began to lighten as the canopy began to pull away. We finally emerged into a large lagoon, and there was sky above us for the first time in at least an hour. The lagoon was full of life. Egrets and other water birds greeted us, and Rico turned the motor off, and we began polling slowly across the wide expanse of water. He told me to get my rod ready. Apparently, we'd be fishing for either snook or baby tarpon. At that point in my fishing experience, I have caught neither. We poled up the left side of the lagoon, and Rico told me to make some blind casts as closely as I can get to the mangroves which lined the banks of the lagoon. After several unsuccessful casts he excitedly pointed out towards the middle about a hundred feet in front of the boat. There was surface activity going on, and it looked almost like a trout feeding in a mayfly hatch. "Baby tarpon, "he said quietly. "Cast beyond it and strip it back near the surface," which I did. The strike was instantaneous and hard, and elicited an immediate jump. My first tarpon! Granted, it was a juvenile. but I'll take it! And it fought like a large trout, jumping and making runs across the lagoon, and finally hunkering down under the boat doing the figure-8 dance that they're known for. Rico got the net, and we figured around 20 pounds. Not bad! Now any pressure was off. We proceeded to go up river above the lagoon into the same dark canopy and managed to pull a couple snook out of the mangroves, and then headed back. All and all, a good day.

Late afternoon the skies cleared, which promised tomorrow would be a beach day for Marti, out in the open water. After dinner at the lodge, a couple Belikans, and a cigar out on the dock, the owner walked up and said, you want to go for a boat ride on the river? In the good boat? Marti and I readily agreed so we headed upstream. We asked him questions about living down here, the culture, the crime, how many Americans lived here, and he pointed to the left bank of the river where we passed a number of homes, some nice, some shacks. He told me about them.

"Most of these houses are owned by Americans. I want to show you a particular one."

About a half mile further, we stopped in front of what looked like an upscale, large residence, for Belize. We commented on the place and he said, "I want you do look a little closer." And he pulled the boat up to the bank. As he did, we noticed it was not a house at all, but the front wall of a house, supported from behind by 2 by 4s. Of course, that confused us so I asked him what was going on, and he smiled.

"That's a life lesson for you, if you would ever consider moving here and building a house. An American real estate guy who just retired bought the riverfront property and proceeded to build his dream retirement home. Nothing but the best inside. Plumbing, electronics, furniture, appliances, all top shelf. But the problem was, he only planned on living here during the winter months, so he decided to hire one of our guys in town to boat by every day to make sure that all was well. And I guess he should have been more specific because that's all the guy did. He drove by in the boat, looked at the place, everything looked OK, and so he went home. He did this for six straight months, all while being paid by our retiree. Unbeknownst to our boatman, local thieves were inside ransacking the place. They took everything, down to the bare walls. And then, they decided to take the bare walls too! They propped the front of the house up so it looked somewhat normal from the river, and dismantled the rest of the house, to the point of what you see now. Nothing but the front of the house left!"

"So what happened?"

"Well, that's the thing. Nothing! He comes back down, it's all gone, goes to the police, they have no suspects, probably because they got paid off by the looters, and the guy loses everything, except for the front. This made the TV news in Houston. Don't know if it did anywhere else. All that's left is what you're looking at. And it stands there as a cautionary tale to anyone else thinking about doing the same thing."

"What about out on the water and on the cays? Is it the same?"

"It's different out there. More money and more security. But inland here it's a whole other world."

As I have repeatedly said, some of the more memorable stories from fishing trips do not involve fishing. The weather was not supposed to be good on the coast. Same rain and wind that had followed us all week. Taking the advice of the lodge owner, we decided to hire a guide/interpreter and do some exploring inland. Ermelo was a bright

Belizean college student who was on break from Texas A&M, where he was enrolled in their pre-med program. We told him we'd like to see some Maya ruins, as well as cross in to Guatemala since neither of us had been there. So off we went on an early Wednesday morning. As we drove inland, we noticed little kids at bus stops waiting for the school bus, all in school uniforms, but it was also apparent that these kids were Mennonite because of the bonnets worn by the young girls. And he explained the history. Most of the Mennonites were of Russian descent and migrated here via Canada, to Mexico, and then in the late 1950s the more conservative of the bunch made the jump to Belize, where now they number around 12,000. Mostly all white, but the kids I saw were certainly of African descent.

Ermelo insisted we drive through Belmopan, the Belizean capital, which he was quite proud of. Not unlike Brasilia, Belmopan was a completely planned city, newly built, still being built actually, from the ground up. To me--and realize back then it was not yet complete—it seemed stark, institutional, and almost seemed not to fit into the geography. But I kept my thoughts to myself as we passed in and out of the city and headed further inland towards the hills and the Xunantunich ruins. I remember very little of the ruin site, other than there was a pyramid, and that was about it. We continued towards the Guatemalan border, following the CA-13 towards the crossing near the village of Melchor de Mencos, Guatemala. Not only was this THE major crossover for mostly big rigs and other commercial vehicles, there was also a footbridge that crossed the Mopan River, which was the method we decided to use to get to the other side, since the road was backed up for miles. And I use this metaphor often, but in this case it was true. The truckers, and other vehicles crossing into Guatemala were driven by people I can only describe as scary. These dudes could have been easily cast into the bar scene in the first *Star Wars* movie. Traffic was moving at a crawl, so Ermelo parked his Toyota in the parking lot, and we walked towards the border crossing, and into the building where people like us would be processed and hopefully allowed to walk over the bridge into Guatemala. Getting through the Belize side was easy enough. Showed some ID, had Ermelo explain what we were doing, and we got waved forward, down the hall to where the Guatemalan processing point was. We're sitting in a small, non-descript lobby, and after a few minutes get called into the office where we thought the process would continue and go fairly easily, based on what happened with the Belizeans.

We seemingly have walked onto the set of a World War Two Nazi movie. We open the door and entered into a small office-type room. Standing there was a version of my father-in-law. Fair skinned, very Germanic-looking, wearing what appeared to be a desert tan military uniform with knee-high jack boots, and the appropriate military head gear. He is flanked by two large, simian looking, similarly dressed storm troopers, each holding a military grade weapon resembling an M-16. At this point, I thought we walked into the wrong room, or even worse, we were being arrested on some trumped-up charges and they'd dump our weighted down bodies into the river, where we'd become Mopan River catfish food.

I looked over at Ermelo and was about to ask him what the fuck was going on, when he motioned for me to be quiet. The jack-booted commandant, or whatever he was, stared at us for a long moment and then rattled something off in very quick Spanish. Ermelo smiled at him nervously, and said, "He wants to see your passports," which we immediately whipped out and placed them on his desk. He looked at them, looked at us, looked at them again, and puts them in his desk drawer. At that point I was surprised the urine didn't start running down my leg. He sat down, lit a cigarette, put his boots up on his desk and again, says something in Spanish.

"He wants to know why you want to go into Guatemala."

I explained that we were on a fishing trip, and we've never been there and had a day, so we decided to take a tour and wanted to cross over just to see his beautiful country. At that, he turned around and said something to the armed Stormtroopers, and all three burst out laughing. Ermelo smiled a bit, but you could tell he was thinking that this was highly unusual and wondered if we could just start slowly backing out towards the Belizean side.

After they got done with their good laugh, he turned to us and again—in rapid staccato Spanish—asks us something else. This made Ermelo's eyes widen, and his retort, without even translating the question for me, was an octave higher in somewhat placating tones.

I turned to Ermelo with a questioning look, and he said, "I'll tell you later, but he needs some money if you want to cross."

I looked back at the Commandant and in English ask how much, which he actually seemed to understand. He looked me straight in the eye and said, "Two dollar. American." I thought to myself, what the fuck? Two stinking dollars? That's all this dude wants? I thought he was going to extort us for some crazy sum, but two bucks? At that point I lost all respect for this guy. I would have given him twenty, easily! Even more if it meant not having by balls blown off by his henchmen. But two dollars American? OK pal! It's yours! For some reason I had several quarters in my pocket, so I count out eight quarters, and place them in front of him on his desk. Again, he looked at me, looked at the quarters, and with one sweep of his right arm, backhanded the quarters into my face, and then stood up and screamed, "No coins! Paper American money!"

Then I realized I was truly dealing with a deranged individual, who was on a power trip, trying to extort a scared American tourist for little to no money. Marti started picking up the quarters from the floor as I fumbled for my wallet, and thank God I actually had several singles with me that I specifically took to tip people with. Most likely with shaking hands, but as of yet, no peeing of myself, I handed over the two dollars, and he mutters something under his breath, took our passports out of his desk drawer, opened them up, stamped them and in English said, "Welcome to Guatemala." We were led from his office, into a long hallway that led to the outside and the bridge that crosses the river. We walked silently over the bridge. I looked at the river and thought to myself, number one, they never would have found our bodies down there, and number two, it was actually quite a beautiful stream, clear water, running through jungle foliage. If we weren't in Central America, I'd be scanning the water, looking for trout holding at the bottom of several of the riffles.

We made it into the village of Melchor de Mentos. On the Guatemalan side, women were cleaning their laundry on the rocks in the river. Right at the river's edge, there were several touristy stands selling souvenirs, so while still in a state of shock, we bought some carved wooden animal figure and another made of woven wool. Then we turned around and walked back. When we got to Ermelo's car, I asked him, "So what did the commandant say to you before he asked for money?"

He said, "I was unable to translate for you because he told me not to. He said he was going to fuck with both of you, and for me just to stand there and shut the fuck up and let him have some fun!" "But two dollars? Why didn't he ask me for more? I would have easily given him twenty!"

"Not a clue. If you want to go back and ask him, be my guest!"

I politely declined. But at least we could say we were in Guatemala and lived to tell the tale.

*Like anything else, you can talk a good game,*
*but once you're out on the stream, it's impossible*
*to hide how really bad you are.*

# 21 A VOLCANO, A GANGSTER, AND WINTER-KILL RODENTS

IF YOU LIVE IN ALBUQUERQUE AND YOU FLY FISH, your true "Home Water" would have to be the streams in the Jemez Mountains. From my house or the radio station, I could be on the river fishing in exactly one hour, which was precisely why I always kept a fly rod and my waders in the back of my truck at all times.

When you turn off U.S. 550 to go into the Jemez, you pass through the little village of San Isidro and then the village of Jemez Springs, two of the most notorious speed traps in the state of New Mexico. I have been pulled over in both but luckily never ticketed. Jer claims he was given a one-hundred-dollar ticket in Jemez springs for going two miles over the 25 mph. speed limit. He probably didn't mention the joint he was smoking.

In between the two villages is one of my favorite places in the state, the Jemez Pueblo. I love those guys. When I worked for 94 Rock, they were probably our biggest fans. The Morning Show did what we called our "Pueblo Tour," where on certain Fridays we would broadcast our morning show from different pueblos around the state, and the Jemez was the first. The outpouring of people was amazing and heartfelt, and we left happy and overfed, feasting on their red chile cheese enchiladas, the best I've ever had and hot! I have attended their dances and feast days and am humbled to this day by their friendship and hospitality, and certainly hope to return sometime. And that's not taking anything away from the pueblos of Zuni, Acoma, Isleta, and San Ildefonso either! You all have a special place in my heart and always will.

The natural history of the area is interesting and still developing. The Jemez lands are still geologically alive. About a million or so years ago, the Jemez blew up. It was one of the biggest volcanic explosions in earth's history, resulting in the formation of the Valles Caldera, one of the world's largest volcanic craters. The caldera itself is awe-inspiringly beautiful. It is a vast area of grassland that sits at over 8,700 feet elevation, surrounded by the walls of the crater which form the mountains. In the center of the caldera is Redondo Peak, an 11,000-foot-high resurgent volcanic dome. This means Redondo was formed by uplift caused by hot magma beneath the surface getting ready to blow again. Geologists tell me it won't for a long, long time—maybe a short time in the grand scheme of things, but none of us will be around to see it erupt.

The most recent eruptions took place between fifty and sixty thousand years ago and hot springs dotting the entire area are evidence of that. One of the more "notorious" hot springs is the "Hippie Hole," which is on the road to the Caldera. Legend has it that back in those days, hippies used to go up there and hang out and get naked and do all the things hippies do when they're naked. One day my buddy Krunch and I, after downing a few samples of his genuine moonshine that he brought back from the hollers of Virginny, decided to go up there and give it a shot. To our dismay, on that day we found it occupied by several gay guys who particularly liked the cut of Krunch's jib, if you catch my drift. Not that there's anything wrong with that, but both of us being proud heterosexuals, left the premises, feeling uncomfortable and a little stupid. Naked hippie chicks. Right.

Another interesting fact (to me anyway) relates to the giant volcanic explosion that formed the area. There was a huge amount of black obsidian or volcanic glass created when it blew. When you're fishing, you can't help but step on it. There is actually an "obsidian mine" where ancient Native Americans would "mine" the glass which was perfect for making arrowheads, and then trade it. The extra sharp black glass was of such good quality, it was traded as far south as Mexico. Even today the obsidian is used to make surgical blades where very sharp and fine cutting is warranted. It can be made sharper than any metal.

The Valles Caldera has a huge resident elk herd on its 96,000 acres, and both in rutting season in the fall and calving season in the spring, they're not shy, and you will possibly find yourselves fishing amongst them. I mentioned that Bob Gerding, up until recently, did flyfishing seminars there, and we who helped him were fortunate enough to be able to spend the night in the only lodge that exists in the Caldera. It's a circular building that sits on a small ridge above the caldera floor, and in the morning and evening you can look out over the grasslands and watch the elk. One morning in May we were lucky to see a calf being born. As we stood and watched, we saw the baby drop, and as it did, a large number of cow elk stood in a protective circle around the mother and baby to protect them from coyotes and any other predators that might be after an easy meal. In the fall it's a different story. During rutting season, which also happens to be hunting season, the elk tend to stay near the ponderosa pine tree lines. The bugling is non-stop, and occasionally you'll see the alpha bulls with their harems thunder across the open range.

In the spring, the grasses get green and wild irises bloom all over the caldera floor, turning it various shades of purple. The Caldera in the spring can be wet, depending on the snowpack. Lately that hasn't been the case as New Mexico has continued to experience serious drought conditions. That said, two of the major Jemez rivers originate in the Caldera, although the term "creeks" is actually more appropriate considering the small size of the waters. On one side, San Antonio Creek's headwaters are spring fed, coming out of the side of a hill; sadly now, through a pipe. The east fork of Jemez Creek seeps out of the ground on the other side of the valley. At least humans allowed that to remain natural. The water is very clear, and the streams range from a foot in width to maybe 20, maybe even 30 feet in width at large oxbows. But both are small streams that were packed with naturally reproducing brown trout, although there are some rainbows there as well. In fact, up until recently there was actually an overpopulation of fish, limiting the size they could achieve. The Caldera was always a catch and release area, but

Me, Bob, and Milt after a day of fishing through torrential downpours.

officials were considering making it limited catch and keep until trage-
dy struck.

As I said, New Mexico has been dangerously dry and finally in 2011,
a huge forest fire erupted that raced through the Caldera. It would have
burnt the town of Los Alamos and the national labs to the ground if it
weren't for the heroic efforts of the firefighters who dug in and saved
both. God only knows what would have happened if the inferno would
have reached the nuclear weapons lab. But the Caldera suffered a severe
setback.

Rains finally came to the area, but it was too soon after the fire.
They sent massive walls of ash rolling down the surrounding scorched
mountainsides with no trees left to stop the progress. The land was
baked into Teflon-like hard pack with no absorption capacity, so the ash
kept going and emptied directly into the headwaters, nearly wiping out
the entire fish populations. It was more than ugly. At times the waters
were flowing jet black. With the scorched mountainsides and burnt-out
grasslands and filthy water, it looked like a hell-scape.

Thankfully, nature's regenerative powers can be amazing. A year
went by, and the officials at the Valles Caldera called on Bob Gerding to
return and test-fish both streams. What he found was almost a miracle.
The grasses had returned like nothing had happened. And somehow,
the fish in San Antonio Creek must have known the ash was coming,
and had fled downstream. On Bob's first cast, he caught a nice brown.
Then another, then another, then another. He had what he described as
a "very good fishing day." The east fork of Jemez Creek did not fare as
well. But it is gratifying to see this area recovering. Now, all they need
to do is figure out the politics.

The land was originally private, then the federal government took
control and made it a national trust with limited access and a plan to
have the area make a profit after five years. That didn't happen. The
state of New Mexico managed it for a while. These days the land is managed by the National Park Service as Valles Caldera National Preserve.

The only thing I hope is whoever takes it over keeps it as pristine
and unblemished as possible, unlike the rest of the Jemez, which at
times can look like a garbage dump because people can be ignorant pigs.
This is the one issue that I could kill over. If you're reading this, I hope
I'm not speaking to you personally. But if I am, how stupid do you have
to be to just leave your trash on the ground when you leave? Pretty
damned stupid. And what kind of dumb-ass would leave a fire smolder-

ing in the middle of a drought because he's too lazy to put it out properly? A loser needledick, that's who. Or even worse, what kind of an unthinking ignoramus would leave dirty diapers on top of a smoldering fire in the middle of a tinder-dry forest? And is this how you're gonna teach your toddler to be responsible and respectful? You shouldn't be allowed to have kids. I have picked up after people. I have put their fires out. I put their fires out and disposed of their stinking dirty diapers. And it's funny because you see this bullshit and think why should I pick up after these idiots? Why should I be their man-servant? They don't deserve it. They deserve to be put in jail! But the jails are too full, so I am now an advocate for the return of public humiliation and corporal punishment. If one of these jackasses actually gets caught, take 'em to the center of the village of Jemez Springs, put them in the stocks, and let people throw crap at them for a day. Or take them out and flog them at high noon. I'll bet they never trash the place again.

Back to fishing the Caldera and Bob's seminars. In the beginning he'd have one in May and another one in September. Like I said, Bob and all of us would spend the night before at the lodge and then the participants would arrive the next morning. After doing several of these, I had come to the conclusion that the only reason Bob put these seminars on was for the "night before" at the lodge.

One thing you can say about this group of fly fishers, and probably all fly fishers in general: We all appreciate good food, a good cigar, and plenty of quality libatious beverages. The way it worked was, someone brought the food, usually in the form of red meat, someone brought the red wine and the bourbon and/or scotch, and if we were lucky enough, someone showed up with the choice tobacco product. We'd all have dinner and then retire to the huge circular open-air common area with a soaring ceiling, punctuated by a giant rustic stone fireplace and oversized leather furniture. Beverages would be enjoyed, cigars would be smoked (outside, if you work for the Valles Caldera and are reading this). Then we'd sit around and listen to everyone tell their personal tall tales of past fishing trips, and everyone would laugh at all the half-truths and outright lies. Another round of drinks, and then we all had to endure Bob's identical twin brother Dick's, and Bill Carpenter's bad jokes! (I say that in a loving way.) Luckily, all the bedrooms ringed the outside of the common room, so if we drank a tad too much, we could crawl back to our rooms and call it a night. The only problem was, since it was a circular room, all the bedrooms looked alike, and on more than one occasion, I made two or three tries before I found mine. The next morning brought hangovers, breakfast burritos, and coffee that Bob got up early to make.

The participants arrived around 9 AM, all excited to be in such a beautiful place, and eager to learn the skills necessary to catch a trout on a fly rod and especially excited to be learning from Bob, whose reputation certainly preceded him. Most were beginners, and the others who claimed to already know what they were doing and just needed a few tips were usually the ones who were the most trouble. Like anything else, you can talk a good game, but once you're out on the stream, it's impossible to hide how bad you really are. In fact, after a couple of these seminars, we'd give the participants a once-over and make bets on who would be the biggest pain in the ass. There's always one.

So outside in an open area behind the lodge, Bob would explain the basics and the equipment, his brother Dick or Bob Widgren would give a casting demonstration, then they'd divide the group into two sections. At one picnic table you'd learn about bugs, and at the other, how to tie basic knots. Then everyone would get a fly rod and the casting lessons would begin. Again, this is probably why you should keep your mouth shut if you've fished just enough with a fly rod to make an ass out of yourself.

Beginners are easier to teach than spin fishermen because beginners have no pre-conceived notions. Spin fishermen always without exception try to power the fly out instead of realizing flyfishing requires a completely separate set of skills. Women are the easiest to teach because they're more open to taking instruction and don't have that testosterone-driven macho thing about having to use their brawn to cast. In all my experience, I've only known one woman who actually did that, and I watched her whip the water to a froth while moving her fly rod back and forth like some crazy metronome. If you're from Albuquerque and listened to 94 Rock, I reveal that female individual to be former TV news anchor and now mother and philanthropist, and all-around good person, Cindy Hernandez. (Didn't think you'd make it into the book either, did you?) After a while, I got her calmed down. Anyway, after casting, we the instructors would be assigned two people and we would be responsible for guiding them on the river.

You might think that two easy flowing rivers running through a treeless wide-open area would be the perfect place to teach neophytes the flyfishing art. You might think. But during the warm months, the grass gets waist high, and being around 9000 feet, sooner or later it's gonna get windy. Combine that with clear, slow-moving water and you get spooky trout and a pretty technical place to fish. All that said, it was our appointed duty to get everyone hooked up at least once, and at times that called for improvisation and luck.

The first two guys I ever guided up there happened fighting a steady 20-plus mph wind. After their casts either ended up wrapped around their legs or caught in the grass, I figured this was either going to be a long several hours, or I'd have to do that improvisation thing. I walked them down to a place where the stream was less than two feet wide. Grass still lined both sides of this little vein of water, but I knew there were fish hiding beneath the undercut banks because every minute or so I'd see one dash out and take a bug on the surface and then retreat back to its hiding place. It was there that I taught them the science of what I call "dink" fishing. I would have them stand, or get on their knees as far back as they could from the water, but close enough so their rod tip would reach mid-stream. They'd have just enough line out so their dry fly would float on the water, with a little spare so the fly could drift a bit. Then they would just "dink" their fly onto the water and let it drift to the end of their line. No casting was required, just lowering the fly and letting it go. We were wildly successful, and these guys gained confidence with every fish they caught.

It was at the end of that day, and as we were walking back towards the trucks, I was watching the stream. As I said, they had caught several fish, but neither had really caught one with a legitimate cast. We came to a bend in the river where it was about 20 feet wide, and I saw a large rainbow feeding right at the bend below a bush growing on the bank that was hanging inches above the water--the perfect hiding spot for this big fish. When I say big, I mean Caldera big. He was probably 18 inches, a great sized fish for that stream. Amazingly, he was unaware of our presence as he leisurely moved out into the current, slurped a passing bug, and then went back to his comfort zone under the shrubbery.

I signaled to the guys to stop walking and pointed to the water where the big rainbow was chowing down. Neither of the guys showed any real promise in casting in windy conditions on a stream surrounded by high grass, so since Greg was standing next to me, he was the chosen one. We crept to the most advantageous position on the bank, which was across and maybe twenty feet downstream. The wind was still blowing, but more of a crosswind than directly in his face. That's when I had the "Come to Jesus" moment with him. I said, "If you ever in your life make a good accurate cast, now is the time to do it. You will only get one shot at this fish, so you absolutely have to put the fly in the perfect spot." I told him to watch the current and see how it was flowing directly to the bend in the bank where the bush was and instructed him to cast about ten to fifteen feet above it and let the fly drift right to the fish. Greg pulled some line off his reel, made one false cast which I winced at and then let it go. It landed exactly where it needed to. We both watched as his caddis drifted right into the feeding lane. The rainbow didn't hesitate. He darted out from under the bush and sucked it in. Greg set the hook, and being a small stream, the fish had little room to run. It darted back and forth and then headed directly back to the bush and held under the bank, and there was no more fighting, just the taut line. I realized the trout had wrapped itself around the roots of the bush and there was a slim chance that it was possibly still on the line. I got into the water, walked over to the bush, reached under and undid the tangle, and the fish shot out downstream still hooked. For a beginner, Greg played the fish well enough, with me barking instructions at him: "Give him line! Don't give him slack! Reel! Reel! Keep your rod tip up!" And he ended up landing probably one of the biggest fish in the river on his first real cast. I was so proud of him.

I am not going to tell you where my other favorite spots to fish are in the rest of the Jemez, unless you bribe me with cash, good wine, or illegal cigars. Then I might. But there are plenty. Most of the time, I will fish the Jemez River above the town of Jemez Springs, although sometimes when I'm in a wacky mood, I'll fish it right through the town. There's a Buddhist monastery near the town center, and I've caught many a trout watching the monks go through their ablutions. There's also a hot spring that flows into the river at the town center, making it possible to fish the river in the winter as it keeps it free of ice and snow, and also gives the fish warmer water to swim around in. If you are into winter fishing, the same can be said for the number of hot springs that flow into the Jemez especially. I never saw a fish in the hippie hole though.

If you like more vertical pocket fishing, the Guadalupe should be your river of choice. It's a little harder to access and it may take some hiking, but not as many people fish it and there are plenty of browns in it. There's also the Rio de las Vacas, the east fork of the Jemez, the lower San Antonio and possibly my true favorite stream in the area, although

I don't go there that often--the upper Cebolla Creek or Rio Cebolla. It's a high-altitude creek meandering through a grassy meadow that is full of little Rio Grande cutthroats that will strike at pretty much anything you throw at them if you don't spook 'em. If you keep walking, you'll come to a series of beaver ponds.

The Rio Cebolla also has a "legendary" history. Lore has it that gangster Al Capone spent some time there. If you go on-line, most people think it's all fable, but a person who I trust implicitly insists on the contrary. That person would, again, be Bob Gerding. These are his words: "When we were young, my brother Dick and I worked in the Jemez above Seven Springs Hatchery at a dude ranch called "The Lazy Ray Ranch." That's the same place where Al Capone stayed at least a couple of times (At that time, it might have been known as 'Rancho Ria.')" The story was told to me by Homer Pickens, one of the first state game wardens. If there was ever a man who I believed to tell the truth, it would be Homer Pickens. He couldn't lie or embellish a story if his life depended on it. This is the story Homer told me: Homer was working at the Seven Springs Hatchery before he was the state game warden. One day he looked up and saw a horse with a saddle and bridle, sans rider. He captured the horse and figured someone had either been thrown or didn't tie up the horse adequately. He walked the horse back in the direction it came from and discovered a rider who was looking for the horse. Homer returned the horse to him and received many thanks. A few days later while Homer was outside the hatchery working, several cars came through the hatchery, big black Packards as Homer remembered. One stopped, and a man got out and came over and thanked Homer again for rescuing him and his horse. When the man got back in the car, one of the other workers asked Homer, "Do you know who that was?" Homer said he had no idea. The other worker said, "That was Al Capone!" Homer later checked with the ranch people, and they confirmed that indeed it was Al Capone.

Bob was still in his teens when he worked at the ranch, and one of his tasks was to go out and catch fish for dinner, helping him refine his skills on the way to becoming Yoda. For those of you who must know, I asked him where he learned to fish, and he told me a little old lady taught him along with his brother Dick on both the Chama and Brazos rivers in northern New Mexico, although that might be a fable too.

The following is no fable: it was a warm day in late March, and the ice and snow were pretty much gone. Jer and I thought it would be a great idea to hike up to the beaver ponds on the Rio Cebolla and see if anything was happening. The beavers up there had been very industrious the year before. It looked like an urban construction site with absolutely huge dams constructed all the way to where the river seeped out of the ground. I was standing on one beaver dam and casting a weighted brown wooly booger towards the next dam above me. It was too early to use any dry flies, and we were having some success but not a lot. My next cast dropped directly onto the dam and then fell into the water. I started to strip in and got a sub- surface snag. Figuring I'd have to break it off and re-tie, I aimed my rod towards the object of my derision and started to pull the line, but then it started to give, just a little bit, but it was slowwwwwly moving towards me. I figured I had hooked one of the submerged logs, and I really didn't want to lose my fly so I just kept pulling and pulling and pulling it in. I got it to within about fifteen feet and I yelled over to Jer, "What the hell is that? That doesn't look like a log! Maybe it's some big clump of crap." When I got it to where I was standing, I let out a startled yelp, recoiling for a second. Jer ran over to see what it was and then started laughing hysterically. I ended up landing a huge, recently thawed, bloated dead beaver. This thing was the size of a bear cub. Apparently, the previous winter had not been kind to him. At that point I figured what the hell. I got him this far, I may as well retrieve my fly, which I did. It was my first and only beaver on a fly rod. And no, I didn't have a camera.

# 22 DON'T CRY FOR ME

*...and when you're being romanced by a large animal with*
*big antlers that's in a hormone-induced frenzy,*
*you tend to rapidly vacate the premises before it either*
*makes sweet love to you, or discovers that you're actually*
*not a female stag...and tramples and gores you*
*into a pile of bloody gelatin.*

EVERY FISHER, AT SOME POINT IN HIS OR HER LIFE, needs to take one big-assed trip. Not just a weekend on the river or lake, you need a trip out of your safety zone that will be true adventure, giving you stories to tell for the rest of your life.

Mine was to Argentina. Twice, once in 2005 and then again in 2006.

As I expected, it was very easy to talk my former boss and now fishing buddy, Milt, to tag along with us. There was a group of maybe ten of us, led by Taos, New Mexico author and fishing guide Taylor Streit, accompanied by his son Nick, who both own the Taos Fly Shop.

Taylor was, and still is, a unique individual. At first impression, you might think he was a painter or actor, or someone involved in the arts, because that's what his demeanor is like. Off-center, a little flighty, impulsive, and on outward appearances, unorganized, yet he is unabashedly creative, and a kind soul. Milt on the other hand is a great guy but all business which caused a little contention in the planning stages. But even though it seemed that Taylor flew by the seat of his pants, he ultimately got things done. It's funny because when you were fishing with Taylor as your guide, he had a very businesslike approach. We'll walk up to an appropriate riffle and he would bark out orders: "We will only spend one minute here. I want you to cast no more than six times. If nothing happens, we move on. We have a lot of water to cover so let's go!"

"Yes sir." Actually, his tactics worked well with me. If I'm good at one thing, it's taking orders.

178 Fishing with My Fly Down

Taylor's son Nick is one of the best fly casters I have ever seen. I learned more about improving my casting from him in one week, than I have from anyone. He is pure artistry in motion with a fluidity in his technique that makes it all look effortless.

The whole group met for the first time ever in the Albuquerque airport terminal, waiting for our flight to Dallas, which would connect us into Buenos Aires. All seemed fine with everyone. No obvious signs of dysfunction with anyone, yet. As with all trips involving groups of strangers, it took a few days in intimate contact for those traits to surface.

We all boarded the plane in high spirits, got into Dallas on time and had an uneventful connection for our overnight 11-hour flight into Buenos Aires. Here's a helpful hint if you can afford it: If you are going to be flying a long way for a long time, do not, I repeat, do not get a seat in coach unless your economic situation forces you to. For obvious money-making reasons, on overseas or cross-hemispheric flights, the airlines like to cram as many people onto their flying busses as possible. My knees were crammed up against the seat in front of me, and it's not like I'm a huge guy or anything. I'm 5'11" and shrinking rapidly! Maybe since this trip the airlines were forced to give more leg room because passengers were dying of deep vein thrombosis. And if you're claustrophobic, forget it! You'll be bat-shit crazy two hours into the flight. Milt had the right idea. He was up in "Business Class," where his seat folded down like a freakin' Lazy Boy. We all would have made fun of him for not sitting with the rest of us, until we realized what a wise man he was and how undereducated we all were regarding the perils of long-distance flight. But then again, at the time, Milt was probably earning multiples of what we were, so we were sitting where we all belonged, back with the unwashed and under-employed.

However, one of our fellow travelers who will remain nameless became a legend on that flight out. Not unlike a tale in some tawdry sex blog, or like one of those letters sent to the Penthouse Forum thirty years back, he became a member of the "Mile High Club" on that overnight flight. It was the perfect set-up. She was a professional on her way to Buenos Aires to finalize some big business deal, and uh, Rooster—I'll call him Rooster—was the consummate opportunist with the charm and greasy slickness to get the job done. It started with a glass of wine, then another three or four. And then in the middle of the night when most people on board were asleep it was a quick trip to the airplane john, which was only a row or two behind them. And of course, being the gentleman that he was, when the deed was done and she was asleep in her seat, he walked across the plane to where I was sitting and said "Dude! You're not gonna believe what just happened! I just banged the chick sitting next to me! I am now officially in the Mile High Club!"

Great. Congratulations. I guess he had to tell somebody, so it might as well be me. Here I am, sitting all cramped up like some bad contortionist, and he made the best of his situation. Way to go. Actually, I didn't mind him telling me; in fact, I was amused. It was his damned shit-eating grin that got to me.

We landed and checked into a beautiful downtown Buenos Aires hotel, better than we all probably deserved: stately with marble floors,

Milt and me at the mouth of an Argentine river that emptied into one of the many beautiful lakes, in northern Patagonia.

exquisitely appointed with a bonus bidet in every room, just in case one of us has to wash up after a night of airline coitus.

The plan was to rest up a bit, get some lunch, and go on a tour of the city. Buenos Aires is a combination of old European style architecture and beauty, combined with wretched third world living conditions. And that says a lot about the politics of the country. Every couple of decades or so, Argentina has a revolution, overthrowing their government and then the cycle begins anew. It had been a while since the last one because it seemed the discontent among the have-nots was starting to simmer again. Everywhere we went there was anti-government graffiti scrawled on the public buildings and statues which I personally found a little unsettling and said so to one of the Argentine guys who was showing us around. He reassured me, saying all of that was ancient history and not to worry.

That said, the city was a delight to walk around, and making it even easier? All the beautiful women. Look, Albuquerque has plenty but I'm telling you, in Buenos Aires they were ALL hot. Maybe it was the blending of European cultures. Spanish, Italian, French, all interbred together in one big gooey hybridized estrogen-soaked gene pool. They all dressed to the max with that sophisticated big city air about them.

And then there's the food. Argentina is big on red meat and red wine. And that's precisely what we consumed for an entire week, and we didn't mind because it was so damned good. Steaks and Malbec over and over.

We planned to do some sight-seeing, and the next morning we would be boarding an early flight and head southwest across the country. But before that, we had our one big night in Buenos Aires. And how were we to spend it?

Milt is a friend of mine, so I can say the following was his fault. He used to be my boss at 94 Rock and was the guy who actually brought me to Albuquerque and was responsible for beginning my illustrious, if somewhat dubious career there. Since then, we have become fishing buddies, and although we haven't fished in a while, we continue to vow to change that. It was our one night in the big city, and Milt insisted that we all go see a tango show. Apparently, he planned this long before we left because we had to get seats in advance or we never would have gotten in. Having no idea what was in store for us, we all climbed into taxis and got dropped off in the theater district, which was very much like being in New York City. We filed into the theater which was completely packed with men in suits and ties and women dressed like royalty. You have to try and picture this: Here we come, ten guys dressed in khakis, jeans, flannel shirts, baseball caps, who look like we're about to go fishing, better yet, who looked like we just walked off the set of "Duck Dynasty," walking into this highly cultural event. People are stopping to watch as we were led to our seats, which were actually great, first row of the mezzanine. The lights dimmed, and this middle-aged guy walked out onto the stage and the crowd went absolutely nuts, screaming and cheering. He started singing and everyone stood up and started singing along, swaying to the music. We're all looking at each other and going, "Who is this guy?" Later we found out he was the Argentine equivalent of Frank Sinatra or maybe Sting, or Elton John, the biggest musical star in the country. At this point people were weeping openly in the theater. Then the dancing began, which was actually interesting. It was kind of like watching foreplay. I saw something like that on the dance floor at the old Señor Buckets bar in Albuquerque once, except the couple was drunk and couldn't dance. This, however, was an artful combination of sex and dance in a socially acceptable way. And when it was all over, we all filed out as a group, feeling kind of self-conscious and out of place. If I would've known, I at least could've put on a cleaner shirt.

The next morning, we got into cabs at some ungodly pre-dawn hour and got dropped off at the airport for our flight to Junín de los Andes, a small village located in Patagonia's Lake District, nestled in the foothills of the Andes. The early hour really didn't matter because it was almost the best part of the trip, being 100 percent pure anticipation. Nothing has happened yet to screw anything up. We all boarded the plane with visions of large trout dancing through our brains, anticipating plenty of red wine and enough red meat to bind up John Wayne's colon.

Remember what I said about the hellish travel conditions on the flight to Buenos Aires? Well, the airline gods must have sensed that I paid my dues the previous night, especially being the one who had to listen to "Rooster" go on and on about his little airline toilet escapade. As all of us were boarding, for some reason the hot, and I mean hot, flight attendant pulled me aside and asked if I wanted to sit in first class. I looked up and did one of those point-my-finger-at-my-chest and say, "You mean me?" Apparently, it was my lucky morning. As the rest of my loser companions were led to the back of the bus, I was put up in luxury. It was actually a little bizarre. There was no one else up there but me. Maybe they were training a new flight attendant on how to properly dote on the privileged class. I was immediately given a glass of champagne (at 5:30 am, mind you) then given a full breakfast with real porcelain dinnerware, real silverware, and damned good coffee, all given to me by one of the most beautiful women I have ever seen. I ain't dwelling on this, but she was one of those women who you couldn't speak to. "More coffee sir?" And you'd turn into Beavis and Butthead, "Uhhhhhhhhh-huh-huh-huh-huh—OK!" I was hoping for a back-rub and foot massage, but I'm sure the thought of her actually touching me would have been far too repulsive. Also, the flight was only about two hours, so it all couldn't be fit in.

The very small Junín de los Andes airport which surprisingly was big enough to land a 737, was perched on a high plateau above the town surrounded by the Andean foothills. It was one of those landings that reminded you why you're not piloting the plane, because if you were, we would have ended up a smoldering pile of charred wreckage that friends and relatives would've seen on nightly news. There was an evil crosswind blowing from left to right and the pilot was obviously having trouble keeping us on the approach path. We would jerk violently from left to right and just when we thought he was going to pull up and abort the landing, we slammed down on the runway with such force that I spilled my second glass of bubbly. How unfortunate.

Junín and the surrounding area very much resembled the high desert of New Mexico, very brown with sparse, desert-like vegetation. Instead of the Rockies rising to the north, the Andes tower over to the west with the country of Chile directly over on the other side. The region was also covered with large beautiful mountain lakes full of fish, and the lakes were connected by some of the best trout rivers I have ever seen. Large powerful rivers like the Alumine and the Chimihuín, along with more manageable and easily wadable rivers like the Malleo. Plus, countless spring creeks and other less famous rivers that are all teeming with trout. Again, if you were blindfolded and not told where you were, and put on a drift boat on the Alumine, you would think you were somewhere on the Madison or the Snake, or even the San Juan, without the hordes of people.

So we got off our plane, collected our gear, and vans picked us up to take us into town. But before we did that, Taylor took us to one of the ranches in the area that he knows, and our week-long red meat/ red wine orgy began. It was like an episode of Anthony Bourdain's "No

Reservations," because we were treated to a lunch of some of the best barbecue I've ever had. Beef ribs, pork, blood sausage, and other wiener-type meats, all cooked over open flames by people who obviously have been doing this for generations. By the end of the lunch, we were fully sated, and Taylor said, "I hope you guys still have some energy because now we're going fishing for the rest of the afternoon." We all changed into our fishing garb, rigged up, and got driven to a river that's about an hour away—not the greatest river in the world, but one good enough to bust our cherry on Argentine trout, which we all did.

Then it was back in the vans for the trip into Junín. As we pulled near the outskirts of town, there was a military check point set up. All vehicles on the road were required to stop, identify themselves, and state their business. This was a little unsettling, seeing guys in fatigues with automatic weapons, but we were told that's the way they do it in these small towns. There's a checkpoint on the road into town and on the road out of town as well. Apparently, we passed inspection, which was good, because it happened nearly every time we left town to go fishing.

Staying in Junín would be the equivalent of staying in West Yellowstone, because it was surrounded by a crapload of excellent fishing opportunities. Some like the Chimihuín are right in town, and others are within no more than an hour's drive.

The Chimihuín must get pounded by the locals because it was the river where I experienced the least luck, but it still held a "Stephen Stills" memory. It was well past sunset, and we were walking with our flashlights up from the river on a narrow dirt path through the willows. It was a cool but pleasant night, very dark because the moon either hadn't risen yet or it was a new moon. After a somewhat arduous uphill walk to where the trucks were parked, I happened to look up into the star-filled night sky and realized it was totally alien because we were in the Southern Hemisphere. And then I thought, Oh yeah! I should look for it! I looked up to the east about 45 degrees above the horizon, and that's when I saw the Southern Cross in all its astronomical glory—a constellation that can be only seen in the Southern Hemisphere. I would have wept, but I was with the other guys, and you know how that goes. It was one of those magical occurrences that let you know you were somewhere cool, somewhere exotic—somewhere you'd never been before.

We got back into the trucks and made it back to Junín for dinner around 9 pm, which was actually early. Most Argentines have their dinner around 10, so the restaurant started to fill up just as we were getting served. And after a long day's fishing, a half a cow and a bottle of red wine for dinner, followed by a fine cigar, it was time to crash and dream about what adventures awaited us tomorrow and the rest of the week.

It was early the next morning and it was sunny but cool. It's the middle of February but that means it's the equivalent of early fall in Argentina. As Milt and I made our way into the motel restaurant for breakfast, we noticed that the same dude that was singing in the tango show that people were having conniptions over is belting one out on the local radio station. The restaurant staff smiled at us, we got coffee, and were asked if we wanted an egg. Apparently, Argentines don't eat eggs for breakfast, so it was an American thing. It's a very European spread—cold cuts, cheeses, hard rolls, and this really super sweet condensed milk product that they put on everything, which was actually very good. Then over our second cup of coffee we learned there was a double murder in Junín while we slept. Remember this was a tiny village where not much goes on besides fishing. Apparently, it happened at the local bakery. One of the employees had a problem, and he tried to solve it by sending two people to hell. They caught him, but the whole town was freaking out. And when the army found out about it, they tightened down on the town even more and stopped every car going in

Taylor and Nick Streit with a fat rainbow. Don't remember if this was taken before or after the "Red Stag Rutting Incident!"

and out, even though the shooter was in custody. On that cheery note, we took off for a float trip on the Alumine.

The Alumine is a big, strong river, similar to the south fork of the Snake in Idaho. To get there we drove through high desert foothills where we saw rheas, which are the Argentine equivalent of an ostrich, llamas, and red stags (which were in rut, and I'll get to that later). We were also very fortunate to see a condor, which was the size of a small prop plane, slowly circling, riding the air currents above a high mesa, looking for something dead to eat. Maybe it should have flown over to Junín, considering what happened the previous night.

We also saw the Argentine cowboys known as gauchos. I wish I had taken a photo because these guys looked like they came right out of some B-grade western movie. Everything you've heard about them is true. They looked like a cross between a pirate and a gypsy, but still a cowboy. The one guy was decked out in all black with a silver concho and spurs, riding his horse slowly along the road we were on.

Like I said, the Alumine was big. It was primarily a float trip with our guide Gabe and Taylor acting as guide as well. We did get out every so often to wade, and we did quite a bit of hiking from riffle to riffle. At one point we all met at a certain point and were told we had to wade across the river to get back to the boats. There were five of us including Taylor and we were instructed to all grab hold of each other and wade, arm-in-arm, across the river. The current was almost unbearably strong, and the thought of "cracking the whip" with the guys on the outside of the chain did cross my mind.

During the day our method of attack was using a six or seven weight and bombing the riverbank with a big green streamer or wooly bugger as the boat drifted us downstream. This was not only very productive, it also produced huge strikes as the trout ripped into the moving targets. I was trying to just hit the bank with my cast, have the fly drop into the water and then start stripping like hell. You could see the fish charge out from the undercut banks and attack.

Later in the afternoon we'd change to dries, using big royal wulffs or caddis patterns. Gabe was insisting that we use heavy tippet, even on the dries. I think maybe he was used to having less experienced guys break off too many fish. I wasn't having too much success until I convinced him to tie on maybe 5x, and then all hell broke loose—all big, healthy rainbows on flies big enough to see on the water. We fished until dusk, and even at the put-out, we continued to cast and catch fish as the boats were being trailered. It was a long exhausting, successful day on the river. Cigars were smoked, maybe a bit of the hard liquor was passed around, and we made it back to Junín around 9:30 pm, just in time for our next steak dinner and a blissful night's sleep.

The Malleo (pronounced mah-*yay*-oh) like many great trout waters in the states, is two different rivers. The lower Malleo is bigger and driftable, and the upper, which is closer to the Andes near the Chilean border, is a smaller, easy-to-wade stream but contains fish as large as their downstream cousins. This might have been *the* perfect trout stream and definitely my favorite river in Argentina. It had enough great water to do a 13-mile drift on the first day, and the next day we waded up top. The lower river was about the size of the Arkansas in central Colorado, but not as vertical. And its upper portions were like the Arkansas below Leadville.

It was a beautiful, warm, sunny day, temperatures in the mid-seventies. As we drifted the lower river, we were using typical Rocky Mountain flies: dry/dropper combinations, maybe a caddis or a big hopper on top, and a prince nymph below. As we drifted, we would cast under the trees in the shadows which is where we got most of our strikes, or we'd use the same flies on the scum lines of fast-moving riffles in the mid-river. These were not huge fish, maybe our biggest was 20 inches, but it was evident that they had not seen many flies because of their willingness to strike if you put your fly anywhere near them.

Lunch on the river was a special occasion. First there was Taylor's rule: We were not allowed to fish after lunch and were required to take an hour-long siesta because according to him, the fish weren't biting then anyway. But lunch was not your typical guide food of cold fried chicken or deli meat and chips. Our guides' wives and girlfriends would each prepare a literal feast the night before. Gabe built a fire on the bank, took out an iron skillet or pot and heated up some of the best native cuisine that was restaurant-quality. This particular afternoon we were having a version of a beef and chicken stew. Before we started eating, Gabe handed me a bowl with cooked meat scraps in it and told me to take it over near the tree line, about a hundred feet away. I asked him why and he said, "We have to feed the yellow jackets."

"Feed the yellow jackets? Are you kidding me?"

"It's true. They are carnivorous here. We need to put some meat down by the river and near the trees so they don't bother us while we're eating."

Holy shit, flesh-eating hornets. And he was proven correct. We noticed yellow jackets on and near the river during the morning, but as we ate our lunch, here they came, hundreds of them, flying in formation, intent on destroying us and everything we owned. As Gabe said, they went over to where I put the meat, and as they flew past us, we saw little chunks of red meat in their mandibles. Scary little bastards. But we managed to finish our meal without any stings, and after a glass or two of Malbec, we ended up not caring much. After lunch, Taylor found a place in the shade under a large tree and was sleeping with his mouth open. Luckily, he didn't inhale a single hornet.

The next day we travelled to the upper Malleo, which was on the road to the Chilean border. The Andes WERE the border, a spectacular awe-inspiring wall of snow-capped granite, with Lanín, the magnificent Chilean volcano acting as the star of the show. It was purely conical, towering above the rest of the peaks. I often found myself staring at it and the surrounding scenery, not watching my fly, probably missing a dozen strikes because of the rapturous beauty. It was going to be a good day. We seemed to use Royal Wulffs a lot, and my first cast of the day, about a 30-footer into a small riffle snaking around a large outcropping of rocks resulted in an immediate strike; and I landed a beautiful 20-inch rainbow.

In an entire week's worth of fishing, this was the only river where we saw anyone else. There were a group of Chileans, according to Gabe, that were in front of us, catching and keeping fish, which was illegal on that stretch of the Malleo, and he let them know it in what I can only describe as enthusiastic Spanish. It must have worked because they promptly left, and he didn't get shot.

Late in the afternoon clouds moved in and the wind picked up, so we decided to call it an early day, and actually got back into town in time for a nap and a shower before dinner.

I just got off the phone with Taylor, and he begged me not to reveal the location or the name of the nearly pristine spring creek that we fished. So I'll call it "Frustration Run." It was a gin-clear sweet little stream that emptied into one of Patagonia's giant lakes, and it held some of the largest trout I've seen this side of Alaska. The problem was, despite the fact that these behemoths have rarely seen a human, or a human with a fly rod, I could see them giggling at me as my fly passed without a strike. And not just once or twice but all afternoon. Some of these fish were as big as logs, facing upstream in the current, occasionally moving to the left and right, depending on what morsel of food would pass their way. It was insanely frustrating watching these guys take real insects and ignoring every single thing I threw at them. The major problem was there was no real cover for them. As you know, lots of spring creeks are almost congested with plant growth, but this one was not. Taylor swears people have caught fish here.

But that's not why I'm writing about this particular creek. I'm writing because it was the location that Taylor and I almost got buggered by a huge rutting red stag. Red stags are big animals, probably as big as a North American elk and just as popular with hunters. It was hunting season, and we had observed the American hunters coming and going at the Buenos Aires airport.

It was late in the afternoon and all day there was one solitary red stag hanging out with us, watching us fish. Initially it kept its distance, maybe a hundred yards off, but it was obviously interested in who we were and what we were doing. As the day progressed, it kept creeping closer and closer. Normally during hunting season, you would expect the stags to be skittish and wary of people, but not this one. He liked us, and to have Taylor tell the story, he liked me. Great. Just what I needed.

It happened quickly, and when you're being romanced by a large animal with big antlers that's in a pheromone-induced frenzy, you tend to rapidly vacate the premises before it either makes sweet love to you, or discovers that you're actually not a female stag (or cow, or whatever the hell they're called) and tramples and gores you into a pile of bloody gelatin.

Taylor, being the matchmaker, started loudly making calls that were his version of a bugling stag, thinking it would be so funny if he actually called it in. Well, he did! The beast lifted its head, and intent on meeting us, started coming towards us at a steady pace. He got to within a hundred feet and Taylor said, "These animals are dangerous, we better get out of here!" He high-tailed it downstream and decided to hide behind a clump of bushes, leaving me to fend for myself. It kept approaching, grunting and slobbering all over itself. It was close enough that I could see strings of drool running down its face, landing on the earth below. That was enough for me. I followed Taylor's cue and took off running, as fast as my middle-aged feet could take me, intermittently looking back over my shoulder, as my "date" followed closely behind. I ended up crawling underneath a barbed wire fence, which was about a hundred yards from our truck. The stag stopped about fifty feet from the fence, and apparently decided I was not worth pursuing. He sauntered off, going back to the business of getting laid, hopefully with someone of its own species. Taylor, by this time, is laughing hysterically. I'm actually surprised he didn't write about it in his own book.

Speaking of large horny animals, the next day we left for our final river destination before we sadly had to return to Buenos Aires and then the states. The Rio Pulmari is not talked about much. Not many people fish there because the fish are generally smaller than the more famous rivers. So why did we go there? Because Taylor had a hot date. This was news to us until the morning of the excursion. I noticed he was a little antsy that morning, and when the news was broken to us, we all knew why! So the crew was divided up into two small groups. Most of the guys went back to the Collun-Cura, which left Taylor, our guide Gabe, Milt, and me, to make that drive to the village of Alumine. We entered into the village itself, and Gabe hadn't even turned the truck motor off before Taylor was out of the door and power walking down the street in the direction of the object of his desire. He yelled back over his shoulder, "OK, start low and fish your way up."

Isn't that what we would normally do?

"I'll be tied up at least until three!"

I hope it's not with scratchy rope. It'll leave burns for sure, dude.

So as Taylor, in a testosterone haze, disappeared down a side street, Gabe took us back onto the road and down to the river. He dropped me off low, and he and Milt took off and started fishing about a mile above, leaving me to fend for myself.

The Pulmari was geologically different than the rest of the rivers we'd fished. It was about the size of the Rio Grande as it flows through the Taos gorge, and similarly, it was strewn with boulders from one side to the other, some the size of Volkswagens, others the size of Volkswagen dealerships. The trick was, to look for the fish in and around these rocks. From the first cast, I was catching one fish after the next but nothing of size, the biggest maybe 12 inches. Wading was not easy because the riverbed itself was also home to an infinite number of rocks of all different sizes, so you really had to watch yourself. I slipped or tripped several times, almost going down once. I came around a bend in the river and it opened up considerably turning wider and relatively shallow, with the same giant monolithic rocks breaking its surface. I sat down and took it all in for a moment, and saw Gabe and Milt WAY up in the distance near a small waterfall. I probably had caught at least 20

fish, mostly rainbows, and had resigned myself to the fact that it would
be quantity today, not size.

In front of me was an absolutely huge rock, probably the size of
a small house. The water was exceptionally clear and the current was
gently flowing around either side, having dug out two deeper holding
areas where I was certain there was a trout or two. On the right side of
the rock, the water ran past a submerged rock shelf that had been undercut by centuries of erosion. With a small caddis on top and an even
smaller pheasant tail about two feet below it, I decided to try the right
side. I cast to the right above the house-rock, and got no response. I cast
again and this time let my flies drift behind me to where the submerged
rock table was. As it reached the middle of the shelf, my caddis stopped
moving. I raised my rod and felt a very heavy weight. It didn't move,
and I thought I was snagged for a moment. Then it slowly started to
move and I realized I had a fish, and it was big. Expecting a dramatic
run or jump, I tightened my line and began to reel. The fish did neither.
Now I'm thinking I hooked a dead beaver or some other large, deceased
rodent. It just kept swimming back and forth, not showing itself, almost like when you hook a shark or a big ray in saltwater. After several

The big brown I caught on the Pulmari in Argentina that caused me to do a face plant in the river and snap
my rod in two.

minutes I got it close enough to see what I had, a very large thing that looked to be brown trout. Now I'm thinking, how am I gonna land this? To make matters worse, the footing was unreliable at best. My one foot was lodged between two rocks and my other foot is sitting on top of a third. The fish is within three feet of me, so I raise my rod and lean forward as far as I could and luckily, it slowly swam directly into my net. This fish was either on valium or had never been hooked before and had no idea what was going on. I lifted my net out of the water, and its head was hanging out one end and its tail at the other. I had landed a hook-jawed monster, I'm thinking at least 24 inches long, and no one around to show it to!

As that thought passed through my mind, I lost my footing and face-planted into the river, barely missing braining myself on a submerged rock. On the way down, I heard a loud snap, and realized my fly rod has just been destroyed. I am now dazed, soaked and humiliated, lying in the river, wondering what the hell to do next. I somehow got to my feet, and did a quick inventory of all my body parts and luckily no major damage was done. Then I realized I am still holding on to my net, and miraculously the brown is somehow still there, my pheasant tail in its jaw, with my fly line leading towards the now-dangling top half of my rod.

So now what?

I sat down on a rock, and keeping the very mellow fish underwater in my net, I contemplated my next move. Most rationally thinking logical people would have gently released the fish, walked to the river bank, and made their way upstream to where Milt and Gabe were. Then, I would tell them my tale of my huge fish that almost got me killed.

"I swear guys, that fish had to be 24 inches. Really! I would've taken a picture but Gabe had my camera and...."

And they would have shaken their heads and smiled politely, expressed the proper amount of sympathy over my broken rod, and continued to fish, believing maybe half of what I told them.

No. That would not be my plan.

I got up and unhooked the fish, while keeping it in the net. I somehow reeled in my line, put the two pieces of my shattered four-piece rod under my arm, and started walking up the middle of the river towards Gabe and Milt with the fish in my net in the water beside me. Did I do this with dignity and grace? No. I would be goddamned if I didn't get a witness and a record of this fish! As I waded up river, I screamed at the top of my lungs, "Heeeeeeeeeeeeeeyyyyyyyy!!!! Gaaaaaaaaaaaaabe!!!! Hellllllllp!!!!" Not once, but about every thirty seconds until in the distance I finally saw Gabe's head turn towards me, and he started walking in my direction.

He was quite a distance away, so it took him several minutes to get to me. I was exhausted and wet, so again, I sat down on a rock and gently moved my beloved brown trout back and forth in the water. I swear the fish dug it. It was almost like I was rocking it to sleep. He didn't fight, didn't try to escape the confines of my net. I actually think we were bonding. In fact, I found myself talking to him as I waited. "Don't worry! As soon as Gabe gets here and takes your picture, I'm gonna let you go and you can go back downstream to your rock table and live out your days undisturbed there."

He didn't answer me, but he did look at me occasionally.

After about ten minutes Gabe arrived, thinking I broke my leg or something worse. When I assured him I was OK, I showed him the fish. His eyes got really big and he said, "That is truly the big fish of the river! He must have been in that place all his life, and you caught him. Congratulations!"

I think he really meant it. He took out a measuring tape and indeed it was 24 inches. He got my camera and took pictures of it from every angle, so I could get a replica made when I got back to Albuquerque. Then as I promised, we gently released the fish, and in keeping with its character, it leisurely swam away. As it left, I swore it waved goodbye with its right pectoral fin.

As we walked up towards Milt, I told Gabe everything that had happened, and he said, "You know, you should write this story in a book."

Not a bad idea.

Milt was fishing on an outcropping of rocks next to a large riffle coming off the waterfall, and having considerable success when we arrived, pulling in trout after trout. I told him the abridged version of the tale, and when I showed him the picture of my trophy, his face tightened up as he forced a terse smile and said, "Congratulations!" and then went back to fishing. Being the competitive sort of guy that he is, I was happy I got that much out of him!

The next morning, we boarded our plane and flew back into Buenos Aires, where we had one more day of sightseeing, and then it was back to the states. When you spend ten days with a bunch of guys, there's at least one whose personal idiosyncrasies begin to surface more than the others. And, yes, there was one individual, who by the end of the trip was almost too weird to abide by. We had finished touring the huge cemetery in the middle of the city which was as big as a city itself, consisting of mostly above-ground mausoleums and graves. The most famous dead person in the place was Eva Perón, the wife of Argentine president Juan Perón. She was beloved by the populace, died early, and the stage musical and movie "Evita" was all about her. Remember Madonna? The song "Don't Cry for Me, Argentina?" The day we were there, her gravesite was covered with fresh flowers, and we were told that's the way it was every day.

Outside the cemetery was a large park with street vendors set up selling mostly art, crafts, leather, you name it, which is where the final straw with our friend happened. Some of us were wanting souvenirs to take home, and as could be expected, the vendors did not speak English well, or at all for that matter. So, to make himself better understood, "Howie" would start asking them questions in English, but with a bad Spanish accent. It wasn't quite Cuban enough for Al Pacino in "Scarface," or Castilian enough for Ricardo Montalbán, but more like an exaggerated Cheech Marin. Witnessed by all of us, we could hold back no longer and had to call him on it; at this point it was too funny to be polite and not laugh at him.

"Dude! Do you hear what you're doing?"

"No. What?"

"Do you really think these vendors will understand you better if you talk to them like an illegal immigrant?"

"What? What do you mean?"

"You're speaking to them in 'Spanglish,' dude! Stop it! You're embarrassing all of us!"

"No, I'm not!"

"Yes, you are! You sound like Cheech gone bad, and you're peeing all over yourself!"

I don't think he spoke another word that day.

*So on the ends of both our lines, we had two large toothsome creatures that were capable of biting us and drinking our blood, and no real way to land them.*

# 23 BIG MEAN BASTARD FISH

THE PROBLEM IS, ONCE YOU DUMP ANY FISH, frog, snail, snake, mussel, microbe, or any other organism into a body of water, that never lived in that particular body of water, doesn't belong in that particular body of water, never would have gotten there unless some dumb-ass human hadn't come along and screwed things up, you're going to have a problem. There are many examples to cite.

Some mental midgets decided to dump their Burmese pythons in the Florida Everglades, and now they are eating everything that looks like food to them. Other morons dumped lake trout in Yellowstone Lake, and they began decimating the native cutthroat population. Somehow, flying Asian carp got into the Illinois River, and not only are they giving people concussions as they fly through the air, Game and Fish is desperately trying to keep them out of Lake Michigan so they don't completely overrun it.

But wait! There's more! Zebra mussels brought in on tankers from Europe are clogging up the water intakes in the Great Lakes. Also from Europe, spiny shrimp are replacing the natural freshwater shrimp in the Great Lakes, and are killing the prized jumbo lake perch. When the perch attempt to eat them like a shrimp they're used to eating, the spines puff up and get caught in the perchs' throats, killing them. God only knows how whirling disease originally got here, most likely a terrorist plot... but it has become a major problem in trout fisheries nationwide. My point is, once you introduce one of these invasive species, it at the very least, changes the environment it was put in. At the worst, it destroys it.

Introducing an invasive species can be as innocent as dumping your remaining live minnows into a lake when you're done fishing. Seems like an innocent act, right? I mean, you're saving the lives of these little guys, not realizing you are the main cause of the glut of goldfish that have taken over several lakes, especially in New Mexico, and other lakes across the country. In fact, it is now illegal to release baitfish into New Mexico fishing waters.

Three lakes in particular were experiencing real problems from the invasive goldfish; Ramah, Quemado, and Bluewater. If you're not from New Mexico, you probably have no idea where these lakes are, and I'm pretty sure you've never heard of them either. But that's not the point. The point is, what do you do to get rid of these fish? According to New Mexico Department of Game and Fish, you put something in the lakes that is much bigger and meaner, something that when it sees a goldfish, it hears a dinner bell ringing in its brain. Some awesome predator that thinks a goldfish is a swimming filet mignon.

That would be a tiger muskie.

A tiger muskie is a sterile cross between a regular muskellunge and a northern pike. These are naturally occurring fish in the Great Lakes, as well as other places muskies and pike cohabitate. Like I said, the off-spring are sterile, not unlike mules, which are a horse-donkey combo. It's been recently discovered that Cro-Magnon humans and Neander-thals actually got together and knocked boots. Unfortunately, the re-sult of that action was not sterile offspring, and it is obvious with the numbers of dumb-asses we have walking around today, particularly in Congress.

But I digress.

Tiger muskies were introduced into New Mexican lakes in 2003 in order to control the goldfish problem. You might ask yourselves why they would introduce another invasive species to control lakes that were already overrun by an invasive species. The key is, they are ster-ile. They will eat as much as they can, get very big, and eventually die without having any little tiger muskies. On paper this looks like sound reasoning. But Bob Gerding and I brought up two points: First, why would the tiger muskies JUST eat the goldfish? Wouldn't they think a small rainbow trout is just as tasty?

This, actually, could be a potential problem.

And secondly, nature is amazing. The driving force in all creation is the desire and ability to propagate one's own species. Wouldn't you think that one or more of these muskies would have a recessive gene that allowed it to reproduce? Or at the hatchery, someone slipped some purebred muskies in with the tigers? Could we have a tiger muskie problem in the future? A tiny, tiny chance, but not so much of a prob-lem. This is probably me thinking about it too much.

But in the meantime, an amazing fishery is growing up in these lakes, and when I say growing up, I mean barracuda-sized fish ap-

proaching fifty inches that actually frighten you when you hook one.
My first experience fishing for these guys was in 2009 with Bob and
Mark Sawyer, the owner of Los Pinos Fly and Tackle Shop in Albuquerque. Mark's shop is tucked away so deep in the city that you almost need
GPS to find it but plans are to move to a newer, bigger and more visible location. I assume by the time this book gets published, he should
be firmly ensconced in the new digs with more customers than he can
shake a stick at, whatever the hell that means.

Truth be known, Mark is a good-old-boy bubba bass fisherman. He
takes his boat to tournaments all over the southwest. His favorite bass
tournament story is the time his boat accidentally drifted over into
Mexican waters while fishing on a lake that straddled the border. Of
course, I don't remember the name of the lake and am too lazy to ask
him. But the border patrol boat with sirens blaring and lights flashing,
ran him down thinking he was possibly bringing illegals into the country or smuggling drugs. But what they really suspected in this post-

Grandstanding with a tiger muskie at Bluewater Lake in New Mexico. The fish are even bigger than this
now!

9/11 world, was that he was a member of a secret terrorist organization intent on overthrowing the state of Texas and then the rest of the country. And his clever disguise? He, along with his compatriots brilliantly matched the look all those bass fishermen in bass boats who fish in tournaments held near the border. After the cops searched his boat, after several body cavity searches, and after interrogations meant to trip up his alibi and reveal his true identity, they let Mark go with a stern warning to stay the hell away from the border. He has not returned to the scene of the crime since.

I had never fished for a tiger muskie before. I had unsuccessfully fished for full-blooded muskies up in Canada with no luck. I hooked one when I was maybe ten years old, only to lose it in the weeds. And I had never tried it with a fly rod either, so this was all new territory for me. Bob was filming the TV show "Wild New Mexico," so with a camera crew in tow, we made the drive to Bluewater Lake on a beautiful warm and sunny morning, getting on the water by about 9:30 am. It was a clear windless early-summer morning, with afternoon thunderstorms predicted. Mark's intent was to first take the boat to the rocky shoreline before you get to the dam and pound the rocks with a large muddler-type minnow. I had a slow-sink line on my eight-weight, the line I usually used when fishing in the surf in Florida. He also tied on a couple feet of about 50-pound shock tippet. I asked him why no wire leaders because these fish have big sharp teeth, and he claimed the leaders scare the fish. We used a length of thick tippet that we could change when it started looking frayed.

This day turned out to be special. My first cast hit the edge of the rocks and dropped into the water. I let it sink for about fifteen seconds and started long steady strips. The strike was hard, heavy, and in triplicate. BAM! BAM! BAM! With each BAM, my rod bowed with the force of the take. Then, just like a barracuda, it did an acrobatic jump, eliciting a "Holy shit!" moment. The tiger muskie had to be at least forty inches long. It then hunkered down to the bottom, swimming back and forth, appearing unsure as to what it should do. I kept steady pressure on the fish, not wanting to lose the first tiger muskie I ever hooked, and on the first cast at that. After several minutes of fighting this bulldog, it tired, and Mark got it into his net. As he reached down to unhook it, it shook its head from side to side and bit him on the hand, causing him to start bleeding profusely. Now with his own blood all over his shirt, and dealing with forty inches of pure muscle, he insisted we get a photo. Somehow, I grabbed the beast, hoisted it over my head and grandstanded for the camera, as the picture in this book shows.

In retrospect, I'm not proud of that gross display of bravado, but come on, man, it WAS my first tiger muskie on my first cast and I was thrilled! After the excitement died down, Mark was still nursing his wound, and while still bleeding, told me there is an anti-coagulant in tiger muskie saliva, causing its victims to continue to gush like a fountain. It probably took a half hour for the bleeding to stop.

Trust me when I say that all fishing days are not like this. It was a day that the heavens opened up, the few clouds that were in the sky parted, and God pointed his finger at us and said, "OK dudes. I'm granted you a day like you've never had. Have a great time but remember, you owe me one!" I can't tell you the number of tiger muskies we hooked or caught. It had to be in the twenty-plus range. They were all about forty inches since they were all put in the lake at the same time, and they all seemed to fight in the same way, initially jumping and then going straight to the bottom, some even doing the typically tarpon-like figure-eight under the boat.

I had caught enough fish and could tell that Mark was itching to get a fly on the water, so we took the boat over to the other side of the lake. Clouds were rolling in and the wind was definitely picking up, so in a medium chop we both started casting around a rocky point that looked promising. Almost simultaneously we got big strikes and both of us had fish on. Both fish jumped nearly in sync, almost like some kind of tiger muskie water ballet, and then per the memo, they both headed to the bottom and fought bullishly. His fish was tiring first, so with my bent rod in one hand, I went to get the net. As I picked it up I realized to my horror that the previous fish had gnawed its way through the netting leaving a gaping hole at the bottom, rendering it useless. So we had two large toothsome creatures that were capable of biting us and drinking our blood, on the ends of both our lines, and no real way to land them. He didn't have a gaff or a shotgun for that matter, so we were left with four options:

—Break one of the fish off and try to land the other without getting lacerated.

—Scan the horizon and look for another boat that might have a net.

—With a spare hand, find a cell phone and call Bob, who was in the other boat somewhere on the other side of the lake and see if they could motor over to us.

—Try to find a creative way to land both fish with what we had, which was a lot of nothing.

We, of course, chose the latter. There was no way in hell that we weren't going to try to boat a double header. We'd have bragging rights for the rest of our lives, and it was possible that someone might actually believe us.

Mark told me to keep my fish on the line, and he'd figure out a way to land his first and then dispatch with mine. Finally remembering he had a set of pliers in his tool box, he got them, and as the fish rolled up onto the side of the boat, he grabbed it with the pliers, not unlike the clamps used in boating saltwater fish. He managed to flip it up onto the deck, and while it proceeded to make a mess out of the back of the boat by maniacally flopping into everything, he ran up to where I was and landed mine the same way, although it was easier since he had two hands. After the mayhem, we somehow managed to get a photo of both us, both fish and the net with the hole in it. Of course, he thinks he deleted it, so it ain't in the book. Tired, but happy, we went back to the other side of the lake, found Bob, and right before a hellacious thunderstorm hit, and we made it back to shore.

There were a couple of unnerving occurrences worth mentioning. As we were fishing, we'd occasionally see a tiger muskie on the surface, swimming with its mouth open and the upper half of its head out of the water, looking like an alligator cruising through the everglades. I've seen tailing fish, spawning fish, fish swimming near the surface, but never anything this weird. Observing this, you got the feeling that you didn't want to fall in, or even have any vulnerable body part dangling over the side of the boat, which made you think twice about taking a leak. Secondly, as I said, we were initially fishing near the dam, and we decided to drift right up to it and make a few casts. As we got closer we noticed all the swallow nests plastered to its side. That's when it got strange. As we slowly drifted in front of the dam and under the nests, we noticed some kind of debris in the water. Then we realized what it was. There were swallow "parts" floating on the surface beneath the mud nests. Heads, wings, feet, you name it. It was a swallow killing field, stretching the length of the dam. We surmised the tiger muskies had learned about the birds and where they nested. As the swallows swooped down to feed on the evening insect hatches, the muskies lay in wait, just under the surface. And as the birds got close to the water, they struck, and carnage ensued. Granted, we did not witness an actual tiger muskie attack a swallow, and someone from Game and Fish might dispute what I just related, but I'd sure like to hear a better explanation of what caused this phenomenon. I suggested to Bob that he go home and tie a swallow fly and come back and fish it.

*I turned back to my brother and yelled "Sharrrkkk!"*
*That prompted a little kid about 9 years old*
*to immediately scream, "Shark! Shark!*
*Somebody help!"*

# 24 FOURTH OF JULY—SPARKIN' ONE UP IN BETHANY BEACH, DELAWARE

IT'S THE FOURTH OF JULY IN 2012, and I'm sitting in 96-degree heat in Bethany Beach, Delaware. It's about one in the afternoon, and the holiday parade just passed by the house. It's what you'd expect from a small beach community—local cheerleading squads, trucks from restaurants, the Elks Club, Miss Delaware, Tom Carper for Senate, a calypso band, several local patriots in their pick-ups all decked out for the big day, along with other local dignitaries and senior citizen groups. At the beach, the Fourth of July is like Christmas Day. It's right in the middle of high season, the town is packed with tourists, and the locals all have out-of-town guests, and right now they're all lining the streets or packed onto porches and balconies watching the parade go by. Houses in town are decorated in red white and blue in various conformities- bunting, streamers, flags, statues of Uncle Sam; all things that make you proud to be an American, goddammit!

It is hot. Oppressively so. Actually, too hot to go to the beach. It's days like this when the sand gets so hot that it turns the beach into a convection oven. Don't even try walking across it barefoot because your feet will turn into something resembling two slabs of seared ribs right off the grill. But at night when it cools down a bit, all the true believers will stream onto the beach or onto the boardwalk near town center to secure a good space to watch the fireworks. I prefer the beach. The boardwalk becomes Times Square on New Year's Eve: there are thousands of hot, sweaty, overweight Americans with unruly kids, screaming because they just dropped their Dickie's frozen custard which was melting all over them and you. At least on the beach you have a fighting chance of not having to get up close and personal with a stranger you'd just as soon not ever talk to.

I like Bethany Beach. I like it because it's small, quiet, and manageable. Going southward, it is fourth in a string of five Delaware beach communities. Lewes is first, a quaint, charming, almost New England-like port town on Delaware Bay, known mostly as a fishing village. It was the first town settled in Delaware in the early seventeenth century by the Dutch. There were plans on making it a huge seaport, not unlike Philadelphia and New York, but it was determined the harbor was too shallow and it kept silting in, so it remains what it is.

Rehoboth Beach is next: Delaware's largest beach community with an extensive boardwalk, and plenty of retail shops and restaurants along Rehoboth Avenue and surrounding streets. It has a large gay community who were responsible for gentrifying a large portion of the town and is where a lot of the interesting shops and restaurants are located.

Dewey Beach is Delaware's party town. It's where all the college-aged kids go to hang out, drink heavily, try to get laid, and throw up in the streets. By the way, a note to all 40- and 50-somethings who continue to hang out in Dewey thinking they're still cool and can keep up with the kids: Dude—seriously—you look like an idiot. The girls look at you like you're the creepy dad of their friend back home who hits on them all the time. You don't stand a chance. Give it up. You're old, you're overweight, and you're an object of ridicule. Go down the beach to Bethany, put on a polo shirt and a nice pair of chinos.

Dewey Beach hosts The Bottle and Cork, the self-proclaimed "Best Rock and Roll Bar in the World." And actually, they probably could back that up. Over the years, the likes of Robert Palmer, Donovan, Dave Mason, Little Feat, George Clinton, Junior Walker, The Hooters, George Thorogood. and others I can't remember performed there. When I worked for 96 Rock in Ocean City, Maryland, it was our go-to bar in Delaware. I remember one particular night when bluesman Junior Walker was performing. After the show we walked back into the dressing room, opened the door, and a huge blue fog bank of pot smoke rolled out the door. We entered, and one of the band members was rolling a joint the size of a small burrito. I don't remember much after that, at least nothing that I plan on writing about.

Bethany is next. Speaking of joints the size of a burrito, the now "Quiet Resort" as it's called, is a little town that now is all about kids and family, and used to have some of the biggest pot-growing operations in the state. As in any resort town, there were, and still are, a lot of houses that are vacant for most of the year, most being second homes or rental properties for the well-off. Interspersed among those were several houses with all the innards ripped out, replaced by hydroponics and lighting systems. One of the guys I worked with at the radio station was paid to be a "house sitter" for one of the growers in Bethany. He got to live in a beach house and made sure that the operation was running smoothly. I know the Bethany Chamber of Commerce will be thrilled to death that I'm including this little tidbit about their town, but as far as I know, that shit happened a LONG time ago and is now past-tense.

Completing our geography lesson, Fenwick Island, which is technically not an island, is a non-descript beach community right on the Delaware/Maryland border. Over the border is Ocean City, Maryland, a behemoth of a town with condo and hotel skyscrapers going on for miles. Not as big as Miami Beach or Panama City, Beach, but too big of a city for me to relax in.

I have been coming to the beach here for over thirty years and have not tired of the area. The rest of the country has no idea Delaware exists, or knows next to nothing about it, even you live in one of the surrounding states. One of the most popular bumper stickers and t-shirts out here bears the one-word slogan in the state's dark blue and yellow license plate colors, "Dela-Where?" I finally saw the local answer to that the other day on a t-shirt. It was a dark blue shirt, and in yellow letters it said, "Right here, Motherfucker." How could you not be amused?

Delaware is a puny state, Rhode Island being the only one smaller, not counting the District of Columbia and all the U.S. territories. Northern Delaware is pretty much a suburb of Philadelphia. There is only one "trout stream" in the state of Delaware and that is White Clay Creek. It's on the extreme northern border, and the stream's headwaters originate in the hills of Pennsylvania. Not only are there stocked trout, but smallmouth bass, bluegills, and these strange shad-like fish.

I have no idea what they are. White Clay Creek runs through heavily forested, hilly terrain consisting of state park land and farms. The farmland is beautiful, looking like an Andrew Wyeth painting. All the barns, walls, and lots of the houses are made of fieldstone, giving it all a look of a distant time gone by.

Southern Delaware below Delaware Bay consists of chicken farms and chicken processing plants, fields of corn and soybeans to feed the chickens, and the beaches. As I said, I like it. Another popular car sticker is one of those white ovals that proclaims "LSD." In small print under the letters it says, "Lower Slower Delaware." Timothy Leary would be proud. Except for the upper northwest corner of the state, Delaware is flat. Totally flat. It's easy to ride a bike because there are no hills at all. Tidal rivers cut through the state, some fishable, some not. Most are surrounded by large areas of wetlands, which, during low tide or on a particularly hot and muggy day, have the pleasing aroma of dead shellfish.

A sizeable shark caught in Bethany Beach, Delaware, delighting the kids who were watching and scaring the mothers!

A popular pastime in these tidal rivers is crabbing for Maryland blue crabs. They could be called Delaware blue crabs, but Maryland thought of it first. To crab, you stand on a low bridge, or get in a boat, or go to the bank of one of these rivers with a rope of some sort and a bag of chicken necks. You tie the rope around the chicken neck, throw it into the water, and wait for a crab to grab it, and then you pull it in. Simple as that. Doesn't sound like much fun? It doesn't matter because a Maryland blue crab is one of the best tasting creatures you can get out of salt water, anywhere. I'm not kidding, they're that good.

I have been fishing in Delaware since 1977, long before I took up flyfishing. In fact, I have the same ten-foot-long blue surf fishing rod that I bought around the same time. I replaced the reel once, because they don't tend to hold up that well in saltwater despite how well you maintain them. For those of you who have never done this, surf fishing is pretty simple: you go down to the beach with your rod, your sand spike, which is a hollow PVC tube with a spiked end that holds your rod, your slop bucket containing ice, bait, beverages, a cigar, and various fishing implements, a slop rag, and a beach chair. You find a suitable place on the beach that's away from swimmers, stick your sand spike in the sand near the water, put your rod in the spike, attach a suitable rig, bait it, cast your line into the water, put the rod back in the sand spike, open up a beer, light a cigar, sit in your beach chair and wait for a bite.

People rig their lines in different ways depending on what they want to fish for. I personally prefer a mullet rig because I'm either fishing for stripers or bluefish. Sharks tend to get hooked too, as does the occasional stingray. A mullet rig consists of a brightly colored float about the size of a wine cork or marshmallow. I like chartreuse. Coming out of the bottom end of the float is a stiff, stainless-steel wire, and on the end of that is a removable double hook. Above that are the line and a swivel you attach to your main line and another swivel that you attach a pyramid sinker. I usually fish with a three- or four-ounce sinker. If it's really rough, I'll put a six-ouncer on. If it's so rough a six-ouncer won't hold you, you shouldn't be fishing.

To fish, you remove the double hook, take a fresh or frozen (thawed) mullet and stick the wire through its mouth, down its gullet and literally out its ass, where you re-attach the hook. Bluefish in particular have sharp teeth, and the wire prevents them from shredding your line. Theoretically, out in the water, the float keeps your bait off the bottom and allows it to move back and forth with the surf action. That's what it's supposed to do anyway. On calm days it just sits there near the bottom gets eaten by crabs. The float also acts as a fish attractant. It must work because the more you fish, the more bite marks you accumulate on the float. Maybe they should design one with a hook in the float.

My problem with mullet rigs is actually the double hook because they do too much harm to the fish, especially if you're releasing a lot of small ones which I tend to do. Bluefish get their mouths ripped to shreds it they've aggressively taken the bait which is what happens at least half of the time. I did a lot of thinking about this, and I finally created a rig which eliminates the double hook and seems to be equally effective. Instead of the removable double hook, I bought some small detachable swivels and attached them to the end of the rig. Then I bought some circle hooks, which have big wide circular bends, making it harder or impossible for a fish to swallow. After using these all summer, I noticed no difference in my hook-ups, so, success was achieved. I should sell them, although I don't think the mind-set of the average Delaware fisherman is ready for this product, or is concerned as I am about hurting the fish they catch and release. I walked into one of the bait and tackle shops and described what I was attempting to do. First, they misunderstood me, thinking I was trying to add another hook to the rig, which obviously was the exact opposite of my intent. Then when I repeated again what I wanted, the guy behind the counter cocked his head to one side and raised his one eyebrow and said, "Well whadaya wanna do that for? You ain't gonna catch as many fish, and you know, and it's a proven fact those bluefish don't feel no pain!"

"Ok buddy, thanks for the help. I'll just find what I'm looking for on my own."

So, back to surf fishing.

It's a great way to fish and enjoy the beach. I fish late afternoon/ early evening for two reasons. First, the town of Bethany Beach doesn't allow you to fish until after 5:00 pm during the week, 5:30 on weekends. Nazis. The other reason is that's my favorite time on the beach. The light is softening and changing with the sunset, making the colors more pastel instead of the harsh brightness of the day. It's not as hot and most people are off the beach, although there's usually still enough to draw a crowd if you hook a big one.

I mentioned that occasionally sharks get in the way of your line when you're fishing for stripers or blues. But in all truthfulness, catching a sizable shark on your surf rod on the beach with spectators is a kick in the pants. I have landed several sharks off this beach, with me being the only witness, and with an entire beach packed with broiling tourists. Two nights ago, I could have sold tickets to the show.

My brother was visiting and is not a fisherman but is more than willing to come down to the beach with me and help me schlep my gear down. He also is handy with a camera if need be. We got on the beach about 5:45 pm, set up my stuff and sat down to shoot the shit and watch the water. For the first hour it was slow. I landed and re-leased one croaker and had pleasant conversations with some lady and her two toddlers who were just fascinated by all my fishing equipment. Three other fishermen had staked their territory up the beach from me and were not having any luck. It was a beautiful early evening. A few clouds were making the sunset spectacular, and there was enough of a breeze to provide a light chop to keep my bait moving. After releasing the croaker, I re-baited the mullet rig and cast it out about 150 feet, and sat down hoping to get one more bite before my wife's strict dinner time of 7:30 pm. Nothing for about ten minutes, and then a steady tap-tap-tap at the end of my rod. Not getting too excited about it, I got out of my chair, walked to my rig, took it out of the sand spike and I kind of half-assed set the hook. Immediately, the rod bowed into a wide U and line began screaming out of my reel as whatever I hooked headed out towards the Azores in the middle of the North Atlantic. I palmed the reel to slow it down a bit, and then the fish stopped moving and gave steady resistance. I could not budge it. I turned back to Ron and said, "This is a big fuckin' fish!" At that point I also remembered I only had 18-pound test line on the reel, so if I was going to land whatever it was, I would have to be very, very careful.

On this beach, there are only two things that fight like this; either a big ray or a shark. It was too early in the process to tell which one it was, but I was determined to find out. I did not want to blow this one--patience was the key. I started slowly reeling it back in. I'd reel a little, lift up my rod and reel some more. The fish again took off for open water taking more line but at a slower pace. This happened three more times, and on each run I could feel my reel getting hotter and hotter. By this time a large crowd had formed, curious to see what was on the other end of my line. I finally got it within about 150 feet of the beach, and it started swimming back and forth instead of making those tearing runs. Now, both the fish and I were tiring. My arms were aching and fatigue was setting in. It was 100 feet away. Now 75. Now 50, and I still wasn't sure what I'd hooked. When I finally got him on the far side of the breaking waves, I saw the dorsal fin and the tail. I turned back to my brother and yelled "Sharrrrkkk!" That prompted a little kid about 9 years old to immediately scream, "Shark! Shark! Somebody help!" This attracted even more people. I shoulda had the kid selling tickets.

I could see by the distance between his dorsal fin and tail that this was a big shark by Bethany Beach standards, and quite frankly I didn't know exactly how I was going to land him. In the past when I hooked a shark, I would get it into the breaking waves and let the surf push him in as I pulled with the line. But because I had light test line on and this was a bigger fish; I knew I couldn't drag him out of the surf and onto the beach because the line would snap.

Then my savior arrived on the scene. One of the kids who was watching came up to me and said, "Do you need any help? I'm a fisherman and I know how to deal with sharks." So I thought why not? His name was Dylan and he was a 13-year-old red-headed kid, and I said, "Look. Let me try and beach him using the waves and if that doesn't work, it's all you." After a few more futile attempts, I said, "OK, what's your plan?"

Waiting for a bite. How many hours of my life have I spent staring at a rod tip?

Another, larger wave rolled in and without saying another word, Dylan ran into the surf and literally jumped on the back of the shark and wrestled him onto the beach, as the horrified, yet fascinated crowd watched. For a moment, he was riding on its back like a bucking bull, then rolled it completely over and onto the beach. I handed my rod to my brother, ran down to Dylan and the shark and pulled it another ten feet onto the beach away from the water. I stood there catching my breath while

Dylan straddled the shark, sitting on top of it like he was still riding a now-vanquished bull. I got my long pliers out of my shorts and removed the hook. People wanted pictures, so I grabbed the shark below its tail and could barely lift it off the beach. By our estimation, it was between five and six feet in length, and it weighed somewhere between 75 and 100 pounds. As I said, there were people taking video and photos of the battle. You could probably find it on YouTube somewhere if you cared to look.

I am the first to admit that I like catching a fish in front of a crowd. Considering the career I chose, I apparently feel the need to perform and be the center of attention. I consider this a fatal character flaw and deserve any ridicule and loathing that comes as a result. I spent hours alone in a darkened room contemplating this, and feel it must be because my stupid older brothers got all the attention when I was a kid, or my mom left me alone too long sitting in the cart at the grocery store when I was very young while she flirted with the guy at the meat counter. Either way, put me on a beach with a surf rod, or on my favorite trout stream with a fly rod, and I'll be your dancing monkey.

I wondered what type of shark I actually caught, so I showed the picture to my friend Holly at the Albuquerque Aquarium, and also consulted Captain Seagull's shark chart. The consensus was that I caught a dusky shark. They get to about 10 to 12 feet, so mine was an adolescent. My brother decided to send the photo that's in this book into the local fishing newspaper with the description, and all the pertinent info. It never got published. About a month later, I called the editor and asked if he received the photo and if he was planning to publish it. There was a short silence on the other end of the line and he finally said, "Well, I would have put it in the paper, but I really don't think you would have wanted me to."

"Why not?"

"Uhhh, a dusky shark is actually an endangered species, and I didn't think you would want to deal with the consequences if Game and Fish decided to do something about it."

I thanked him profusely for not publishing it, apologized for my ignorance about not knowing it was endangered, but then I started thinking:

"OK, number one, I certainly didn't go fishing specifically to catch a dusky shark. Number two, I DID release it alive and unharmed. And number three, and what I consider the pivotal question, how in the hell am I supposed to know what species of shark I hooked until I have it beached, and by then it's too late to do anything about it anyway?"

He said, "You're right. You actually did the right thing. It's true the law reads that it is illegal to hook and land a dusky shark, but Game and Fish are more concerned with charter boats that will gaff it and most likely kill it when they boat it. But just to be safe, we kept it out of the paper."

Thank you. It's bad enough that Bethany Beach doesn't much like me fishing out on their beach. I don't need the law after me too.

I just found out recently why Bethany Beach is not too fond of sharks being caught off their beach. The obvious reason is they don't want their money-spending, beach-going tourists to have the crap scared out of them. But another and more valid reason is a practice that they banned several years ago. Apparently, a fishing outfit got the bright idea to take people shark fishing on the beach at night, but with a twist. They'd rig up and bait the hooks for their clients, and then with jet-skis, would transport the business end of the fishing lines WAY out to sea, farther than anyone could ever cast.

Man, did it work.

Very large sharks started to be caught off the swimming beach on a regular basis, some ten-feet or more in length, with the biggest being a twelve-foot black-tipped beauty. When the town heard about this, they immediately wrote a law or something, banning this practice within city limits.

In conclusion, this is something I've continued to ponder: Over the years I've been releasing every shark that I've caught, meaning, they've all had a chance to grow up and get a lot bigger, and have had a lot of time to think about the jackass that hooked and beached them. So they're all waiting. Waiting just off my beach for me to go swimming, or to take a boogie board out and ride the waves. And when I do, they'll devour me, leaving behind only my testicles, which will fall to the ocean floor, only to be gnawed at by the same Maryland blue crabs that the tourists will eventually eat. *Bon appétit!*

And finally, a postscript, referring back to the beginning of this chapter: The Delaware state legislature just legalized the growing and distributing of medical marijuana in the state, and they say that either full legalization, or at least decriminalization might be coming soon, making the state one of the first eastern states to do so. Hmmmm, I DO have some unused rooms upstairs.

# 21 LIGHTNING WILL KILL YOU

*We were an equal distance between the vans
and the creek when the lightning and thunder began.
Catherine...turned and thrust her rod towards me,
asking "Is my rod supposed to do this?" I took her rod
and it was vibrating like one of those "neck massagers"
you can buy on-line.*

I WAS PROBABLY SIXTEEN OR SEVENTEEN and hanging with my friend Ed up in Mount Clemens, Michigan. It was a hot summer day in maybe 1972, and we decided to take Ed's boat out on Lake St. Clair, which is the small, not-so-great lake below Lake Huron that empties into the Detroit River and then into Lake Erie. It's a very small lake compared to the other Great Lakes, but still big enough to get us into trouble. Ed had a 12-foot aluminum boat with a 10-horse Evinrude clamped to the back. This wasn't any boat with a fancy center-console or anything like that, just a sit-in-the-back and hold on to the motor deal. We drove the boat down to the launching ramp near Metro Beach Park and puttered out onto the aqua-blue waters of the lake, not really noticing that some pretty formidable storm clouds were building to the west. What did we know? It was sunny, hot, and there just might be some fish biting. We were about two, maybe three miles offshore looking for the shoal where everyone fishes, when the sky turned too dark for comfort and the wind picked up forming a moderate chop. The sound of thunder rumbling in the distance and the occasional flash of lightning told us we'd better get moving.

Unfortunately, that thought came too late.

Instantly, almost like someone flipped a switch, the wind began really gusting from the west and it took no time for the swells to reach three feet. Ed turned the boat towards shore just as a flash of lightning hit the water about a quarter mile to our left, followed immediately by an ear-splitting crack of thunder. Ed gunned the engine; as much as you can gun a 10-horse Evinrude, and we headed directly in towards land, which meant directly into the waves. We'd hit a crest and then slam back onto our seats, holding on as best we could. The rain began, and we were both having a hard time seeing where we were heading. We crested another swell, and as we slammed back down, there was a loud sickening crack and splintering noise. The wooden plate that the motor was clamped to broke in two and flew out of the boat, meaning, the running Evinrude was airborne. Miraculously, Ed somehow saved the motor from going to the bottom of the lake and was desperately holding onto it. As lighting flashed all around us, I crawled into the back, and tried to get the motor clamped down against the back of the boat, while Ed kept one hand on the throttle, and tried to keep the prop in the water. I was having a difficult time trying to screw the bolts back on when lightning struck at close proximity and an angry clap of deafening thunder followed, startling us both and causing us to let go temporarily. Somehow again, we got the motor under control. We were now several hundred yards from the marina, and holding on for dear life, we finally pulled into the safe waters at Metro Beach. True story. I don't remember if we told Ed's mom about it. Probably not—that would've freaked her out too much.

I was thinking just the other day about how many times I've come close to getting nailed by a lightning bolt and reduced to a pile of smoldering ashes—all while in pursuit of some kind of fish, usually a trout. I would bet that everyone reading this has at one time or another, had to seek shelter, run for the car, or just plain hunker down and pray when a big thunderstorm passed overhead.

Lightning is the great equalizer. It doesn't matter if you're Tom Brady, or some homeless guy on the streets. If you get hit, it ain't gonna be good. So let's have some fun and do a little bit of catastrophic thinking. Most of these facts and figures have been harvested from Wikipedia.

About 24,000 people are killed by lightning strikes around the world each year and about 240,000 are injured. According to the NOAA, over the last twenty years, the United States averaged 51 lightning strike deaths each year. Again, according to the NOAA, the chance of an average person living in the US being struck by lightning in any given year is estimated to be around one in 500,000, while the chance of being struck by lightning in your lifetime is one in 6,250, with an estimated lifespan of eighty years.

AND, the major statistic we all need to worry about? According to government weather officials most lightning deaths happen while people are enjoying outdoor activities, which seems obvious, but there ARE cases of people getting struck inside their houses as well, standing by windows, even working on the computer. But what's the number one deadliest thing you can do outside when it comes to getting flash-fried? Wait for it.

While fishing.

Yep. Even tops golf, especially now since virtually all golf courses have installed those lightning detectors with sirens that go off if there's lightning within a five-mile radius. And to make matters worse for me and the guys reading this, 82 percent of lightning fatalities are males.

What happens to you when you're a direct hit? Again, from Wikipedia: Lightning strikes have a mortality rate of between 10% and 30%. Of those who survive, around 80% of them sustain long-term injuries. You would think those injuries would be caused by severe burns, but apparently the current is too brief to cause a major heating-up of bodily tissues. The major problem is that nerves and muscles may be directly damaged by the high voltage, which causes holes in cell membranes to form, and that again, ain't good. The lightning also generates large electromagnetic fields which may induce electrical surges through the nervous system, which in turn can mess up your heart function, possibly causing cardiac arrest or seizures. A direct hit can also result in internal burns, organ damage, and my favorite?

Explosions of flesh and bone.

Look at it this way: If you explode into little bits and pieces, it'll be a lot easier for what's left of you to be eaten by forest creatures and vultures. At least they'll be happy, and your last thought, if you're capable of thought after all that, will be the satisfaction of knowing your thoroughly prepared-and-cooked-by-nature remains were a tasty treat.

After reading everything above, it would seem logical to take steps to avoid being struck by lightning. You see lightning and then hear the thunder. Everyone thinks they know how to gauge distance by counting the time between seeing the lightning and the hearing the thunder, but you may not know the correct method. You can thank me because the following is the right way to do this, according to the National Lightning Safety Institute. They recommend using the F-B, or flash to boom method and it takes a miniscule amount of math to do it properly. Lightning and thunder occur roughly at the same time, but light travels far faster than sound does, so the lightning is seen before thunder is heard. Very simply:

— Count the seconds between the lightning flash and thunder.

— Divide by five to determine the distance in miles.

For instance, you see the lightning flash, then it's thousand-one, thousand- two, all the way to, say, thousand-ten. Ten divided by five is two, meaning that lightning was two miles away. Pretty easy.

I knew all that, except the divide-by-five part.

They also warn that even this could be inaccurate because there could be multiple flashes of lightning happening at the same time, and that lightning can occur out of a clear blue sky because the storm clouds could be behind the mountains. AND, it does not have to be raining for there to be lightning.

And finally, what's the best thing to do if you can't make it to your car or cave or some form of shelter? If there is no other alternative, the safest thing for you to do is lie prostrate on the ground. They don't mention if praying, or chanting, or making deals with the devil helps.

Ever been fishing when there's lightning and thunder present, and your rod starts "buzzing?" Bad sign. That means that positive charges are rising through you, trying to meet up with the negative charges in the storm, which is basically what lightning does as it tries to neutralize the charge. What to do is obvious. Put your damned rod down! And if you can, get to shelter. This happened to me three times. The first time was in a boat on Heron Lake in New Mexico during threatening weather, luckily with no ramifications. A friend of mine who was boating even told me of once seeing an arc of electricity shoot from his rod down his line which was still out in the lake. The second time, it was September of 1995 and I was fishing above Crede, Colorado with my friend Bill as the thunderstorm was about to hit. We had just hiked up from Clear Creek, and were sprinting across an open meadow towards the truck when my fly rod began to vibrate, almost hum. Immediately we both threw our rods down and then lightning struck VERY close to us. It was like a bomb went off. The thunder was instantaneous and deafening, and scared the crap out of both of us. Instead of hunkering down, which we should have done, we picked our rods up and continued our run to the truck as we began to get assaulted by marble-sized hail. We made it back cold, drenched, somewhat pockmarked, but not barbecued.

Another time was in 2008 during one of Bob Gerding's seminars at the Valles Caldera in New Mexico's Jemez Mountains. It was after lunch and the sky was cloudy but didn't look threatening yet, so we took the group up to near the headwaters of the east fork of Jemez Creek. Realize that the Caldera is a huge volcanic crater, and rim being the surrounding mountains. It is a huge flat meadow covered with grasses where both cattle and elk graze. We began the walk down from the parking area to the stream and as it often happens at high altitude, the storm was moving in quickly and the sky turned an evil black and greenish color. Normally windy up there, it was dead calm, telling all of us that something not good was about to happen. We were an equal distance between the vans and the creek when the lightning and thunder began. Catherine, who was one of the two people I was guiding, turned to me, thrusting her fly rod towards me and asked "Is my rod supposed to do this?" I took her rod and it was vibrating like one of those "neck massagers" you can buy on-line. All of the guides realized at the same time that it was time to go into protection mode. Bob yelled out, "Everyone put your fly rods down and get as low as you can to the ground!"

Fear swept through the group, but all complied, and within a minute, the storm was upon us, unleashing a hellish fury of electricity. Lightning flashed all around, and some of the closer strikes resulted in high decibels of explosive, even crackling thunder, and the definite smell of ozone wafted through the air. Just when we thought we were goners, the strangest thing happened. Almost as suddenly as it hit, it was over. It took maybe no more than ten minutes for the worst to pass through, and after a few more minutes of making sure it was all clear, we all got up and continued walking down to the stream. It really didn't rain or hail either, maybe a sprinkle but that was it. The sky lightened up, the sun even came out and we had a delightful afternoon fishing. And, and best of all, nobody died!

Jer and I finished fishing and were walking down the trail from the upper portions of Cebolla Creek, again in the Jemez Mountains, probably in the late 1980s. There was lightning and thunder in the distance, but we were confident that we'd make it back to his truck before hell broke loose. We were still about a quarter mile from his truck when there was a blinding flash and a huge explosion. It wasn't just the sound of thunder but something worse. Right in front of us, not more than a hundred yards away, a large pine tree had been directly hit, splitting it in two, causing sawdust and wood splinters to rain down from above. A strong smoky turpentine scent was in the air, and as we came upon what was left of the tree, half of it was lying across the road, and the surrounding ground looked like it had been snowing sawdust and pine parts. The tree grew directly next to the road, and if we had been two minutes earlier, well, bye-bye Jer and TJ.

And finally, I have nothing but respect and admiration for fishing guides. There is no doubt that most of the techniques I have learned over the years have come from listening, watching, or being instructed by one of them. If I'm on a new river that I'm totally unfamiliar with, I always try to hire a guide for at least one day because it's their home water and they know all the little quirks and idiosyncrasies of the place. Like I said, most of these guys are great, except the one guy who tried to get us killed.

It was 1999. Milt and I were fishing the Madison in Montana and our name-withheld guide was older, gruff, even wizened. It was obvious he'd spent a lot of time on the river, probably too much time. In our case, probably one week too long. If he would have retired the week before we got there, it probably would have been better for all of us.

The first day was not bad, except that his social skills weren't that great. Before we got close to the water, he took one look at the way my rod was rigged and summarily tore off my loop-to-loop connection I had on my fly line. All the while, he was berating me for being an amateur as he tied on a new leader with a nail knot. Granted a nail knot makes for a better stealthier presentation, especially when casting in still water, but did he have to make me feel like a doofus fifth grader?

My first mistake was trying to defend myself: "Yeah, I use a loop-to-loop because if you're in the heat of the battle and need to change leaders quickly, it's a lot easier just to loop one on than try to tie a nail knot. It takes less time, and if you're in diminishing light conditions you can…"

"Aw that's bullshit! You just ain't tied enough of 'em! If you're gonna fly fish, you gotta learn how to do this shit or you don't belong on the water."

That hurt. Bile was rising up in me, but I figured I'd let it pass.

"Now if I'm gonna guide you, we're using a goddam nail knot and you watch if you don't catch more fish."

OK, fine. He had a point that probably could have been made more judiciously, and even though I thought there was some merit to my argument, I let it pass.

He took us to Hebgen Lake first because as many guides do, he wanted to see if he had two imbeciles in his boat before we hit the river. That was fine with us because we experienced the biggest caddis fly hatch that either of us had ever seen. At one point we were covered in caddis flies. There were so many that they were getting up our pants legs and under our shirts. Needless to say, the fish were going crazy with so many bugs rising off the water. We threw dry caddis imitations all morning resulting in a strike on nearly every cast. Our guide was probably unhappy with this because a rank amateur could have been pulling in fish on that day, so he really couldn't tell if we knew what we were doing.

For those of you unfamiliar with the area, the Madison flows into Hebgen Lake, and then out, flowing downstream into Quake Lake, which was formed by a landslide during an earthquake in August of 1959. It registered 7.5 on the Richter scale, and the landslide killed 28 people, burying them in the slide. Out of Quake Lake the Madison resumes its travels, flowing through Ennis, Montana, eventually dumping into the Missouri River. After the caddis-fest on Hebgen, we would float the Madison the next morning.

The next day broke beautifully, with a cool sunrise and a few clouds but with thunderstorms forecast for the afternoon. Even this perfect morning did not put our guide in a better mood. Maybe he was hung over from the night before, but we weren't going to let him ruin our trip. And we were catching fish. He actually lightened up a little after

Milt in Montana....A thumbs-up before the lightning storm hit, and we were nearly incinerated by the wrath of the gods!

he saw that it wouldn't be necessary to give us casting lessons. Using a large caddis imitation with a pheasant tail dropper, we pounded the banks and cast to the mid-stream riffles pulling in brown after brown, along with the occasional whitefish.

After lunch, the storm clouds were building, and our guide must have remembered why he was pissed off. I was in the front of the boat and because of my aging back, I have a tendency to occasionally shift my weight from foot to foot. I must have been doing this for a while, because he finally had enough.

"Will you please...STAND STILL?" he bellowed. "I'm trying to fucking navigate this boat through the rocks and you're making it hard as hell!"

"Sorry! I didn't realize that I was doing that."

"Well, you do now!"

And almost on-cue, the first ominous roll of thunder was heard. We figured we had about twenty minutes before it hit, so we got our rain parkas on and continued downstream, still catching fish, as the lightning and thunder became more frequent and nearer.

Then the deluge began. The rain was relentless, coming down in sheets and the wind made it difficult to stand in the moving boat. Lightning and thunder was all around us, and yet our guide kept rowing at the same leisurely pace, matching the Madison's flow. Milt and I fully expected him to pull over, but he never did. Finally at the height of the storm's fury, I turned and yelled back to him, "Shouldn't we get off the river and find some shelter with all this lightning?"

"No, goddamit!" he snarled with a half-crazed look in his eye. "We're on the river, right? Do you see where the river bank is?"

"Well yeah, it's—"

"It's above our heads is where it is! And what are you supposed to do in a lightning storm?"

"I would go and find somewhere to get out of the weather, and..."

"Wrong!" he screamed. "You go to the lowest place you can find, and the lowest place around IS the river! Are we catching fish?"

"Yeah we are, but—"

"Well keep fishing! I ain't stopping, and the fish love to feed during a thunderstorm, now cast your fly!"

Milt and I looked at each other with a mixture of bewilderment, confusion, and fear that this guy was going to turn into Quint in the last scene of "Jaws." So, I yelled back to Milt, "Hey! It's a good day to die!" and made a cast towards the bank. It was immediately met with a huge heavy strike on my bottom fly. It was a big brown, and through the wind and blinding horizontal rain, punctuated by strobes of lightning, I fought the fish through successive runs and head shakes, constantly wiping the water away from my face. I eventually landed a healthy twenty-incher. Our guide was cackling with delight, partially because of the fish, but mostly because he had been vindicated.

"What the hell did I tell you? They love thunderstorms, and we ain't dead yet, are we?"

Again, he had a point. Milt also was having success, and finally when the rain stopped after about a half hour, the sky cleared and as the sun broke through during the storms final drizzle, a double rainbow gaudily stretched across the eastern sky.

I thought about what the guide said, about how the river IS the lowest point around, which was true. But we were still holding up a nine-foot-long rod, made of highly conductible graphite and waving it in the air. I don't know, man. I'd like another fishing professional to weigh in on this conversation.

The day was done, and on the way back to the fishing shop, our guide asked if we wanted to get a cocktail to celebrate a successful day on the river. That sounded like the perfect plan, so he pulled into the parking lot of a roadside bar, but instead of parking, he drove around to the side of the building.

I asked, "What are you doing?"

"I'm in kind of a hurry so if you all don't mind, we'll go through the drive-thru."

"A drive-thru at a bar?"

"That's right. It's legal in Montana. You can drink and drive at the same time, but you can't drive drunk. What do you want?"

What a strange land this Montana was.

"I'll have a scotch and soda."

And the way the day ended. Maybe the old bastard wasn't such a bad chap after all.

*The only rod the son in the ad ever touched was back in college when he was going through his "experimental stage."*

# 26 AD AGENCY MORONS

I'LL BE BRIEF. THIS IS FOR ALL THE IDIOTS who work in the creative departments at ad agencies who think it's cool to include flyfishing in their TV commercials for whatever product they might be pushing: YOU MONEY-GRUBBING DOUCHEBAGS! EITHER GET IT RIGHT, OR STOP!

Granted, what we do IS cool. In fact, I'll go as far as saying, a fly cast when done properly, and when filmed well, is a work of art. And where we fish is usually quite scenic. But then you and your ignorant prop people who know absolutely nothing about the sport, completely ruin it on a number of levels.

Maybe the general public doesn't know the difference, but you idiots are annoying fly fishermen (me) to the point that even if I needed your product to save my life, I would gladly die first! Most of the time you get the location right, but usually the guy you have in the middle of the stream can't cast to save his mother.

There have been many, but I will cite one example that was particularly annoying, probably because it ran virtually non-stop for at least a year. This forced me and other fly casters to watch it over and over again, which resulted in over-analyzing it to the point of acquiring an obsessive/compulsive disorder. And to the detriment of my blood pressure and general health, I'd get angrier each time I'd see it.

I have nothing against Symbicort®. I'm sure they make a necessary and effective product for those who suffer from asthma. But for all that is good and holy, why didn't you hire a consultant who at least had some rudimentary knowledge of flyfishing? Before you read any further, go on You Tube, watch the Symbicort® ad, and then continue. Done? Good. By now you realize I probably have WAY too much free time on my hands, but I got so agitated every time I saw this abomination, I scared my wife. Here's the breakdown of what's wrong:

—The old guy with asthma: if he were a true fly fisherman, would never wear that goofy fishing hat. Most fly fisherman I know wear some version of a ball cap. His son is wearing the same old-man hat too. The grandkid looks more like a fly fisherman than either of these posers.

—What the hell kind of rods are they using with those long handles behind the reels? Upon closer inspection, I think those are spinning rods with fly reels attached, because they seem too short. Plus, the fly reels look like they could hold big saltwater line. Dumb, dumb, and dumber.

—I will give them a break for attaching a bobber to the fly line, since it's all about the grandkid. And the old coot's backhanded cast with the bobber is kind of cool and requires some skill.

—HOWEVER, as Grandpa is casting the bobber, check out the adult son, who's standing to the left. He's holding his rod with one hand above the reel and one below, with a giant loop of fly line drooping down, as he's about to cast. No back cast, just sidearm. It is obvious that this guy has never fished with a fly rod in his life, most likely never fished with a spinning rod, and, this was probably his first time on a stream, or even in in the woods, having never left his cubicle at the office! And at the beginning of the commercial, Grandpa says, "Before COPD, I took my son fishing every year [yeah, right!]. We had a great spot, not easy to find, but worth it." After watching the ad, I am convinced it wasn't THAT son. The only rod the son in the ad ever touched was back in college when he was going through his "experimental" stage.

At least at the end they practiced catch-and-release, and when the little kid showed that the fish was "this big" with his outstretched arms, at least THAT is somewhat endearing, although you can tell the kid initially blew the move, before he did it for real.

All I'm sayin' is, if you don't know what the hell you're doing, find someone who does, or don't do it because, at least in the flyfishing world, you have just lost your street cred.

# 27 BIRDS, BIRDS, AND MORE BIRDS

*Greg screamed at me to watch out as it kamikazeed out of the sky, intent on plucking both eyeballs out of my skull and feeding them to its offspring.*

I USUALLY GET ALONG QUITE WELL with members of the animal kingdom. Dogs love me. As do cats. Even hamsters, rabbits, and gerbils seem to be attracted to the pheromones I give off. Why, then, are birds my arch nemesis? I don't know if these marginally embellished tales of bird-dom happen to you all, but I've had my share of encounters that have not turned out so well.

It was a cool Canadian late spring morning in June with a healthy breeze blowing out of the north, pushing bands of cumulus clouds southward, covering and uncovering the sun. We were fishing for pike in a secluded bay of Lake Ontario, and my fishing partner Greg and I decided to beach ourselves on a tiny island surrounded by weedy water that looked promising. It was a small, windblown, craggy spit of land with a large dead pine tree dominating the center, standing guard over it and the choppy water. So confidently, we grabbed our 8-weights, I with my popper, and Greg with his 8-foot-long purple streamer (OK, exaggerating, but not by much), and we headed to find the swimming toothy bastards we came for. Walking along, we began to notice fur balls and various small bones that looked like the digested remains of various Rodentia. Of course, neither of us even thought to look up in that dead tree, where there sat a monumental owl's nest with hungry chicks inside, waiting to be fed. Admittedly, there's something to be said about living in blissful ignorance, until there's a giant winged flying beast with large talons dive bombing your head. Greg screamed at me to watch out as it kamikazeed out of the sky intent on plucking both eyeballs out of my skull and feeding them to its offspring. I hit the ground and missed being impaled by inches, hearing the sound of the beating wings and feeling the wind it generated on my neck. It flew back up, circled the island preparing for another aerial assault. We didn't have to be asked twice. We sprinted back to the boat, pushed off shore and headed out into the bay, positive that if we had stayed, our bones and hair would have joined the open-air graveyard that was already present.

So that night we returned to our cabin and related our story to our host Alex, whose wife was preparing dinner in the main house. Alex was a slightly built, gentlemanly man of about 70, who spoke with that charming Bob and Doug Mackenzie Canadian dialect. He got a tight smile on his face and said, "Yep, had a run in with old Gert, aye? Tonight, at dinner. I was going to tell you fellas to stay off that island, but I guess you learned that on your own."

Yeah, we did. Thanks a pant-load, pal.

Then, there's the tale of the osprey ignoramus, who apparently had difficulty discerning fantasy from reality. This happened on the same trip I caught my first permit. After a long day of bonefishing the saltwater flats near Ascensión Bay, Mexico, it was time to unwind with my favorite Mexican beer, and kick back, and do some fun fishing. As always with me, there's serious fishing, and then there's fun fishing. Serious fishing is fun as well, but that's when you're out all day in the hot tropical sun, hunting down your quarry, and every cast, every triumphant hook-up, or every tragically stupid missed cast results in a celebration or indictment of your self-worth. And when the day is done and you're back at the lodge or camp, you re-live the day with either a feeling of smug, confident satisfaction, or you relentlessly beat yourself up over your comically bumbled misdeeds. Now fun fishing is when the serious fishing is over, and you grab a beer and a spinning rod and head out to the beach to see what might be out there.

The sun was setting behind my back. I could feel its warmth as I faced the open Caribbean. It was a beautiful white sandy beach, its back end speckled with palm trees and the little cabana huts that the guests, including my wife were staying in, nestled a couple hundred feet back in the palms. There I stood, spinning rod in hand, a Rapala with a wire leader dangling from its end, a cold beer coozied in the sand. Perhaps I could coax a local barracuda to bite and end up with some fine barracuda ceviche after I delivered it to the kitchen. Properly armed, I flung that Rapala out into the warm, azure blue water and started retrieving it with a jerky motion, hoping for a strike. What happened next was not was I was hoping for, nor was it remotely in my stream of consciousness.

Behind me in one of those palm trees ringing the beach sat a juvenile osprey, intent on finding an evening meal out in the water. I must have been doing a good job mimicking a fish in trouble because the osprey launched itself into the air and with talons extended, nimbly plucked my Rapala out of the water and began to fly away with it. This was one of those "What the fuck?!" moments. Here I was with a large predatory bird attached to the end of my fishing line that could easily rip my face off, and I had no idea what to do. I started to tug at the Rapala, trying to dislodge it. This only managed to confuse the osprey, and it decided to land about 100 feet down the beach from me. I gingerly tugged as it stood there, watching its right leg move as I tugged. Visibly confused, it looked at me, looked back at its leg, looked back at me, and then decided to take off. It did a beeline for another palm considerably farther away from its original roost. I loosened the drag, pointed my rod at the bird and my line screamed out of the reel. Finally, it landed and managed to extricate itself from my Rapala and flew back into its original palm tree. Cursing, I trudged back to where my Rapala was stuck in a palm frond and managed to shake it loose. I walked back to where I had been, took a long drag on my beer and figured I'd have a great story to tell around the dinner table tonight. I looked back at the palm tree behind me, and the osprey was still sitting exactly where the whole scene began.

I still had time before dinner so I figured, what the hell, he's not gonna do that again, so I cast the Rapala back into the water. In retrospect, I don't know who was more of an imbecile, me or that bird because here he came again, swooped down, and again, grabbed my Rapala and took off! This time I started screaming at the bird at the top of my lungs, calling it profanely foul expletive-filled names, insulting its progeny and accusing it of making an incestuous, even oedipal choice of a mating partner. Hearing my cries and thinking I was having a coronary episode, my wife ran out to the beach and surveyed the scene, watching as the bird, again, made a beeline for the same back palm, got free again of the Rapala, and went back to roosting where he originally was. I got the lure, reeled up the line, grabbed my beer, and utterly defeated, retreated to my cabana.

I can't make this stuff up.

Seagulls are otherwise and correctly known as "flying rats," especially by members of beach communities that feature boardwalk food fare including beach fries, those delectable caloric treats that are the most likely to get dropped and then consumed by those throngs of screeching, fighting, and ultimately defecating birds. You've seen gulls on the beach. Pleasant to watch at first, then not unlike bears in Yellowstone who have grown accustomed to human contact, they will hang out on the perimeter of your little beach camp, waiting for the opportunity to eat just about anything you drop or leave behind.

Gulls like hanging out near surf fishermen as well because they know that eventually you will get a bite and miss a fish, and you will reel in remnants of the bait that you flung out—mullet heads, for example. Then you, being the charitable sort that you are, will take the mullet head off your mullet rig, and fling it in the air, seeing if one of the begging gulls will actually catch it in mid-air.

This story has nothing to do with French fries, or mullet heads but relates how I became a seagull murderer, with witnesses. It was quite the windy day on the Delaware shore in the late summer of 1997, and as I am likely to do when no flyfishing opportunities present themselves. I will walk down to the beach with a surf rod, sand spike, slop bucket, a beach chair, a beer or two, and a fine cigar. I will put a mullet rig on my line, skewer a previously frozen mullet onto the rig, cast it out into the surf, put the rod in the sand spike, sit down and smoke my cigar and drink my beer, and watch for a bluefish, shark, or depending on the season, a striper to take my bait. My favorite thing, being somewhat of

Netting one on the San Juan River in New Mexico, back when neoprene waders were the fashion of the day!

a show-off, is to hook a sizeable shark while there are still small children on the beach. There is usually one of two reactions from the kids when they see what I've caught. The first is fascination, which is fine, but the second, which usually involves mom, is pure fright. My favorite was the frightened kid accompanied by the mom, who angrily stomped up to me and said first, "This is a swimming beach, not a fishing beach!"

"No, actually, after 5:30 pm, I'm allowed to fish."

"Well, there are still small children on this beach! And I just got done telling little Billy that there were no sharks in this water! And you've just ruined all of that! What am I supposed to do now?"

"Ma'am," I said, "a little dose of reality might be good for the kid and look at it this way. It gives you a prime opportunity to have another meaningful conversation with little Billy, and explain to him why mommy lied."

That's about the time she turned in a huff and took the little whining miscreant by the hand and stormed off to the safety of their rented beach house.

Then it was windy and the gulls were moving to wherever they go at that time of the evening, flying along right at the surf line. One of the gulls did not see my line and ended up flying into it, wrapping the monofilament around its neck. It dropped to the sand and struggled to get loose. I ran up to, let's say his name was Eddie, and frantically tried to unwrap the tangled line from around Eddie's neck. But clearly, his goose or gill was cooked. Now here's the weird part. As I was trying to save this poor bird, all of his buddies, maybe eight other gulls, were hovering in the air directly over the crime scene, watching the events intently. These birds were literally flapping their wings, remaining stationary above us, watching their unfortunate friend breathe his last breath. Finally, when all hope was lost, and I swear this happened, Eddie looked up at me, looked me directly in the eye, uttered a final miserable "Squawwwk" and died. At that exact moment, all his buddies saw what had just happened to their pal, and deciding there was nothing else they could do, flew away. I was bummed. Thinking I should give Eddie a proper burial, I picked up his limp, still warm corpse, and being too lazy to dig a suitable hole on the beach, and not finding another alternative, walked him over to the nearest beach trash can and dispatched him. Defeated again, I gathered up all my stuff and walked back to the house. Bummer.

Then there are bird encounters that border on the surreal. Often mistaken for bats in the evening, swallows, depending upon the variety, are actually beautiful little birds, building their mud nests right along their favorite stretches of water, as at the San Juan River in northwestern New Mexico. A desert tail water, the headwaters begin far up in the San Juan Mountains of southern Colorado. The river runs into Navajo Lake where its flow is impeded by Navajo Dam, and then flows out the bottom of the dam, assuring that the water in the river below stays between 41 and 42 degrees, year-round, providing an incredible habitat for growing large trout. The river cut a canyon through sandstone deposits, resulting in impressive sandstone cliffs, which are especially close on the northern river bank. And in these cliffs, countless numbers of swallows have taken up residence, and dine off the same menu that the trout do, which are the large and prolific hatches of mostly midges and mayflies, and downstream, caddis.

Hopefully, most of you have been out on the river when you finally have that one spectacular day that normally you only dream about. Everything goes right and you end up having one of the best fishing days of your life. That happened to me in the fall of 2011 on the San Juan. We got to the river that morning around 8:30 am on a sunny but again, windy day. Mo and I were drifting with John our guide through the quality-water stretch of river, starting at Texas Hole. Fishing had been good for the past couple of weeks, so the river was full of people. As I've said on numerous occasions, you don't go to the San Juan River for a wilderness experience, you go there to catch large trout. As we got on the river, we noticed an unusually large number of swallows dive bombing the water, which was a very good sign that a big hatch was in progress. It took me two casts to hook up and land my first trout. Then another, then another, then another one. After Mo's slow start due to his mechanical dorkiness, he soon caught up and we realized this was going to be one of those charmed days. But we also noticed that the number of swallows on the water was increasing. And as the hatch continued, the birds continued to send in re-enforcements and by about 10 am, the sky was so thick with them, it was becoming difficult to cast without hitting one. I am not exaggerating when I tell you there were legions of these little bastards. It was an incredible, all-day midge and mayfly hatch, and the assault on these bugs was relentless. To our delight, the trout were coming up in a feeding frenzy from below, gorging themselves, and the gluttonous swallows did the same from above.

The problem started when we started not only hitting swallows with our casts, but actually hooking them. Pardon the pun, but it turned into actual "fly" fishing. We'd hook a swallow, it would try to fly away, and we'd be forced to reel it in, unhook it, untangle the line which usually wrapped around the bird, and then release it unharmed where it flew away to resume feasting. As I said, in hand, the birds were actually quite pretty with bright sky-blue underbellies. They'd initially struggle, and then I think they realized we were actually trying to help them, so they just sat there patiently while we extricated them from the mess. The trout continued their bug orgy as well. We stopped even trying to count fish after we had lunch. But, I did catch, land, and release four swallows and hit probably twenty others with my casts. And as I'm writing this, it just occurred to me that none of us got shat upon, not even once.

*This might be my only chance in my entire life to land a marlin, and I wasn't going to screw it up. About this time, I started cursing myself for not going to the gym more, because I was getting seriously worn down.*

# 28 IT WAS HARD

IT WAS 18 DEGREES IN JANUARY OF 2012. Too cold to fish, hike, ride a bike, play tennis, or even do yard work, so I decided to join a gym, at least for the winter. I was on one of those hamster wheel-type cardio machines where you walk or run or peddle or do some form of torturous motion to stay alive and functioning and came up with a brilliant idea to save the planet and wean us off the teat of Big Oil.

All these stupid perpetual motion machines in gyms all over the world should be hooked up to the local power company to generate electricity. Gym membership should be absolutely free, and the profits would come from selling the energy back to the local power utility. With millions of people creating all this kinetic energy, we'd solve the world's energy crisis instantly and cut health care costs because we'd all be in better shape. Brilliant! Someone should give me the Nobel Prize. I'd take it one step further and say that each citizen would be required to do at least 15 minutes of cardio a day for the good of the country, but you'd all accuse me of being a socialist.

So, I was on this machine, and it's one that had your own private TV monitor hooked up to it. I was watching the Outdoors Channel to keep myself from constantly looking at how much time I had left to go and trying to keep my mind off the pain I was causing myself. They had a program on about fishing for marlin and sailfish, which harkened me back to Yucatán again, where I found out that hooking and landing a marlin is the most difficult thing you'll ever do while fishing. Well, maybe that, or being stung repeatedly by jellyfish as you're trying to land a fish while wading off a beach, but that's another story.

It was 1993 and we were staying on the island of Cozumel, which is just off the Mexican Yucatán coast within sight of Cancún. This was actually not a fishing trip. It was a vacation for me and the Little Woman which involved beaches, snorkeling, eating and drinking, exploring, and, oh yeah, if we have time, maybe one fishing trip.

The hotel we stayed in was right on the water, and the water surrounding Cozumel is spectacularly clear with that bright Caribbean blue. They built a man-made sandy beach in front of a coral rock wall that lined that part of the coast. This was actually a good thing because the reef ran close to where we were staying, and there was a chrome swimming pool ladder that was bolted into the rock so you could enter the water and immediately start snorkeling in about six feet of water. The underwater life was spectacular, and I spent many hours blissfully paddling around. One morning I decided to snorkel my way to the south end of the property where a small stream entered the open water, and a white PVC pipe jutted out from the side of the hotel. Just as I reached the stream, a bilious river of brown effluent began to vomit out of the pipe, and it was coming towards me. Appalled, disgusted, and fearful of contracting salmonella, E. coli, hepatitis, or any number of insidious Mexican hybridized gastro-intestinal viruses, I finned my way back to the ladder as fast as I could, never to return to the water for the rest of our stay, at least not anywhere around there. So much for clear blue water.

The Little Woman and I also seem to have strange things happen to us when we go on sightseeing trips. There was a Mayan ruin on the island, so we rented an old, barely running Volkswagen Beetle, which in Mexico was, more often than not, the only rental car choice. We drove about a half-hour through the jungle to the ruins. Apparently 1,500 years ago, this particular area was a Mayan fertility site. When the young Mayan girls came of age, they would take them there and do to them what is done to Mayan girls when they reached puberty. I have no idea what that was.

The ruin was literally cut out of the jungle, surrounded by a wall of green that the groundskeepers did battle with constantly to stop the place from being overrun. There were several large trees that grew throughout the site, keeping it in dappled sunlight and shade, which made the tropical heat and humidity more tolerable. There was a small pyramid surrounded by several out-buildings and an ancient well. Back when we did this trip, they would let you climb the pyramids, so we did, which was fine, except Marti was afraid to climb back down, so she unceremoniously "sat" her way down the entire way, sliding her butt from step to step. I do have a photo of this somewhere. Then, to make matters worse, after the fear and exertion, she really had to pee, and there was not a toilet to be found. She took the only perceived option. She went around to the back of the pyramid, squatted down, and let it flow.

This must have angered the Mayan gods because on the way back from the pyramid we stopped at the well we saw on the way in. Wondering if it still contained water, she peered in, and as she did, she must have startled the well's inhabitants because about a hundred bats flew up into her face, causing her to scream and instinctively recoil in horror, which caused even more bats to fly up and around. After they figured out that she was no threat, they returned into to the safety and darkness of their sanctuary. I don't have a photo of that. Shaken, but at least with an empty bladder, she and I returned to our VW Beetle and made our way back to the hotel. We showered and went down for happy hour, which we spent on the deck overlooking the water to the west and the Mexican mainland, where each night we watched a spectacular Yucatán sunset while enjoying several fine alcoholic beverages. It was a good day. And tomorrow was my fishing trip.

The next morning was warm and sunny with very little wind. We found our boat at the marina, met the captain and first mate, who could speak just enough English to get by, and met our traveling partners, a charming couple about our age from Biloxi, Mississippi. It's always a good thing when you get along with or actually like the people you'll be in a confined space with for an entire day because if you're teamed up with a couple of morons, the day will prove to be very long.

I had rarely gone deep-sea fishing, so the prospect of battling something much larger than me was very exciting. There was no flyfishing to be done here. The fishing would be accomplished with heavy equipment perfectly matched to its task. I actually have a problem with these guys who go out and insist on getting a marlin with a fly rod. Come on, man. Really? When it comes down to it, it's really not flyfishing. They're still drawing the fish in with their bait and attractors, and then when they get the marlin close enough to the boat, you put your "fly." I use the word fly loosely because that thing you have on the end of your line ain't no fly in the water and pretty much troll your "fly" behind the boat. Then the fish that has already been lured in by all the other stuff, happens to see your "fly," and goes for it. It is a contrived, artificial way to catch a marlin with no real basis in reality, other than the paid customer insists he needs to use a fly rod to stroke his ego. Again, there are some sorry flyfishing purists out there.

We headed east for about an hour into the deep blue water where the big guys swim and hunt, and there was nothing. It'd been two hours and not a fish to be seen. We had lunch and began again. We got a bite, and a fish was on. But it was obviously not a marlin and then we saw the glowing, almost phosphorescent green under the water. It was a mahi-mahi, and it was other-worldly beautiful, as it flashed from green to yellow to blue as it battled us. We landed it, and then another, and another, and then, nothing again. At this point everyone's satisfied with mahi-mahis, except me, of course. I wanted to be possessed by the ghost of Hemingway. I wanted to pitch battle and vanquish a large sea-beast. I needed to prove my manhood to myself and to those who might bear witness. This, by the way, had nothing to do with my penis size. Oh, hell. Maybe it does.

It was late afternoon and we turned to head home. The captain and his first mate felt bad that no marlin was had, so they kept us rigged up and trolling on the way in, explaining that the closer we got to land, the less chance we'd have of getting one. Despite that, we persevered. The coastline of Cozumel was well within site, and we saw the outlines of the beachfront hotels. Marti and our new Biloxi friends were on the bow of the boat making dinner plans for tonight, and I stood in solitude at the back watching the outriggers, when the one on the left side went down. The first mate yells at me in his best English, "Sit in the chair and take the rod! Now!!!" I was seated, strapped in, and the rod was in front of me in the rod holder. I looked out to sea where my line was pointed and it was like all the fishing shows you've seen but never witnessed for real. The marlin did a spectacular leap, almost dancing on its tail, and the fight was on. By this time, Marti and our new friends had run to the back of the boat for the show.

This, my friends, was serious business.

The fish was pulling harder and harder, making screaming runs as the first mate poured water over the reel to keep it from overheating. I was warned to keep my hands away from the spinning reel handles unless I enjoy broken fingers. Sweat was pouring off of my body, and I actually felt the pulsing muscular strength of this fish. Each time the fish stopped running the first mate screams "Reel-reel- reel! Do not let the line go slack!" And I did my best. My arms were aching, and I was getting aerobically tired, but I vowed to myself not to give up. This might be my only chance in my entire life to land a marlin, and I wasn't going to screw it up. About this time, I started cursing myself for not going to the gym more because I was getting seriously worn down.

Then the battle started to turn in our favor. It had been about an hour and the runs were becoming less frequent as the fish began to tire. The captain was doing a great job of positioning the boat to make it easier. It appeared that we would win the day. And at that point, the first

mate was no longer barking out instructions. His conversation now became, "Hey man that is a great fish! My uncle has a good cheap taxidermy service for you. I can get that fish stuffed real cheap and shipped to
you!"

Realize at that point, I was still fighting the fish while barely remaining conscious, but I did know that I don't want this fish stuffed. I
didn't even want this fish boated. So between deep wheezing gasps of
air I said, "No. What I want you to do, [gasp] is when the fish is at the
boat, [gasp] unhook it, [gasp] and let me get one photo of it while it's in
the water. [gasp] Then revive it, and let it go."

He looked at me like I just murdered his entire family. Apparently,
no one had ever asked him to do that before. It was obvious he was
counting on the money from the taxidermy job and cash from selling
the meat. I said, "Do whatever you need to do to revive it, get water
running through its gills. I want this fish released alive." He had a few
words in Spanish with his captain, in a short conversation in Spanish
that probably went... "Hey, this asshole actually wants us to let it go!"

"Shit! That means less money for us! I knew when he got on the
boat he was 'one of those guys...'"

"So, what should we do? We could throw him overboard and say it
was a rogue wave."

Fighting my marlin off the coast of Cozumel, while the Little Woman gives encouragement, and hoping I'll
get it over with and land the damned thing so she'll have time to get back and freshen up for dinner!

"Yeah, but then we'd lose any tip money. Just do what the stupid gringo wants."

He turned to me and said, "OK, whatever you want. It's your trip!"

We landed the fish, and it turned out it wasn't a huge marlin, maybe about 200 pounds, but I have to tell you, it was the hardest thing involving fishing that I have ever done in my life. I got my picture, he released it unharmed, and he handed me an open beer in a gesture of congratulations and good will, and all was well with the world. I sat down for the remainder of the boat ride, drinking my beer, completely covered in sweat, my muscles worked to the point of dysfunction, but happy as hell.

As a side note, if you're like me and you want your billfish released, I would suggest you tell your captain up front, especially if you're in a foreign country, specifically Mexico. I was fishing for sailfish out of Puerto Vallarta couple years after this trip, and these guys spoke English, even less than the Cozumel guys. I hooked and landed a decent sailfish, and before I could get the words out of my mouth about releasing it, out came the club and they bashed its brains in. It was like, "Hey, before you—oh no! Oh god, did you have to do that?"

They understood not a word. They just looked up and smiled at me and nodded. At least the poor fish fed some hungry people.

# 29 ALASKA...BEARS, TROUT, AND WALRUS PENIS BONES

*I didn't realize how big Alaskan brown bears were until
we were face-to-face with one. Sniffing the air,
it emerged from the trees, and made a beeline for
the smorgasbord we had set out for it, and began to feast.
I was fascinated but completely scared shitless.*

I'VE BEEN LUCKY ENOUGH TO HAVE GONE TO ALASKA twice with different results. The first trip was in 1994 with my buddy Bill and Michelle, a platonic female friend. She went along because she was the long-distance girlfriend of Frank, the guy who owned the lodge, thus guaranteeing us a severely discounted rate, since he'd be getting laid on a regular basis for a week. This trip was at the end of September, the last week that Frank's lodge would be open. His lodge was on the Kvichak River, about a two-hour Cessna flight from Anchorage, and we'd be fishing for huge Alaskan rainbow trout since the salmon had come and gone by then. We would fly into Anchorage, spend the night, and then fly out to the river the next morning.

We arrived in Anchorage early in the afternoon, giving us plenty of time to check in at the Hotel Captain Cook and tool around the town before dinner. Bill was responsible for filming all of my TV commercials back in the old days of 94 Rock, so he insisted on bringing a video camera and trying to film some kind of twisted Alaska fishing travelogue. Of course, we had no script or outline, or any idea of what we were attempting to do, so we just kept the camera rolling, hoping that something funny or interesting might happen. I'm also thinking he did this just as an excuse to make this a "working vacation" so he could write the entire trip off. I WAS one of his clients, so it wouldn't have been too much of a stretch.

Bill was an old hippie and was still sporting a ponytail that went halfway down his back. He was a large man, maybe six foot three and very handsome with the look of a hippie-fied Sam Elliott, which made him very popular with the ladies. He's had an interesting, if sordid past involving the ingestion of a wide variety of pharmaceutical substances in quantities that would have killed a normal person. Plus he had an avid interest in the same substances genesis and transport, which also could've had killed him or at least landed him in jail. He gave all of that up long ago along with his four pack a day cigarette habit, after the birth of his beloved daughter. He is part Cherokee and has always been an avid fisherman and explorer and because of his skewed way of looking at reality, we bonded immediately.

While Michelle was in her hotel room, Bill and I strolled down the streets of Anchorage, camera rolling, as I commented on what we saw and interviewed tourists and shop owners who would let us. Our favorite was the guy who owned the souvenir/pawn shop a couple of minutes down the street from the Captain Cook. I forgot his name but he was a paunchy middle-aged black man who, thinking we were filming a segment for the Outdoor Channel, gladly showed us around his shop, which was actually quite interesting, filled with native artifacts and quirky touristy stuff, along with the watches and rings of people who were down on their luck. Suddenly his eyes got wide and he told us to wait right there while he got something from the back room that we absolutely needed to see. A minute or two later he returned with something long and large and wrapped in a white sheet. He unwrapped the sheet from around it and proudly proclaimed, "This beauty is the penis bone of a walrus! Now not many people know that walruses have bones inside their penis but they do, and you're one of the few people to ever get one on film!"

I can't tell you how happy he was to show us that.

After we walked out, we realized that we would find nothing that would beat what we just filmed, so we packed it up, walked back to the hotel, had dinner, and ended up where every single fisherman tourist who comes to anchorage spends their night before they fly out the next morning; the Captain Cook Lounge on the top floor of the hotel.

This legendary lounge is the common point of both my Alaskan adventures. It is one of those bars that had windows ringing its outer walls, with spectacular views of Cook Inlet and the surrounding mountains that framed the city. The bar stayed open late, very late to the point of it being early, especially if you come in the middle of summer when it never truly got dark. It was a place of hopeful inebriation, meaning, everyone there was on their way somewhere else—to fish, hunt, sightsee, and all are drunkenly giddy with the promise of adventure to come. We drank, and kept drinking, safe in the knowledge that the following day would begin a week full of endless possibilities.

Years later on my second trip there, it was the middle of July in 2000 and as I said, the sun never really set. We were somewhere else in town eating and drinking. We noticed it was 12:30 am and it seemed like maybe 7:30 pm. People were out and in the streets like it was nothing. We were driving to the Kenai early next morning so we figured 12:30 am was a good time to call it a night until someone said, "Hey! We can't go to bed without having a nightcap at the Captain Cook Lounge!"

So up we went and spent two more hours drinking dirty martinis until we finally staggered--and I literally mean drunkenly, sloppily staggered, back to our hotel, and got all of two hours sleep before it was time to pack up and go.

Now, back to the original trip.

Dawn came early on a dreary, rainy, cold late September morning. After our night of drunken revelry, we made it to the airport to meet our plane. The weather was bad enough that they were considering canceling the flight, but at the last minute decided to go. We loaded up our gear as well as supplies for our lodge and a lodge at Clark Fork, which was on the way. Now I certainly know nothing about flying or the load capacity of a single engine Cessna, but it seemed to me that we were taking on far more weight than seemed sane. But like I said, I was ignorant of any of that, so we loaded up, Bill sat in the front next to the pilot, and Michelle and I sat in the two back seats. I had bags of groceries under my feet and Michelle had a couple sacks of potatoes. We taxied down to the end of the runway, turned into the wind and light rain, and started down the runway. We slowly gathered speed, and as we began to lift off, a loud, persistent, "Beep, beep, beep," was heard along with a flashing light on the dashboard of the plane. Somewhat alarmed I asked what that was, and the pilot said, "Oh, don't worry about it. That's just the stall light and buzzer."

"Just the stall light and buzzer?"

"Yeah, we might stall, but we'll probably be OK in a couple of seconds."

"Holy shit." So apparently there IS a weight limit to these planes. We seemed to struggle and kind of hang in the air for a few seconds like the engine was consciously debating whether or not the take-off was worth the extra effort. As we collectively held our breath, it must have decided it was actually possible to become airborne, and it haltingly lifted us into the sky. Bill, who had flown planes, later said, "Yeah, I didn't want to scare you guys, but it was about fifty-fifty whether or not we were gonna make it."

I replied, "It's probably good you didn't say anything because it would have been a long flight if I would have shat my pants."

It was about a two-hour flight from Anchorage to the lodge, and since we were in a small plane and loaded down, instead of flying above the mountains, we flew below the peaks, following the river valleys and glacially carved canyons to get to our destination. This proved to be unbelievably exciting and scenic, as we got close-up views of glaciers and their ancient, almost alien looking bright blue ice, whose melt fed the rivers below us and flowed either the same blue color or ran white with glacial silt. We followed these craggy rock-lined canyons until we reached Lake Clark, where we dropped off supplies and then took off again for the Kvichak. Our flight took us over Iliamna Lake, Alaska's largest freshwater lake and over the world famous upper and Lower Talarik Creek, which we never did fish.    Finally, at the base of Iliamna Lake the Kvichak emerged, and we landed on a dirt airstrip next to the native Alaskan village of Igiugig, pronounced "iggy-ahggy," which translates roughly, "Like a throat that swallows water." It was named for its location near the mouth of the Lake Williams River where it feeds into the Kvichak. As we flew over the village we noticed the

Bill and me in the boat on the Kvichak River in Alaska. He's smiling because Michelle just peed in the water and he magically caught a fish!

wooden fish stands covered with salmon that the native Alaskans were drying for the winter, as they've done for thousands of years.

I don't know if you could call Igiugig an actual town, or village for that matter. In the 2010 census, its population stood at fifty, losing three of its inhabitants since the census in 2000. It, like the rest of this area, had no roads that lead to any civilization, making it totally isolated, except by plane or boat. The inhabitants got around on ATV's and their small boats and pretty much needed to fish and hunt to live. Supplies were flown in on an intermittent schedule, and surprisingly, Igiugig hosted a post office/general store, which was open for only a half-hour each day. No kidding. Interestingly, the village was originally settled by the Russians back in the 1800's and still has a tattered yet functioning domed Russian Orthodox church which today seems like an historical edifice that dropped down from outer space.

The area surrounding us was tundra, with large areas of low-lying brambles and bushes. The mountains were off in the distance in pretty much every direction. Specifically, we were in southwestern Alaska. If we would have kept flying in the same direction, we would have ended up in the Aleutians. The Kvichak drains into Kvichak Bay, which is an arm of Bristol Bay. Bristol Bay is fortunate to have the largest sockeye salmon runs in the world, and it also has runs of chum, pink, silver, and king salmon. This makes Bristol Bay a huge commercial fishery and the Kvichak is a popular sport fishing destination, primarily during salmon season. The river is also host to some of the largest native rainbow trout in Alaska, possibly the world, which is why we were there.

Which briefly, brings us to the controversial Pebble Mine project.

The proposed gold, copper and molybdenum mine, proposed by British/Australian/Japanese groups, is projected to produce ten billion tons of mining waste that will have to be permanently stored in the area, which is an active earthquake zone. And the part that frightens all of us? The area where the mine will be located drains into the Bristol Bay watershed. If you've been to any fishing shows, or read any fishing magazines, you are most likely aware of the coordinated efforts to prevent this mine from being approved.

It's quite simple, really. The mine is a horrible idea and needs to be stopped. I won't get into the politics of it here, but any idiot can see how bad of an idea this is. Waste storage in an active earthquake zone? I don't think so. This is a prime example of douchebags with a whole lot of money trying to make a whole lot more money despite the potentially grave peril they could put the environment in, not to mention the possibility of wiping out a thriving commercial and sport fishing industry. Think of how few healthy salmon runs are left in the world, especially the western United States. How many have been wiped out by over logging and dam building? And now plans are in place to put the biggest sockeye salmon fishery in the world in danger? Give me a break. If you haven't checked it out yet, Google "Pebble Mine" and see what you find.

The plane landed, we got our gear, and walked over to the riverbank where Frank's boat was waiting, as his lodge was across the river and maybe a quarter-mile downstream. Frank's lodge was perfectly situated on the river, across from an island and close to the lake with easy access to the braided waters downstream that held monster rainbows, arctic char, and grayling. I pulled out many rainbows averaging around six pounds without having to leave his property. Downstream and separated from Frank's by a tiny slough and seated on a small berm was another lodge which was recently raided by the feds, apparently over copious amounts of cocaine that were being processed and distributed there. More on that place later.

Frank is tall, lanky, and according to Michelle, hung like a mule, which apparently was a major part of the reason for flying thousands of miles for a reunion. He is not your typical lodge owner. Bill and his wife had stayed with him one time several years ago, back before he swore off ingesting legal and questionably legal intoxicants. He had stories where once Frank would make sure all of his guests were of the same mind, he would lock the doors and the frat-style parties would ensue. Frank had an intimate relation with the guys who owned the world-famous strip bar, the Great Alaskan Bush Company (more on that place later too), so you can only imagine the hijinks that occurred. Bill got so out of control one night that he decided it would be really funny if he got about two feet of monofilament with a lead bell sinker attached to the end, tied it around his member and swung it around like a Ron Jeremy windmill. Don't know if he got hurt or hurt anyone else with it. I guess you had to be there.

Frank is also a pilot and had recently crashed his plane twice and walked away from both wrecks without a scratch. This was the primary reason we never made it to Talarik Creek, which was only about a fifteen-minute flight from the lodge. He also owned a large boat with which he took his guests out onto the lake for some "Gentlemen's Fishing." We did it one evening after dinner. Frank and the three of us went out with a couple of his guides, who rigged our lines that were slowly trolled behind the boat as we all sat in the cabin enjoying a fine cocktail and a cigar. If one of the lines went down, we'd get up, go outside and land what was usually a rainbow in the six-pound range. Not "real" fishing by any means, just an excuse to go out on the water and get lit and possibly catch a fish or two.

The real fishing was on the river. The current on the Kvichak was stronger than any river I've been on. We were warned not to wade over our knees because they'd never find our bodies, or they'd find the gnawed-on skeletal remains years later further downstream. There was a constant background hiss that you heard while fishing. Our guide told us it was the sound of rocks, pebbles, and sediment being pushed along the bottom by the flow. Don't know if I totally bought that explanation, but I chose to believe it because it sounded so cool.

As I said, it was the end of September, Frank's last week before he closed the place down, winterized it, and left for warmer environs. It was chilly, not cold, and when it wasn't cloudy, the autumn sun hovered at a constant thirty degrees above the horizon where it passed from morning to dusk, our daylight cast in muted yellow hues. You always hear horror stories about hoards of Alaskan insects that will fly up your nose, get inside your clothing, and strip the skin right off your bones. We were hoping that since it was this late in the season the bugs would all be dead. Most were, but not all. There were still enough of the little bastards around that I kept a cigar constantly burning, the smoke keeping the bugs away just enough to keep me sane.

Michelle did not fly fish, and Bill decided not to, so they were given spinning gear, while I steadfastly kept to my 8-weight, generally fishing with egg-sucking leeches or orange flesh flies, which mimic shreds of dead salmon. Our guide also insisted that I use this silver gizmo shaped like an oval strike indicator, with wings that rotated—a garish whore of a fly that looked like a miniature spaceship out of a bad sci-fi flick. Because of the powerful current, we had to get the flies down quickly, so Randy, our guide, would not use BB shot, but a small bell sinker about a foot above the fly. As we drifted, you knew you were on the bottom by the tap-tap-tapping of the sinker against the rocks. So many of these fish had never seen a fly or a lure for that matter, and almost seemed surprised that they were hooked. Once they figured it out, they jumped more and fought harder than any rainbow I have fished for. But the thing that astounded me the most was Michelle's secret ritual that made us catch fish.

As you know, the only way to relieve yourself in the middle of the wilderness is whip it out and let it flow. In fact, even environmentalists say if you're in a boat and have to pee, don't get out of your boat and use a convenient tree or shrubbery. Pee IN the river. It is diluted almost immediately and does virtually no harm. And that goes double for the Alaskan wilderness because who knows if there's a mama bear with her cubs within sniffing distance from you just as you have your waders around your ankles and are in mid-stream. I don't like the survivability odds of such a scenario. Every time Michelle felt the call of nature, she'd go to the back of the boat, shimmy out of her waders, stick her bare behind over the stern, and let it flow all while the boat was drifting downstream. And every single time she did it, we got a fish. By the end of the trip, we were insisting that she drink more water.

It took me until the day before we left to hook and land my biggest rainbow, and this one had nothing to do with Michelle's bladder. As I said, I was using an 8-weight which most people would think too heavy of a rod for trout fishing. Not so. Even with a six-pounder, the fish would take me to my backing and sometimes to the end of it. Bill and Michelle were trolling with large silver lures off the back of the boat, and I was pounding the shore with an egg sucking leech with a small sinker described earlier, a foot above it. I would cast a little ahead of the boat, let it get to the bottom and strip back. The trout came out from under the bank where there was a bunch of scrub brambles. It made a pass at the leech, swiped and missed, and after nearly defecating in my waders, I quickly regained my composure and continued stripping. It hit like a freight train, immediately jumped and then took off up-stream like a bullet. I was into my backing almost immediately as Bill and Michelle frantically reeled their lines in. Then I was at the end of my backing. I was wondering what to do next other than just hold on, and then it stopped. The give and take began. The trout would allow me to reel all my backing in and then take off again. As the fish tired, the runs eventually got shorter and shorter until we finally boated a beautiful silvery thirteen-pound wild rainbow. After we landed it, we saw there was something on its anal fin, and then realized it had been previously caught and tagged by Alaska Game and Fish. Apparently, when you catch one of these tagged fish, you're supposed to remove the tag, measure and weigh the fish, and let them know when and where you caught it. All that was interesting enough, but it kind of bummed me out too because I was hoping my biggest trout was one that had never seen human hands. Oh well. It was a fight for the ages.

It was after lunch and we were all sitting around in a food coma debating on the merits of either taking a nap or getting back at it with the big trout, when Randy said, "You guys tired of catching trout?"

On any other day that would have been a ludicrous question, as we never get tired of catching trout, but that morning we had hooked and landed countless big strong rainbows, again all in the six-pound range or bigger, as well as several arctic char and even a couple graylings. It was also the morning we mistook a porcupine about the size of a Prius for a brown bear until we saw the quills. I said, "I wouldn't say were tired of catching 'em, but what did you have in mind?"

"Well, there's a backwater about a mile downstream that is full of northern pike. Wanna give it a go?"

It took us about two seconds to agree to this sideshow, so we climbed back in the boat. Randy started the motor and off we sped downstream, holding our breath at times as he navigated us through labyrinthine narrow veins of water through marsh grass and scrub as fast as he could. It became evident to us that he either knew this river like the back of his hand, or he was psycho-crazy, intent on killing us. We survived, which gave credence to his knowledge of navigating the river.

The backwater was a small dead-end slough, fed on top by a riffle that went completely across its mouth, creating a large, wide pool behind it. It was full of vegetation, and Randy said the pike were hiding under the weeds, mostly at the top of the slough. We would cast to the top where the water was still moving, and let the fly drift down and drop into the slower water below. Randy tied on a flesh fly, and my first cast resulted in a vicious surface strike before the fly had a chance to sink. We landed it, and it didn't look like the big healthy pike I used to catch in Canada as a kid. This one was about five pounds, skinny, almost sickly looking, dark green but with a sallow yellow coloring to it. I asked Randy about them and he said, "They're all like that. There's a million of 'em in here, actually too many to sustain the area, so they get stunted like that, but I guarantee you, you will at least get a strike on every cast."

He was right. It was like fishing for brookies in a kiddie pool. Every cast resulted in a strike and a fish. We could have stayed there for the rest of the day and probably caught a hundred of these mutants. But an hour or two of this was enough, and we headed back upstream before it got dark. Also, Michelle had to pee again, and she wanted to use the bathroom at the lodge this time. But, we wouldn't let her, and as a result, Bill ended up landing a nine-pounder before we called it a day.

Bubba was one of the more colorful guides working Frank's lodge. He is a large burly man with a full beard and lots of guns. An avid, almost fanatical hunter, he proclaimed that his motto in life was, "Stop a beating heart each day." I hoped he didn't mean a human heart. And he did his best to accomplish that. One late afternoon after we were back at the lodge and were sitting around drinking beer and talking about the day's fishing, Bubba stood up, whipped out his .44 Magnum and proclaimed that he was going caribou hunting right then. He walked outside and disappeared into the brush, returning a couple of hours later with no caribou, or anything else for that matter. At least he tried.

Over the past week we had been noticing very large bear tracks followed by two sets of tiny tracks all around the lodge and near the abandoned DEA-busted lodge as well. It was obvious that this was a mother bear with her two little cubs, but nobody had actually seen them; so being the mental midgets that we were, we decided to hatch a harebrained plot.

The DEA lodge was on a braided sinew of the river and behind the structure was a large grass- covered open area surrounded by the surrounding forest. The back of the building was a single story with a metal roof that sloped down to about eight feet off the ground. After drinking one night, we decided it would be a great idea to "bait" the yard behind the lodge, and then right before dark climb up on the roof with a camera and get some great photos of mom and her kids. The guides all liked to eat any arctic char we caught, so we would bring them back. There were lots in the fridge and freezer, so Bubba thawed a bunch out, and along with table scraps, vegetables, apples, and anything else that a bear might find appealing. All got hauled into the middle of the clearing about an hour before dusk. We ate an early dinner. Fueled by alcohol, Bubba, Bill, and our guide Randy left Frank's and began the one hundred yard walk over to the DEA lodge. Michelle thought we were totally insane and refused to go. Bill was a great photographer and brought his Olympus with a telephoto lens, and Bubba brought a very large rifle with equally large bullets. I'm not sure of the caliber but I would imagine they could have easily brought down Frank's plane. I was given the task of carrying a large spotlight.

The four of us walked slowly and as quietly as possible, following the river and then using a narrow dirt path through some scrub, with Bubba and his big gun leading the way, just in case the bear showed up early. There was already an aluminum step ladder at the DEA lodge which we used to climb up on the metal roof. Randy was the last to make it up, and he dragged the ladder up on the roof when he was safely up, not knowing whether a motivated bear would be compelled to climb up and devour us. We kept the noise and conversation to a minimum, having mapped out the battle plan back at Frank's. The bait was in a pile directly in front of us, maybe 75 feet away. We would keep as perfectly quiet as possible. If and when the bear appeared and was onto the food, I would turn on the spotlight and Bill would start snapping away. Bubba would have his gun at the ready, just in case the bear decided she didn't like us.

We all looked at each other, nodded we were ready, and I shut off the flashlight. We waited in muted silence. It took a couple minutes for our eyes to adjust to what was a very dark night. The moon hadn't risen yet and being a clear, cold night, the curtain of stars swathed across the sky was our only light. We sat and waited. And waited. And waited some more. After what seemed like an hour sitting there in silence, we heard a twig snap in the distance to our right. Bubba looked at us and pointed to where he thought it came from and shushed us silently. Then came another crackling noise and more twigs snapping. Something was walking toward us and as it got closer, we could hear the exhalations and grunts of what was obviously a large animal. Personally, my heart was beating like a Keith Moon drum solo after he did several lines of Peruvian white. It was absolutely huge. You don't realize how big Alaskan brown bears were until you were face-to-face with one. Sniffing the air, it emerged from the trees, and made a beeline for the smorgasbord we had set out for it and began to feast. I was fascinated but completely scared shitless. So scared that I forgot it was my responsibility to turn the spotlight on. Bubba looked over at me with a look that plainly said, "You big pussy! Turn on the goddamn light!"

I did, not knowing that it might have been the absolute last task I would ever perform. The light, of course, startled the bear. It stopped eating, looked up, turned to face us, and the it did what brown bears do when they want a better look. It stood on its hind legs trying to figure out what the problem was.

That's when we all started doing the math. The lowest part of the metal roof was maybe eight feet off the ground. So, we looked at the bear, looked at the edge of the roof, and looked at the bear again. Damn. With arms outstretched, that bear could easily have reached it. We were frozen in time, afraid to move an inch, afraid to even breathe. The only solace we had was knowing Bubba had a bullet in the chamber, ready to go if necessary. The mother bear decided she didn't like this turn of events at all, and was curious as to what was going on. She started ambling towards our position, again sniffing the air. Bubba's had enough. Instead of shooting the bear, he fired a shot into the air, startling her. She stopped. Then, as our collective lives are flashing in front of us, she decided maybe she should retreat into the woods and come back later when there was no one around, so she turned around and headed back the same way she came, possibly reuniting with her two cubs who either didn't come with her or were told to stay behind until Mom gave them the all-clear. We sat there in stunned silence as we heard the sounds of her walking through the brush get softer and softer. At that point Bubba decided she was far enough away to make a break for it back to Frank's. This time, making as much noise as possible, we climbed off the roof and high-tailed it back to the lodge, this time with Bubba trailing behind, another bullet in his chamber.

I looked at Bill and asked, "Did you get any good shots of all that?" He shook his head no, and then I looked around his neck where the camera had remained untouched for the entire incident.

All good things must end, so on the morning of our last day at the lodge, we said goodbye to Frank, boarded the bush plane just as the first snow that we'd seen started falling lightly and took off to the east towards Anchorage. We made a brief stop at Lake Clark again, where they loaded two large kitchen grade plastic bins full of bloody caribou meat, one of which was unceremoniously put between my legs in front of my seat in an already overloaded plane, and the other, between Michelle's legs who was sitting in the seat next to me. This time the stall light and buzzer did not go off and we were airborne. The snow and the wind picked up right when we got into the canyon, and the wind blew the plane like a pinball back and forth between the canyon walls, causing us once again to see Jesus and at least some of his disciples.

Frank stayed at his lodge to finish closing it up and flew to Anchorage the next day, promising us the best sushi we'd ever had, along with another surprise before we boarded our overnight flight home.

It was late in the afternoon when he picked us up at our hotel in his beater of a car, held together by bailing wire and duct tape. He swore it was road-worthy, so off we went on the twisting, turning road that followed Cook Inlet, with the mountainside to our left and then a cliff that dropped precipitously into the inlet on our right. At some point we turned off to the left, right where a large, greasy, and ancient looking moose was nibbling on some roadside vegetation. We ended up at the local ski area, whose name escapes me. At the sushi place, Frank introduced us to the sushi chef who happened to be a world class ice sculptor and had won a crapload of awards. He pulled out his photo album and while we drank Sake and Tsingtaos he proudly showed off his art. And then as Frank promised, he brought out the best, freshest sushi I've ever had. It was one of those deals where he wouldn't let us order off the menu, he just kept bringing it until we had to stop.

So with a raw fish hangover and a little buzz, we headed back onto the highway. It was now totally dark, and on the same Cook Inlet road, Frank's headlights died, just like that. Realize that this trip was before cell phones. Frank pulled over on the shoulder, and not wanting to shut the car off in fear that it wouldn't start again, got out with a flashlight and fiddled around under the hood to no avail. He walked back, got behind the wheel and said "Fuck it. I always said I've driven this road so many times I could do it blindfolded, so I can sure do it without headlights."

Again, this was a road with a cliff leading to a watery grave on one side and a large imposing chunk of granite on the other. What choice did we have? Probably a few, hitchhiking or walking were two that I thought of. Despite the protestations of Bill and me, Frank put it in drive, and under a pitch black, moonless sky, we moved forward and downhill and lightless, on a road that had more than its share of blind curves and switchbacks. We had run out of gods and deities to pray to, so our only choice was to white-knuckle it for the last fifteen miles and pray that a semi driver that was hepped up on crank wasn't coming the other way.

Somehow, again, we made it. And once again, it was one of those incidents that when it was over, we all laughed about it, happy that we just dodged another bullet. We had several hours to go before we got on our plane to head back home. Our luggage was already in the back of Frank's car. Michelle was back at the hotel, and Frank was probably planning to go back there, knock one more off for good times, and then pick us up where he dropped us off. He pulled in front of the Great Alaskan Bush Company and opening up his wallet, handed Bill and me each a hundred-dollar bill and said, "Have a good time on me! See you in a couple of hours."

What choice did we have? As Frank sped away for his last carnal rendezvous, Bill and I walked into the joint, found a table and ordered drinks. Soon enough, two unbelievably hot girls slinked up to us and decided they are going to be our friends for the night. My new friend was beautiful, petite, exotic, and Korean, with garishly large breasts. She put on this shy attitude, almost like it was our first date. Bill's new friend could not have been different. She looked like Liv Tyler, except she was probably six feet tall, athletic, and had a nasty crazy attitude. Mine apparently saw me for the mark that I was. She would sit next to me making small talk in barely understandable English, not that I could hear her anyway, and every fifteen minutes or so she would ask, "You want dance?"

"Uhhhhhhh, OK!"

"Twenny dollah."

I forked over the cash and soon enough, I had blown through all of Frank's drinking allowance. As I handed her my last twenty, she said, "I be right back!" And never came back.

Bill's friend was another story. When my little companion ditched me, Bill's decided she was going hang with us and see how drunk all three of us could get. After several shots of who knows what, we were all tanked, and that's when her charming bipolar side kicked in. It soon became clear that she needed somebody to abuse, verbally and physically, and for some reason, she chose me over Bill. It started with witty banter and repartee—you know, subtle jabs and put-downs that you and your buddies engage in. It was all fun and games. I was dishing back as much as she was giving me. Then she was silent for a minute, walked over and stood in front of where I was sitting and said, "How long have you had that ponytail?"

This was obviously back in the day when I HAD a ponytail, which today, I am quite embarrassed by, being a bald man. Nothing could have been more pathetic.

Anyway, at that point, Bill knew something was up. Something that could prove to be very entertaining and he sat back, relaxed and prepared to enjoy the show.

"I don't know. I've had it for a couple years I guess."

"I like it!"

Usually, I didn't get many compliments on it because as I just said, I looked like an overcompensating balding dork.

"Thanks!" I said.

"You know why I like it?"

"No but I imagine you're gonna tell me."

"I need some love and affection!"

With that, she reached down and grabbed my tail and screamed at the top of her lungs so that everyone inside the bar and probably on the sidewalk outside could hear, and repeated herself.

"I need some love and affection!!!"

Using my ponytail as a convenient handle, she smashed my head into her breasts which smelled like roses and sweat, bellowed, "Tell me you love me! Tell me you love me!!!"

Again, what could I do? I yelled "OK! I love you I love you!" At that point the whole bar is cheering, and Bill is laughing so hard tears are running down his face.

"So, you love me Ponytail Boy?"

"I said I did, didn't I?"

"Well prove it!"

With her hand still securely attached to my tail, she rammed my head down to her crotch and yelled, "Tell me you love me again! Do it!!!!"

Despite the fact that I could barely get my jaw to work since it was crushed against her pubic bone, I yelped, "I love you!"

At this point, Bill was pounding his fists on our table, laughing at my predicament with wild abandon. The crowd again erupted in cheers, and I fell back onto my chair as she released me in triumph. She then sat next to me and whispered in my ear, "Now that was fun, wasn't it? Buy me a drink!"

That I did, and the bar, in appreciation of the performance also bought us a round. Bill was completely spent from laughing so hard, I was exhausted from the booze, adrenaline, and humiliation. Frank finally arrived with Michelle, we said goodbye, headed to the airport, bringing to a conclusion a week that would live on in my memories, mostly all good.

As a postscript to this story: Right before this book went to print, the Pebble Mine project lost one of its major investors, a HUGE victory for all the people who have worked long and hard to stop this project.

At this time, there is one major investor remaining, who said they still intend to go forward only if they can find another deep-pocketed investor. Obviously, this is a major positive step to securing the future of the Bristol Bay watershed, but more work may be required. Again, Google "Pebble Mine" to stay up to date.

# 30 FROM BULL REDS IN FLORIDA TO STEELHEADING IN CLEVELAND

*So each night, roving bands of drunken miscreants,*
*both male and female, would stagger up and down, back*
*and forth, screaming, yelling, swearing, puking, pissing,*
*trying to get laid, you name it. It was truly a parade*
*of despair.*

IT'S 7 AM AND I'M IN BUMPER-TO-BUMPER standstill
traffic, travelling on I-480 westbound, heading towards Cleveland.
Construction is causing us to lose two lanes at the I-271 North inter-
change, where there is always a backup during rush hour, hence the
construction trying to fix it. I have the radio on. I'm tired of Sirius XM
and of most commercial music radio. Because of the present political
climate, I avoid listening to Talk Radio, opting instead to tune into
Sports Talk. Always plenty of angst to talk about involving the Browns,
Cav's, or the Indians. The current topic involves baseball and how the
Cleveland Indians are eliminating Chief Wahoo, their mascot, citing
complaints from the Native American community. Considering that
Chief Wahoo is a leering, huge nosed, beet red-faced caricature of a Native American with teepee-shaped eyes, I agree wholeheartedly. There
is, however, overwhelming support to retain him from Cleveland fans,
who use history and tradition as their reasoning. One of the on-air guys
makes a point. The test is, he says, would you feel comfortable wearing
a Chief Wahoo hat onto a reservation? Personally, no. The other guy
makes another valid point. What if there was a team from Detroit called
the Detroit Negroes with an exaggerated mascot of a black man with
bulging eyes and huge lips? Or a team called the New York Jews with
the same stereotypical mascot? Or the San Francisco Chinamen? You
get the picture. Most of the phone callers continue to be idiots. But I
keep listening.

It's February, it's 25 degrees, and it's snowing, further complicat-
ing driving. And not just pretty little flurries, but a series of passing

heavy squall lines causing near blind-out conditions at times, despite the forecast for a warming trend. And I am going fishing.

Strangely, I am not heading out of the city to fish but into it. Ultimately, I'll be about a half-hour east of Downtown on the Chagrin River. I'm meeting my friend Ron to fish for Lake Erie steelhead, which at this time of year are swimming upstream to spawn. As I sit in traffic, I begin to reflect upon how in the hell did I get into this situation? I lived out west for over two decades with access to the best trout streams in the country. And even after I quit my job, I was still pretty much set. But now I'm sitting here, in traffic, in the snow, on my way to fish in a gritty urban area for transplanted steelhead. What the hell happened? A lot. On a number of levels. I described a lot of my situation at the beginning of the book, but bear with me.

Life has a way of fucking up all of your best-laid plans. Man...I thought we had it all figured out. The Little Woman and I retired early from our radio jobs in New Mexico after meticulously mapping out the rest of our lives. And we were damned excited! We already owned a nice house about a block from the ocean in Bethany Beach, Delaware. We also bought a modest but nice place across the street from the beach in Destin, Florida. We would be spending half of our time up north in Delaware, and then like every other geezer who could manage, would drop down to Florida for the colder months. Both areas, but Florida especially, promised great fishing, plenty of sunshine and a stress-free existence.

We arrived in Florida after New Year's Day and noticed immediately that we were considerably younger than the people surrounding us. Pale-faced, wrinkled, doddering, bad-driving, SLOW-moving senior citizens, mostly from Canada, shared the town with us. We made the mistake of going to the 'Welcome Snowbirds' party at the town hall. As we walked through the front door, it was quite evident to us that we didn't belong there, at least yet. There was a huge line of the walking dead, looking not unlike the security line at an airport. All were anxious to get any freebies that were being handed out. Some even brought their own bags for the occasion. Many of these people knew each other from winter's past, and if you were a stranger, you were greeted with, "So, where you from?" Then talk usually turned to discussing each other's various pains, ailments, diseases, which prescription drugs you were on, and who just died. After enduring a few minutes of this, we retreated to the house, and then to Camille's up the street for an early start on Happy Hour.

As the weeks wore on, we learned NOT to get behind any of these oldsters in lines at the grocery store, or the bank, or Target. And God forbid you got behind one of them driving up the two-lane road along the beach, which happened to be the only way to our house—10 to15 miles an hour was common, not just for a block or two, but for a mile or two, or three, or four. And some had no problem with coming to a dead stop in moving traffic because they liked that pretty boat out on the water, or they forgot where the gas pedal was. Leaning on your horn did no good. In fact, most times they would drive even slower just to spite you. And a few of the spunkier ones would flip you off, and that usually came from the wife in the passenger's seat.

The only win for us was, each day, sometimes several times a day, the EMT's would come screaming down the street, sirens blaring, and then return slowly and quietly with no lights, delivering another ancient stiff to the morgue. Such is the way living amongst the elderly. After reading this, you might think I am an unfeeling, even selfish douchebag, and you are probably justified for feeling that way. But let me assure you that as you continue reading, my feelings on the subject would change dramatically.

Then at the beginning of March, not unlike a caravan, or better yet, a funeral procession, all the Snowbirds left town at once, not to return until the following winter. With that, we thought we were free and clear of any stress-filled situations, but how wrong we would be. Not too long after they left, we encountered another situation that was the polar opposite of living with the fossils, and if possible, was even more infuriating—Spring Breakers.

When we bought the house, our realtor neglected to inform us that the street we were living on turned into Fraternity and Sorority Hell for two months. And it wasn't always that way. Several years ago, Destin was a quiet little beach town with nice restaurants, gorgeous beaches, and great fishing. But a couple of years ago, Fort Lauderdale decided to crack down on the Spring Breakers and actually started enforcing their laws about drinking on the beach or in public, and their noise ordinance began to get enforced in earnest. All of this was great for Fort Lauderdale, but not for us.

All of these entitled, college-aged alcoholics decided that both Panama City and Destin were the new best places to be, so they started coming in droves. And look, I know what you're thinking again. I'm just an old jerk-off who doesn't remember what it was like to be that young.

I say to you, fuck off. Yes, I was young once. I drank more than my share. I smoked a LOT of weed, and I'm sure looking back, there were times that I was just as much of an asshole. But guess what? I ain't 19 or 20 anymore, and my tolerance level for people like my younger self has completely disappeared. Now, all I want is a decent night's sleep. If you're in the house next to me screaming your nuts off while blaring hip-hop at 150 decibels at 3AM, I'm calling the cops. If you're poolside drinking beer through a plastic tube held by your idiot buddy on the second-floor balcony who is emptying a 40 into the funnel attached to the tube, I'm calling the cops.

If the same shit-faced idiot on the second-floor balcony decides it'd be a great idea to jump two stories down into the swimming pool while screaming at the top of his lungs, I'm calling the cops. If you decide the shrubbery in my front yard has a sign on it that says, "Free urinal! I invite you to piss in my yard!" I'm calling the cops. If you're a 19-year-old sorority girl who decided she's had too much to drink, and you walk over to my front yard overlooking my kitchen dinette where my wife and I are trying to enjoy our evening dinner, and you get on your knees while sticking a finger down your pretty little throat and puke all over my hibiscus, you guessed it, I'm calling the cops.

This became a real problem. After about three weeks of this, we were both in a state of what I can only describe as battle fatigue. Especially at night. We KNEW all the noise and debauchery was imminent, and we knew there was really nothing we could do about it, so we were stressed. I bought earplugs and we moved to the bedroom that we considered the most sheltered from all of it. Nothing worked. Even if we 'called the cops' and the houses surrounding us quieted down or they arrested all the under-aged drinkers, the street we lived on was a main corridor to the beach from a large group of rental houses about a quarter-mile away. Each night, roving bands of drunken miscreants, both male and female, would stagger up and down, back and forth, screaming, yelling, swearing, puking, pissing, trying to get laid, you name it. It was truly a parade of despair.

When it was finally over around the end of April, I was at the Publix talking to a local woman around my age who lived nearby. I was complaining about what we just went through, expecting some commiseration, and she looked at me quizzically and said, "I'm sorry, did you say you stayed here during Spring Break? All the locals know to leave town no later than the second week in March and return at the end of April. That's what we all do!" Why didn't anyone tell us?

There was only one incident during the three years of putting up with this crap that anything positive happened, but only for me, not my wife. One year a sorority rented the house next door where the guy was drinking out of the tube the year before. It was mid-afternoon and all the young, beautiful college girls were out around the pool in the backyard. My back bedroom on the second floor has a window that overlooks the pool. This was the bedroom where I set up an office and did all my writing. This particular afternoon, after several beers, or wine coolers, or whatever sorority girls drink, they all thought it would be the best idea ever to remove their bikini tops and cavort in the pool. Of course, they had no idea that a fifty-something guy was upstairs trying to write this book. But there they were, in all their glorious nakedness. You may think of me as some kind of pervert. The proper action on my part would have been to close the blinds on the window or even leave the room. Yeah right. Like THAT'S gonna happen. For next half-hour or so, I reveled in watching the floor show. I did call my buddy Dan and told him what I was observing, and he said "Take some pics, dude!" I declined. At least I had some morality left in my voyeuristic soul.

After three years of this, I found myself torn in two, my brain despairing with existential angst. I LOVED the area...beautiful beaches and water with plenty of fishing opportunities. But I DESPISED those two months, those months being the major reason we decided to spend winter and spring there. And those supposedly idyllic months were being desecrated by idiots. Should we bag it and sell the place? Would that be admitting defeat? Would the little fuckers actually win the war? Sadly, the decision would be made for us.

As I described earlier, Marti's parent's health was failing, and they couldn't maintain their condo or physically take care of each other anymore. Thus, we were required...wrong word...needed...back in Cleveland. Both of her sisters were living and working in California, and we were pretty much jerking off. We were the logical choice to take care of them. Now mind you, this was something we wanted to do. We viewed it as a natural part of life, the kids taking care of their elderly parents. We forgot to have kids, so I have been drilling into my friend Al's daughter's brain that she would be changing our adult diapers when the time comes. Lucky her.

Despite all of that, the house in Florida was a money pit. It had been through several costly hurricanes, one that blew the roof off the year Katrina hit. Then another year, wood rats decided they liked the HVAC ductwork in the crawl space underneath the house so much, they decided to move in. That required the "Critter Gitters" exterminators to pay us a visit with their rattraps, snares, and every other implement of destruction. After they were done with the killing and maiming, we replaced every shredded, rat urine-soaked inch of our ductwork with impenetrable sheet metal.

The moving truck was arriving the next morning, and my brother Jim and I had boxed up all our precious belongings, including two giant boxes of fishing accoutrements, but not everything. It was a beautiful sunny late afternoon in early fall with temperatures in the low 80's and for some strange reason, not humid, and I vowed to get one more fishing day in before we abandoned ship. I left my surf rod out with my sand spike and a slop bucket. I had some leftover shrimp in the fridge that was going in the trash the next day, so with those, a couple Coronas and a fine Dominican cigar, I headed towards the beach. There were still several beach-goers near me, but unlike the Delaware shore, I was not only graciously, but enthusiastically welcomed. As I've said, the sand on this beach is pure crystal white making the water Caribbean blue-green. The bottom very gently slopes outward, so to get any beyond waist high, you need to wade out and chuck it pretty good. I baited my hooks with yesterday's uncooked dinner leftovers, waded out, and threw it out into the blue. I walked back onto the beach and stuck my rod into my waiting sand spike. As I turned around to find a beer and cigar, my beach companions immediately started yelling, "Hey! HEY! You have a bite!" I turned around just in time to see my rod bent almost in two, then knocking down the sand spike and making a beeline for the water. This was no pompano. I grabbed the rod before it launched into the water, reeled a couple times and set the hook as hard as I could. Whatever was on the other end took off for open water as I frantically adjusted my drag. Then it stopped and started swimming back and forth parallel to the beach. A shark, I thought. Maybe a ray, but something seemed...different...so I wasn't really sure. A crowd included the beaches two lifeguards gathered to watch the show as I fought the beast. As it got closer, I was still trying to guess what it could be...Too close in for a billfish...or a king mackerel for that matter...or a mahi...a big jack maybe? Then I finally saw the red flash about fifty feet beyond the beach. It was the biggest bull redfish I had ever seen, actually too big to keep, since the limit size was far smaller than this monster.

As has happened in the past, there are times I have difficulty getting larger fish beached because I can't get them out of the surf if I have lighter test line on, which I did. The fish was obviously tiring, and I didn't want to snap the line, nor did I want to wear it out to the point of killing it. As my luck would have it, there happened to be a guy in the surf about twenty feet down shore of the battle, completely oblivious to what was going on. I looked at him and shouted, "Can you give me a hand with this?" He looked at me quizzically and I pointed towards the red and said "The fish! Can you either grab the fish or the line and get it out of the waves?" I could tell he'd never done anything like this before, but I will give him credit for being game. He waded over, grabbed the line, and pulled the exhausted red through the waves onto the beach, to the roaring approval of the crowd and me! I didn't have a scale or a measuring tape, but this fish was maybe forty inches, fat, and beautiful. Everyone pulled out their phones and started snapping, and one guy emailed me the photo that's in this book, which looks like I'm having an intimate moment with it. I unhooked it and gently revived and watched it swim away to fight another day. With that, I put my rod back into the sand spike, sat down, cracked open a beer, lit a cigar and was done fishing. A fitting end to my life in Florida, at least for now. Now, where was I?

Cleveland, Ohio. My hometown. The place of my birth. Even after my prolonged absence, I still have family and friends here. I still am a Cleveland sports fan, something that is beat into you from infancy. Honestly, it's a pleasant place to live-for six months out of the year. The remaining six months can be challenging, unless you enjoy slogging through all forms of snow, sleet, freezing rain, and at times, sub-zero temperatures. If you like that kind of thing, fine. I don't happen to. Another charming aspect is the copious use of salt on the roads. I have owned my truck for 13 years...bought it in New Mexico and proudly has not a speck of rust on it, and I'm desperately trying to keep it that way. I look around at the cars on the street next to me that are rotting from the ground up, some tied together with bailing wire to keep the rusted-out bumper from falling off.

Now I'm sitting in a Cleveland traffic jam during a snow squall, trying to get to the Chagrin River for my first attempt at catching a steelhead. All my years of fly-fishing and never had the chance.

The snow squall has diminished somewhat as I pull into the town of Willoughby and park in a small park near the river behind the Willoughby Brewing Company. I make a mental note that this is where we'll go after the fishing is over. Ron is already there, rigging up his newly acquired 8-weight. Ron is a large man with a scruffy brown beard, a baker by profession, who works at a local boutique grocery store with Al. An avid outdoorsman, he gets his deer every year, usually in Pennsylvania, and attempts to get a turkey in the spring and fall. He is the proud new owner of a classic 26' Chris Craft, with a cabin underneath to overnight in. He just spent the fall re-furbishing it and can't wait to get out on Lake Erie for some walleye and perch fishing. But now, as the snow changes to snow pellets, he's putting on a large garish steelhead fly with a trailing egg pattern.

"You know, I've never done this before," I say.

"One of two things will happen," he replies. "We'll get down to the river and they'll be thick as shit, or we'll end up blind casting and hope for the best."

I had visited the local fly shop the day before and let the owner pick out what he thought I'd need. I showed the box to Ron and he picked out what appears to be a crystal white wooly bugger with orange flash. "Put that on, and trail it with a yellow egg pattern."

The snow temporarily stopped as we started our descent down to the Chagrin, which is a wide, tree-lined river that has both a railroad and street bridge running over it. Several businesses and houses back up to it on our side, and the other is a wide expanse of woods and open space. Traffic noise is ever-present, so any illusion of having a 'wilderness experience' is quickly squashed. We choose to enter where Erie Street crosses the river. We walked down a short but steep partially snow-covered embankment. The bridge supports and to some extent, the bridge itself is covered in graffiti. As we arrived at the pebble-covered high-water wash, I noticed not all are pebbles, but some are artifacts of urban decay, including ancient bricks worn smooth by centuries of rushing water, and broken ceramic sewer-pipe shards among the stones. The river bottom is rocky but also strewn with logs and branches, washed downstream from years of flooding, virtually guaranteeing several lost rigs.

We enter the river and notice that the steelhead are not thick as shit. As we scan the water, we see none. "That doesn't mean they aren't here," Ron says. "Just cast towards the far bank and let your fly swing

through the current. Then walk a few feet downstream and do it again."
Okay then. Something I'm very familiar doing with trout.

For some reason and I don't know why, when I'm fishing for something new, I tend to have immediate success. That often pisses people off or at least pisses off those who are highly competitive. I caught my first ever permit on the first cast, making me wonder what all the fuss was about. That was damned easy, I thought. It was a long time before I caught my second. I made my first cast to the bank upstream about twenty feet and let it drift downstream to the end of my line where it began to swing across the current, as I was told to do. At the bottom of the swing, my phone buzzed, so I stopped, put my rod under my arm, and dug my phone out of my top vest pocket to view a text from Marti telling me to pick up dinner on the way home. I put my phone back in my vest pocket, and lifted my rod to start stripping in the line. That was met with a large pulsing, rod bending strike. Totally NOT expecting it, I instinctively set the hook. The large silver fish jumped and then took off downstream on its first of several runs. Ron was upstream with the large net, too far to be of any help, while I unlatched my insufficient rubber trout net from the back of my vest. The fish was tiring and I successfully led it towards the pebbly bank, managing to get about half of it into my net. My first steelhead. About 10 pounds, still silver and shining brightly, not beat up yet by the rigors of the spawn. And caught on my first cast with absolutely no skill whatsoever, an exercise in pure luck and happenstance. Ron finally trudged downstream to congratulate me, and since he didn't see the strike or any of the battle, I could've lied to him about how it took on the perfect drift at the perfect point, but I told him the truth, that my wife's text was more responsible for the catch than I was.

The rest of the day was not successful. Ron maybe landed two more and quite frankly, that was it for me. In a late-afternoon light snow squall, we headed back to the truck and since we were in an urban area, made a two-minute drive to a local microbrewery where we finished the day warming up, eating burgers and enjoying an adult beverage or two.

Switch to spring, two years later. I've been out several times now with mixed results. Now I'm on the Grand River, which is about a half-hour's drive east of Cleveland. The weather is beautiful-sunny, 70 degrees, and the steelhead are definitely in the river. But so are the other fisherman. I've written about combat fishing before, and this is the urban definition of it. Anglers are lined up in the water, each marking their territory, and each making endless casts into the current, some catching fish, most not. Me, thinking that I'm this big-time expert fly-fisher, I decided that I would use lighter tippet and leaders this time, thinking I had the level of skill required to land these fish. I'd show them all! Look at me! I am Mr. Pro! Yeah, right.

The first strike came quickly, almost immediately as my flies hit the water. The other thing that came quickly was how fast the fish destroyed my ego. It was gone after a very short fight. As was the next, and the next, and the next. I started counting. I lost eleven steelhead in a row, broke them all off. I ran out of flies in the process. Disheartened, disgruntled, defeated, and humiliated, I left the water, vowing to return. I immediately drove to the fly shop in Chagrin Falls, and re-stocked my supply, as well as purchasing several 0-weight leaders and 15 lb. test tippet. As it happened, exactly a week later, the weather was again, uncharacteristically spectacular for northeast Ohio, so I ventured back to the same river, at the same time. For some reason, the throng of anglers was not as bad, so I had a little more room to roam. I geared up, locked the truck in the parking lot and trudged upstream to nearly exactly the same place I was the week before. As I said another beautiful day. The leaves on the trees were bright green, birds were singing, but I was laser focused on revenging my failures from the week before.

I cast upstream to the bank and let the fly drift down and swing below me. Boom. Big strike. Again, didn't take long. But this time, I was armed for bear, or at least big steelhead. The fight ensued and—finally—landed my first fish. Beautiful silver, hadn't been in the river that long so it was still strong and fresh, maybe 10 pounds. Another cast. Another big hit, and another fish. This one somewhat smaller but that was two in about fifteen minutes of fishing. And then, another. With the heavier line I was able to bear down a whole lot harder during the fight, and the line weight did not seem to matter to the fish, since they struck just as readily as they had when I was underpowered. My third fish in less than a half hour. Now the other anglers on the river started to take notice. I've explained the 'San Juan Creep' that happens on the San Juan River in New Mexico. You start catching fish, and then slowly, everyone else starts moving towards you until you are shoulder-to-shoulder with a bunch of inconsiderate knuckleheads. Same here. I said screw this and moved downstream. After a couple minutes, another strike, another fish, and again: it was like I was the Pied Piper, because now the creep was happening again! I could have led these dudes off a cliff! I started counting fish again, and when all was said and done, I landed 12. I could have landed more, but I was actually getting tired, it was late afternoon, and I hated driving in Cleveland rush-hour traffic. I packed it in, leaving all the other guys to fend for themselves. I'm sure they caught a fish or two.

*It's gotten to the point if someone comes up to me on the stream and asks me if I'm going to keep the fish I just caught, I'll say "No, I'm practicing torture and release!"*

# 31 THE END—MAYBE

AFTER ALMOST TWO YEARS OF WORKING on this book, I'm finally at the finish line. It's not as long as I would have liked, and I have found that I probably don't have the discipline and work ethic to be a writer of books. I have a newfound respect for those who do have the talent.

I have fished all of my life. It is the common thread that runs through my existence. My earliest memories involve fishing and the most enjoyable, even profound experiences have happened to me while on a stream, in a boat, or on a beach. Flyfishing in particular, insists on the perfect amount of skill that makes you concentrate just enough to stay completely in the present. The stresses and problems of daily life are at least temporarily forgotten as you strive to make that perfect cast upstream so your fly floats by that big rock where you know a trout is waiting to ambush it.

Fishing has allowed me to see the world and how other people live. I have seen some of the worst slums in the world where desperate people were begging in the streets for their basic survival. I have also been fortunate to have stayed at places where only the wealthy could afford. I have learned that there is great inequality in this world, but have also learned that money, or lack of it, does not make you a good or bad person.

As it often happens, conversation with fellow fisherman can be wide-ranging; at one point the subject turned to organized religion and my buddy Milt thought for a minute and said, "You know, being out on a stream in a beautiful place on a beautiful day is my way of going to church." I have no argument with that.

I have felt the presence of creation, of the infinite if you will, while wading a sand flat in the Caribbean, surrounded by brilliant blue water that changed colors almost like a kaleidoscope while I stared out towards the horizon.

I was humbled by the beauty of it all as I watched the spectacular oranges and reds in a sunset over the Tetons while fishing the Snake River.

I watched stunned and amazed as a herd of elk during rutting season on the Upper Brazos River in New Mexico, thundered down from out of the tree line on a hillside and crossed the river maybe two hundred feet in front of me, and time literally slowed down to a crawl, making it seem like they were running in slow-motion.

I've watched an osprey circle high up in the air over the Deschutes River in Oregon, and spotting its prey, go into a nearly vertical dive and snatch a trout bigger than I'd caught all day.

In Alaska, I've seen a large chunk of a glacier break loose and crash into the sea, hearing the deafening roar and feeling the percussion of hit hitting the water. Also in Alaska, I've watched brown bears fishing for salmon on a glacial stream that was coming off a volcano, as we flew low over it in our sea plane.

I remember a particular night while on the dive boat in Bimini. It was a beautiful warm evening with a full moon, and I was standing on the back of the boat with my fly rod as I often did, casting a streamer, not for anything particular. It was quiet--the only sound I heard was the waves gently lapping against the hull of the boat. I was facing towards the moon and its light was reflecting off the ripples on the water caused by a slight tropical breeze. Something made me stop casting, and I stood there with my eyes slightly unfocused. The moonlight on the water became an infinite number of dancing diamonds. The surface of the water had become alive, almost fairy-like, with life. As I stood there, I became aware that my consciousness had shifted. I was acutely aware of sights, sound, even the smell of the water, and for lack of a better term, I experienced the interconnectedness of it all. Everything in that moment was absolutely perfect, and occasionally in my mind, I will go back to that experience and still recall the feeling.

OK, so maybe it's all bullshit.

Could be. It just might be a combination of endorphins, a few glasses of wine kicking in at the same time, or a bad shrimp I ate a couple of hours before. But needless to say, life with a rod in my hand (so to speak) has been pretty damned awesome!

On a more down-to-earth level, I've felt the camaraderie and good will with a bunch of guys who after experiencing a great day of fishing were now around a campfire or sitting in front of a fireplace, enjoying a fine cigar and an intoxicating beverage, reliving the day and telling tales of fishing trips from days past.

Again, the feeling BEFORE a fishing trip is also unmatched. All the anticipation and excitement of what is to be...the preparation, the packing, all of that is special. Before a trip, I still get my fishing vest out of the garage and put it on the kitchen table to take inventory. I'll re-arrange the flies, discard any that are damaged, make a mental list of what new flies I might need. I'll remove the half-smoked cigar butts and trash from the pockets, make sure I have enough leaders and tippet, and sometimes if I'm really geeked, I'll even throw the vest in the washer to get all the ground-in river crap out of it.

Memories are plentiful. I find myself frequently replaying the ones where the big fish got away, fish that actually won the battle of strength and wits. I don't remember these with frustration but with a strange kind of satisfaction knowing we don't always win!

And lately—actually, for the past several years—I've been experiencing a feeling that I'm finding is more common than I thought among some fishermen. I've been practicing catch-and-release for years, not only with flyfishing but with other types as well. As I stated before, I've altered rigs even on my surf fishing gear so they do less damage to the fish I hook. Believe me, I am not above catching and killing a fish. Nothing is better than a freshly caught brown trout dredged in cornmeal and pan fried in butter or a just-out-of-the-ocean bluefish that has been properly cleaned and filleted. But in over 90 percent of the time I'm fishing, I'll let 'em go, and if most fisherman think about it, the majority of the fish they catch are usually too small to keep anyway

Another beautiful day in Destin, Florida. I fly fish near the pilings of a pier destroyed by Hurricane Opal, while pelicans watch.

and get thrown back, so everyone practices catch-and-release to some degree. But now, I'm starting to weigh the pros and cons of even doing this, and at times I've been having moral existential angst over the practice. It's gotten to the point where if someone comes up to me on the stream and asks me if I'm going to keep the fish I just caught, I'll say, "No, I'm practicing torture-and-release!" Then they kind of chuckle and walk away thinking I'm some kind of lunatic.

Am I overthinking this? Probably. But here's my thought process anyway: Catching and killing is understandable, IF you eat the fish and not let it sit in your freezer for two years to get freezer burn, dehydrated to the point that it looks like some form of Scandinavian desiccated herring gone bad. But catch-and-release is pretty much deriving pleasure by torturing a fish, making it fight for its life.

Damn.

Have you ever seen any of those underwater shots of a trout, or any other fish for that matter being hooked? Trout swim frantically trying either to dislodge the hook or find a suitable place to hide from whatever is trying to hurt them. Of course, you've heard the argument that because of the way that fish are wired, they don't experience pain like we do. Well, watching those videos convinced me that they certainly know stress and most likely, fear. A saltwater experience I had nearly broke my heart. There was a school of false albacore feeding in the surf in Florida. I made the perfect cast and hooked a nice one, and then I really started paying attention to what the fish was doing. Instead of running out to sea to get away from me, it continually tried to get back into the school where all its friends were. Every time they would swim close, it would desperately take off in their direction and try to join them, even swim with them awhile, until my line pulled it away. I finally landed and released the fish, and feeling totally bummed, got my gear, turned and walked back to the house.

Is it morally acceptable that we get pleasure from causing another creature discomfort? When we finally end our time on the planet and if we find that karma is real, will we spend eternity being tortured, caught, having our picture taken with some higher (or lower) life form, and then let go to have it happen all over again? Or maybe when we die, our eternity will be constantly fishing, and to our horror, mis-hooking and killing fish after fish? My buddy Al and I always joked that in another existence, we'll be walking down a city street and there will either be a bag full of money or maybe a picnic basket with some great food inside. One of us bends to pick it up before we notice the large treble hook underneath. The hook is set by something above, and up we go to some interdimensional lake surface on which floats an interdimensional boat.

This is the stuff of my nightmares.

I have an old friend who apparently is having similar thoughts, but loves everything about flyfishing. He still goes but now cuts the hook off of his dry flies, and claims he is just as happy getting the strike as he was catching and landing the trout. It got to be too much for him. "Trout are beautiful, noble creatures," he said. "I can sit for hours and watch them feed in the stream, moving out from their hiding place under a large rock into the current, taking a bug, and then moving back. They are full of grace and the wildness of nature itself. Who am I to cause them distress?"

He makes a valid point. And every once and a while I vow that I, too, will stop this barbaric practice and either follow his lead, or walk away from fishing completely.

But I can't.

Something in my nature will not let me. Is it the life I've led? My father teaching me how to fish at a very early age? How almost every vacation we took when I was a kid involved fishing?

Is it an addiction to the thrill of the initial strike which shoots directly to the pleasure centers in your brain, not unlike heroin, cocaine, or the lights and bells and whistles on a slot machine?

Is it the competition between man and beast? The primal feeling of having something wild and alive at the end of your line?

Is it the stuff? All the equipment, rods, flies, lures, boats, clothes, travel, camaraderie, the lifestyle itself?

Or is it something deeper, something that is actually ingrained in our DNA? Are some of us so biologically programmed to be hunter/gatherers that it's impossible to stop?

Maybe a wiser man has these answers. But in the meantime, tomorrow's going to be a nice day. The weather is finally breaking after five days of continual rain, and I'm going fishing.